TRANSLATION SERIES

TRANSLATION OF
CONTEMPORARY JAPANESE
SCHOLARSHIP
ON
SOUTHEAST ASIA

THE JAPANESE IN COLONIAL SOUTHEAST ASIA

EDITED BY SAYA SHIRAISHI AND TAKASHI SHIRAISHI

VOLUME III

Southeast Asia Program
180 Uris Hall
Cornell University
Ithaca, New York 14853-7601

Project Leader
George Kahin

Participating Researchers
Saya Shiraishi
Takashi Shiraishi

Translation
EDS (Tokyo)

Editing and Production
Donna Amoroso
Audrey Kahin
Roberta Ludgate
Dolina Millar

Published under the auspices of the Toyota Foundation

© 1993 Cornell Southeast Asia Program
ISBN 0-87727-402-9

CONTENTS

Acknowledgments

This is the third volume of the series of translations of contemporary Japanese scholarship on Southeast Asia. This project has been headed by Professor George McT. Kahin and funded by the Toyota Foundation. We would like to thank Ms. Yoshiko Wakayama who patiently saw the book through to publication; Dr. Hajime Shimizu who provided us with valuable intellectual assistance; Ms. Suzanne Trumbull and her colleagues at EDS (Editorial and Design Services) in Tokyo who put so much work into the translation effort; Ms. Roberta Ludgate and Dolina Millar who contributed to the publication in many and valuable ways; and above all Dr. Audrey Kahin without whose effort and guidance this book would never have been published.

rise of the Japanese state as an imperial power improved the Japanese position in colonial Southeast Asia in many tangible ways. In the Dutch Indies, for instance, before 1898 the Japanese as foreign orientals had been subjected to the residential and pass systems, along with the Chinese. With their elevation to the status of honorary Europeans they were freed from such restrictions and could engage in whatever trade they wanted, as long as they obtained official permission from the Dutch Resident. Those who visited the Resident's office were now invited to seat themselves on the sofa in the waiting room, while Chinese visitors sat on a bench outside the room, and natives squatted on the floor. If they had fights with Chinese or natives, they were thrown into a prison for whites, and if they died, they were buried in the European cemetery.[9] A prostitute later recalled those days in the following words:

> It is a big mistake to think that the rising sun is the flag for big men to use in diplomacy. When I ran away to Shanghai without even a piece of kimono and with only five yen in hand, I really came to see it. Running into a foreigner's house and saying to him, "I am a Japanese, please let me work for you," I really saw it. The man saw me as the rising sun.[10]

Before World War I, however, the Japanese communities in major urban centers such as Singapore, Batavia, and Surabaya remained prostitution-based, and the situation only started to change toward the end of the 1910s. Cut off from the European metropolitan centers by the war, colonial Southeast Asia provided readily accessible markets for cheap Japanese products. Those who had been hitherto dependent on prostitutes for their livelihood seized the opportunity, opened grocery shops in the cities and the countryside, and began to move into "respectable" jobs. In his autobiography, Iheiji Muraoka captures the essence of this transformation of the Japanese community:

> However remote the place in Nanyo [South Seas], once a brothel is opened, a grocery is also opened. Shopboys come from Japan. They become independent and open their own shops. Companies open branch offices. Brothel owners, who hate to be called pimps, also open shops. In a few years, the number of people increases to develop the area. In due course Japanese ships come. The area increasingly prospers.[11]

Certainly it was not simply because the shopboys became independent and brothel owners hated to be called pimps that this transformation was brought about. More important was because opening grocery stores and dealing in cheap Japanese goods for native customers proved very profitable.[12] There were demands for daily

---

[9] Interview with Sadaaki Kondo, December 5, 1978. Kondo was an agricultural produce dealer in Lumajan, East Java from the mid-1910s to the late 1930s.

[10] Kazue Morisaki, "Karayuki-san," in *Kimin*, ed. Ken'ichiro Tanikawa et al. (Tokyo: Gakugei Shoin, Document Nipponjin 5, 1969), p. 15. For more on Japanese prostitutes in Southeast Asia, see Tomoko Yamasaki's seminal *Sandakan 8-ban Shokan: Teihen Josei-shi Josho* (Tokyo: Chikuma Shobo, 1972) and *Sandakan no Haka* (Tokyo: Bungei Shunju, 1974).

[11] Iheiji Muraoka, *Muraoka Iheiji Jiden* (Tokyo: Nampo-sha, 1960), pp. 57–58.

[12] See *Interview Kiroku: Nihon to Ajia, Kondo Sadaaki* (Tokyo: Tokutei Kenkyu "Bunka Masatsu," 1979).

necessities, which metropolitan economies in Europe could not meet. Japanese ped-dlers, gamblers, and bookmakers who knew the area found good places to locate and opened small stores, brought in Japanese goods on credit from larger Japanese shop-owners in port cities, and sold them to natives. Those who had earned their liveli-hood by catering to Japanese prostitutes also moved into the countryside and opened stores. Japanese goods sold well. Larger shopowners moved into the import-export business. Large Japanese companies opened branch offices in major cities. Japanese banks and shipping companies followed them and also opened branch offices and agencies.

The transformation of Japanese communities was most evident in Java and British Malaya. In Java, peddlers, wandering gamblers, and bookmakers, as well as divers who had drifted back from Australia, opened *toko Jepang* (Japanese stores). In British Malaya, the number of Japanese grocers increased from 121 in 1913 to 350 in 1919.[13] Large Japanese trading firms, banks, and shipping companies also opened branch offices. Mitsui and Mitsubishi trading companies opened their offices and agencies in Singapore, Surabaya, and other port cities. The Yokohama Specie Bank (now the Bank of Tokyo) and the Kanan Bank (subsidiary of the Bank of Taiwan) soon followed. The first shipping company that came to Southeast Asia was Nippon Yusen (with Mitusbishi capital) which had been in regular operation on the Kobe-Manila line since 1892 and on the Bombay route since 1894. In the 1910s, Nanyo Yusen also opened a new regular Java-bound line, and toward the end of the 1910s, Nippon Yusen, Nanyo Yusen, and Yamashita Kisen opened branch offices in Singapore.[14]

During World War I, large Japanese firms as well as individual Japanese began to invest money in the development of plantations. In Davao, jute plantations were pioneered by Ota Kyosaburo, who leased land in 1906 and started to produce jute for the Japanese market. Small planters soon followed his example, and in the mid-1910s large firms such as Furukawa Takushoku (with the backing of Marubeni) joined in developing jute plantations. In 1914–1918 alone, 65 plantation companies were established in Davao and the number of Japanese there, most of them plant-ers, plantation workers, and their families, shot up from 700 in 1913 to 7,000 in 1919.[15] In British Malaya, it was rubber that attracted Japanese planters. The pioneer was San'go Koshi established in 1907 with Mitsubishi capital, which was followed in the mid-1910s by large firms such as Nanyo Koshi (with Okura capi-tal), Fujita-gumi (owned by Fujita Heitaro), Nan'a Koshi (owned by Morimura Ichizaemon), Furukawa Rubber Plantation (owned by Furukawa Toranosuke), and

---

[13] See the table in Shimizu, "Nihon-Tonan Ajia Kankei no Bunmei-shi teki Ichi." Japanese small traders and shopowners were hit hard by the post–World War I recession in 1920, and their numbers declined accordingly. But this occurred after the process of transformation had been set well in motion, and Japanese could not therefore go back to their prewar prostitution-based economy. In those days, small traders and shopowners could not borrow money from Japanese banks and had to rely on mutual financing (*mujin*) to keep their businesses going. Once one of the members of *mujin* went bankrupt, quite often all the rest also went under. For the tough life in Singapore in those postwar recession years, see Takeomi Kikuchi, "Kaiso-ki," pp. 75–79, in *Interview Kiroku: Nihon to Ajia, Kikuchi Takeomi* (Tokyo: Tokutei Kenkyu "Bunka Masatsu," 1978).

[14] Shimizu, "Nihon-Tonan Ajia Kankei," pp. 300–301.

[15] See chapters 4 and 7 in this volume. For the kind of dreams "Davao" evoked among young poor Japanese, see Lydia N. Yu-Jose, *Japan Views the Philippines, 1900–1944* (Quezon City: Ateneo de Manila University Press, 1992), pp. 48–50.

Mitsui, as well as by small independent planters. In the post–World War I recession, many independent planters went bankrupt and were absorbed into larger plantations owned by Japan-based *zaibatsu*, which dominated Japanese-owned rubber plantations in the 1920s in terms of the area leased and cultivated, and the amount of production.[16]

Expansion of "Japanese interests" in Southeast Asia in the late 1910s and 1920s drew the attention of the US Department of State, and we can get an interesting snapshot of Japanese interests in Central and East Java in 1924 from the report the American consul in Surabaya, Rollin R. Winslow, sent to Washington.[17] According to this report, the Japanese population was 627 in Surabaya, 135 in the Residency of Pasuruan, and 23 in Malang, and "in practically all districts the Japanese rank next to the Dutch in numbers." This was a recent development, for there had been an influx of Japanese to the Indies during the war years. They opened many small shops and settled down, and in the 1920s showed increasing interest in rubber and sugar plantations. One mill, "Gedaren," near Semarang was owned by Nagai Seito (Nagai Sugar Refinery), which had 666 *bouws* under cultivation and produced 96,000 piculs of sugar in 1923.

There were two Japanese banks in Surabaya: the Bank of Taiwan, which had branches in Batavia and Semarang as well as in Surabaya; and the Yokohama Specie Bank. Both these banks were established because of the sugar trade with Japan. There were twenty-five Japanese trading companies with offices in Surabaya, including Mitsui Bussan (now Mitsui Corporation), Mitsubishi Shoji (now Mitsubishi Corporation), Arima Shoten, and Toyo Menka. In addition, there were "four of the inevitable Japanese photographers," two Japanese jewelers and watch repairers, one small Japanese lantern shop, eight Japanese retail stores, and four Japanese barbers. In Semarang, there were sixteen Japanese firms, including Mitsui Bussan, Nanyo Shokai, Nanyo Soko, Nippon Menka (Japan Cotton Trading), Nomura Trading, and Toyo Menka.

Many large firms were interested in the sugar trade. According to the American consul's report, of the total 27 million piculs of sugar sold by the United Java Sugar Producers in 1924, 8.67 million piculs or 32 percent were purchased by Japanese firms. Local brokers also reported that Japanese firms bought 10.3 million piculs out of the 1924 crop, including Suzuki Shoten (2.8 million piculs), Mitsui Bussan (3.66 million piculs), Mitsubishi Shoji (1.7 million piculs), and Arima Shoten (1.05 million piculs). Cotton piece goods, matches, tea, novelties, and earthenware were the principal imports from Japan, while sugar, petroleum, tin, quinine, shells, and ebony represented important exports to Japan. What is more important, US Consul Winslow wrote:

> All the products which we purchase are collected and sold to us by Dutch, English, German and Japanese firms all of which derive good profits which might well be avoided to some extent if American purchasing agencies were established. Japanese goods are shipped to Netherlands India in Japanese ships, discharged into Japanese warehouses by a Japanese transfer company,

---

[16] For the development of Japanese-owned rubber plantations in British Malaya, see Yano, "*Nanshin*" *no Keifu*; Kikuchi, "Kaiso-ki."

[17] Rollin R. Winslow to the Secretary of State, Surabaya, Nov. 28, 1924. We thank Anne Foster for making this document available for us.

sold by local Japanese importers and even to some extent sold retail by Japanese shops. American goods are shipped largely on foreign steamers discharged into Dutch, English or German warehouses and sold by Dutch or English importers.

The same is true of exports from Netherlands India; sugar destined for Japan is purchased by Japanese firms established here and shipped to Japan on Japanese bottoms. Japanese capital is being invested in sugar estates and Japanese rubber plantations are increasing. . . On the other hand, the large quantities of rubber, kapok, coffee, hides, tapioca, sisal, shells, tin, etc., which are purchased annually by the United States are purchased by Dutch, English, Japanese and German firms from estates in which not one single American dollar is invested, then sold to American firms in the United States and carried almost entirely on Dutch, English and Japanese bottoms.

His complaint about "a very poor showing" by American firms sounds familiar, but the point more important to note for our discussion is that Japanese trading networks were in the making, extending from Japan down to the retail level in Java's countryside in the early 1920s and that *kimin*, people abandoned by the state who drifted down to Java as small shopkeepers, medicine peddlers, wandering gamblers and bookmakers, photographers, barbers and so on were now being re-integrated into these expanding networks as Japanese.[18]

This new era also saw the emergence of a small *zaibatsu* from among Southeast Asian Japanese: Ishihara Sangyo, established by Ishihara Hiroichiro and his two brothers, which, building its business empire in British Malaya, eventually succeeded in establishing its presence back in Japan. The reasons they came to British Malaya in the first place were not very different from those of other Japanese. Hiroichiro's brother, Shinzaburo, was first sent to Johor in 1911 as an agricultural expert by San'go Koshi. He quickly saw a chance to make money in rubber plantations, and the brothers started their own small plantation in Batu Pahat, Johor, in 1915. The next year, however, they incurred heavy losses from the waterworks they contracted from the Johor government and were forced to sell their plantation in 1917 and establish an import-export business firm in Singapore. Nonetheless, they went bankrupt in 1919. But luck was with them. That same year they found rich iron ore in Sri Medan, Johor. With technical assistance from the State Yawata Iron Works and financial support from the Bank of Taiwan, Ishihara Sangyo with its local subsidiary, Nanyo Kogyo, headquartered in Singapore, began exploiting the mine in 1920.[19] At the same time, Ishihara Sangyo obtained a long-term

---

[18] Winslow's complaint about the poor showing of American firms is exaggerated. Though he says that only five American firms maintained offices in his Consular district, they included Standard Oil Co. of New York and Vacuum Oil Company, which operated in a business denied to Japanese firms.

[19] The pessimistic opinion of the Japanese Consulate in Singapore notwithstanding, the Ishihara brothers had no trouble in obtaining permission to exploit the mine from the Johor government. In the post–World War I recession, the rubber market collapsed, which led to the decline in export tax income for the Johor government. The government therefore welcomed a new source of income as well as the prospect that the company would create new employment opportunities for those laid off by rubber plantations. The British authority in Singapore also did not raise any objection, most likely because British capital was not interested in the exploitation of iron ore in Malaya. In contrast, the Dutch Indies government was more nervous about Japanese exploitation of mineral resources. In the early 1920s, the Indies government purchased the coal

1

THE JAPANESE IN COLONIAL SOUTHEAST ASIA: AN OVERVIEW

Saya Shiraishi and Takashi Shiraishi

1899—the closing year of the nineteenth century.

Japan gets more interesting. This admirable nation gets more surprising. In my diary is written: Holland and Japan signed a treaty of friendship about half a century ago. One after another European countries started to regard it as an exceptional Asian nation. And about five years ago, I read in an article: Japan enters the arena, does not want to be left behind by the white nations; joins in dividing the world for itself: invades Manchuria, attacks China, Chinese territory. And Holland, automatically including the Dutch Indies, announced its neutrality toward the war that has broken out [. . .].

Three years ago, it was reported in the newspaper, an agreement was signed between the Dutch Indies and Japan. Japan again! In it: the Dutch Indies has the right to regard Japanese residents in the Indies as Foreign Orientals. This was three years ago. A year after the agreement: the Indies hurriedly prepared the bill that would give Japanese residents a legal status equal with Europeans [. . .].

And now, at the moment of my writing, Japanese residents in the Indies are already equal in status with European residents.

How proud the Japanese nation is. How proud Maiko is. Why not: it is the only Asian nation that is recognized as equal in status with white nations [. . .].

Not on paper alone, but in practice too. It is said that on plantations and in workshops, entrepreneurs and foremen started to call them not *koh* or *engkoh*, but: *tuan*. Though I am an admirer of Japan, I won't feel good either calling them *tuan*. And Maiko really disturbs the good picture of Japan [. . .].[1]

Thus says Minke, a native student at the European high school in Surabaya at the turn of the twentieth century in Pramoedya Ananta Toer's great novel, *Anak Semua Bangsa*. He is forming a picture of Japan, while reading the world through news-papers and books and observing the only Japanese national he personally knows, Maiko, a prostitute suffering from fatal syphilis and "owned" by a Chinese

---

[1] Pramoedya Ananta Toer, *Anak Semua Bangsa* (Jakarta: Hasta Mitra, 1981), pp. 38–40. The translation is ours. *Koh* and *engkoh* mean "you" and were used when addressing an older person, while *tuan*, "you," was a form of address for European adult males.

taukay. What troubles him and his "good" picture of Japan is the discrepancy between the Japan he imagines through his reading of newspapers and books and the
image of the Japanese he gathers from his acquaintance with Maiko, for Maiko
does not fit well with the image of a Japanese nation accorded equal legal status
with the whites in the Indies.

This discrepancy between the imagined realities of Japan as an imperial power
and the reality of those of its nationals one saw in daily life remained a riddle for
many natives in Southeast Asia, because the link between the Japanese state and
its nationals was hidden from their eyes. Yet it was this link that made a Japanese
prostitute an honorary European, while a native aristocrat remained a native (the
son of one of the highest-ranking native aristocrats-turned-bureaucrats was called
Minke, monkey, by a European school teacher), and a wealthy Chinese tycoon a
foreign oriental. Natives came to see this connection only at the start of World War
II, when their countries were invaded and occupied by the Japanese military and
they themselves saw with their own eyes the transformation of the local Japanese
from being *orang Jepang* (Japanese) to *orang Dai Nippon* (Great Nipponese). Togashi Takeomi, who was the owner of a grocery shop (*toko Jepang*) in Cianjur, West
Java, before the war, recalled years later how he was "welcomed" by his former
native clients when he returned to the town at the start of the war as an interpreter
for Captain Yanagawa. "When we [Captain Yanagawa and Togashi] finally
reached Cianjur and stepped out of the car, Indonesians said, 'Ow [Aduh], it's
Togashi!' 'That's right.' And people crowded around us." It is this "ow" that
signified Indonesians' finally coming to realize the connection between the Japanese they knew and the Japanese state.[2]

The Japanese in colonial Southeast Asia had, however, long been well aware of
this linkage. They put it in words when they said they had "the rising sun [*hino-
maru*] on their back." And the connection, as well as their awareness of it, significantly shaped their life and the nature of their community in colonial Southeast
Asia.

Studies on the Japanese in colonial Southeast Asia have usually been carried
out with one central question in mind: Why did virtually all the Japanese return to
Japan after the war, even though they were not state-organized immigrants?[3] The
explanation has been sought in what we may call the shallowness of the Japanese
communities in Southeast Asia: in the fact that these communities existed in
Southeast Asia as an extention of Japanese society in Japan in its search for wealth;
that no "Nanyo [South Seas] Japanese" were ever deeply rooted in Southeast Asian
societies; that once the Japanese state opted for an expansionist drive into the
South in the late 1930s and early 1940s, the Southeast Asian Japanese were easily
carried along with this policy drift, eventually being uprooted when the Japanese
state was defeated in World War II.

This explanation, however, only invites a further question: why were the Japanese communities so shallowly rooted in colonial Southeast Asia? We will argue
below that it was precisely the linkage with Japan, both real and imagined, that
gave the Japanese communities this shallowness. Certainly Southeast Asian Japa-

---

[2] *Interview Kiroku: Nihon to Ajia, Togashi Takeomi* (Tokyo: Tokutei Kenkyu "Bunka Masatsu,"
1978).

[3] For the most clearly formulated question, see Toru Yano, *"Nanshin" no Keifu* (Tokyo: Chuo
Koron-sha, 1975), p. 175.

nese were not state-organized immigrants. Many of them in the earlier decades were *kimin*, people abandoned by the state who were smuggled out of Japan without passports and, looking for jobs abroad and often cheated or even kidnapped, eventually drifted to Southeast Asia. But this does not necessarily mean that there were no links between the Japanese state and the Japanese in Southeast Asia. They maintained their ties with their families and relatives, dreamt of retiring to their home towns, were aware of being Japanese nationals, and behaved, insofar as they could afford to, as "first-class" nationals. The Japanese state exploited the social and "spiritual" ties they maintained with Japan in its attempt to Nipponize and exert control over the Southeast Asian Japanese.

In this essay, then, we want to explore how the linkage between the Japanese state and the Japanese in Southeast Asia was established and how it shaped the life of the Japanese and their communities in colonial Southeast Asia. In discussing these questions, we will primarily focus on the Japanese in island Southeast Asia— British Malaya (our shorthand for British Malaya, the Crown Colony of the Straits Settlements, and British Borneo), the Dutch Indies, and the American Philippines in the interwar years.

*****

Let us first look at the growth of Japanese communities in Southeast Asia, especially British Malaya, the Dutch Indies, and the American Philippines. Japanese migration to Southeast Asia began in the early Meiji period, and the number of Japanese grew from 2,800 in 1907, the first year for which passably reliable data are available, to 19,900 in 1917, and to 36,600 in 1936.[4] Admittedly their numbers were small, smaller than the small European population in Southeast Asia, let alone the Chinese whose numbers in the Straits Settlements alone reached 224,000 in 1911.[5] Yet Japanese formed sizable communities in many urban centers—Singapore, Batavia (Jakarta), Surabaya, and Manila—as well as establishing concentrated pockets in small towns in Malaya, Java, and above all Davao and its vicinity. The predominant majority were *singkeh*, Japan-born Japanese, though in the 1920s and 1930s a second generation of locally born Japanese began to appear.

The nature of Japanese communities underwent sudden and marked changes toward the end of the 1910s. In the first phase, from the start of Japanese migration in the early Meiji (in the 1880s) to the late 1910s, prostitutes formed a majority among Japanese in many urban centers, especially in British Malaya and Java. In the next phase, from the late 1910s to the late 1930s, it was white-collar workers (in British Malaya, especially in Singapore), independent shopkeepers and clerks (in the Dutch Indies, especially in Java), and planters and plantation workers (in the Philippines, especially in Davao) who formed the majority.[6] Why did such sudden and marked changes take place in the 1910s and what was their signifi-

---

[4] Haime Shimizu, "Nihon-Tonan Ajia Kankei no Bunmei-shi teki Ichi," Yonosuke Hara, ed., *Tonan Ajia kara no Chiteki Boken* (Tokyo: Libroport, 1986), pp. 294–95. See also chapters 3–5 in this volume.

[5] There were 208,000 Europeans in the Dutch Indies in 1930. Amry Vandenbosch, *Higashi Indo*, translated by O'e Sen'ichi (Tokyo: Kaizo-sha, 1943), p. 8. For the Chinese population in Singapore, see Yoshihiro Tsubouchi, *Tonan Ajia Jinko Minzoku-shi* (Tokyo: Keiso Shobo, 1985), p. 128.

[6] See chapters 3–5 in this volume.

cance for the creation of the linkage between the Japanese state and the Southeast Asian Japanese?

In contrast with the Chinese communities in colonial Southeast Asia where there were far more men than women, among the Southeast Asian Japanese population women far outnumbered men, and, with the notable exception of the Davao Japanese, prostitution formed the social and economic foundation of many Japanese communities, especially in British Malaya and the Dutch Indies, until the end of the 1910s. These prostitutes, mainly coming from the southwestern Kyushu, were the pioneers of the Japanese communities. In 1882 when there were only 22 Japanese in Singapore, 14 of these were women, most if not all of whom catered to Chinese, Indians, and Malays at two Japanese brothels already existing there. And in 1903 there were 83 Japanese-owned brothels with 611 prostitutes in Singapore alone, and 101 brothels with 601 prostitutes in 1905. The situation was not very different in the Dutch Indies, where in 1898, when Japanese nationals were accorded equal legal status with whites, there were 166 Japanese men and 448 Japanese women, the majority of whom were prostitutes.[7] It is not surprising that Minke was troubled at the discrepancy between the emergence of the rising sun as an imperialist power and the realities of the Surabayan Japanese community as he personally perceived them, where Maiko was indeed the representative Japanese.

In those days, Japanese men were thoroughly dependent on women, either directly exploiting prostitutes as pimps and brothel owners or catering to their daily needs as rickshaw pullers (*jinrikisha-fu*), barbers, laundrymen, photographers, dentists, masseurs, drapers (*gofuku-sho*), owners of jewelry (especially tortoiseshell-work) stores [*bekko-saiku ten*]), inn, restaurant, and bar owners, medical practitioners, and so on.[8] Those who earned their livelihood by dealing with natives in the countryside—owners of small shops (mainly grocery stores), medicine (*jintan*) peddlers, wandering gamblers and bookmakers for target shooting with guns (*shateki*) or blowpipes (*fukiya*), or for games such as *wanage* (ringtoss), and *bun-mawashi* (spinning tops)—also found themselves on the margins of the prostitution-based Japanese community, often dependent on brothel owners and prostitutes for loans. Drifting into the Southeast Asian Japanese communities without any money and connections, they borrowed money from prostitutes, brought in cheap Japanese goods such as daily necessities, medicines, and fake watches from larger grocers in the cities and peddled them around the countryside.

Before the Sino-Japanese war in 1894–1895, the Japanese had the same legal status as the Chinese and other non-native Asiatics. In British Malaya, they were placed under the supervision of the Chinese Protectorate, and in the Dutch Indies they were "foreign orientals," the legal category in between the Europeans and the natives. They could not and did not expect protection from the Japanese state, for Japanese consulates had not yet been opened there except for one in Singapore, where its presence was more symbolic than real. Japanese associations (*Nipponjin-kai*) did not yet exist and there were as yet no Japanese schools. The day-to-day affairs of the Japanese community were handled by a few local bosses, many of them brothel owners who dominated the community.

The Japanese victory in the Sino-Japanese war and in the Russo-Japanese war (1904–1905) markedly changed this situation. As Minke writes in his diary, the

---

[7] Yano, *"Nanshin" no Keifu*, pp. 18–19, 41.

[8] Ibid., pp. 85–86.

Moreover, because regions assume concrete form only upon being named, that is, upon the verbal definition of space, their existence depends upon an essential affiliation with language. This, too, reveals the arbitrary nature of regions. According to Saussurist linguistic theory, words are not copies of things but are themselves the basic power that defines and imparts reality to things; the world perceived through language "is not a real world whose aspects differ according to the viewpoint from which they are perceived, but a world of relations that is objectified only upon articulation of a point of view."[8] This linguistic function is nowhere revealed as clearly as in the concept of region.

Furthermore, the defining action of language works in two directions: in addition to verbally defining objects, language defines the perceptions of the linguistic subject, so that "language is the expression of concepts and worldviews or ideologies."[9] Thus regions, which take form by being named, are expressions of some kind of worldview or ideology. We may recall, in this context, that as soon as the Japanese cabinet decided, on December 12, 1941, upon the name Greater East Asia War (*Dai Tōa sensō*) to indicate the "revolutionary" nature of the war, which was to liberate Japan and the rest of Asia from Western domination, the government prohibited use of the regional name "Far East" (*kyokutō*) in all written materials: government documents, newspapers and magazines, propaganda materials, resolutions, and so on.[10] The reasoning was that the regional concept of Far East reflected a Eurocentric ideology that disparaged Asians and therefore did not appropriately express Japan's ideal of revolutionizing world history by establishing the Greater East Asia Co-Prosperity Sphere.

In this paper I will demonstrate that a regional concept of Southeast Asia existed in Japan in the post–World War I period, before it did in Western countries, and will also attempt to elucidate the worldview and ideology reflected by this concept as well as the linguistic context within which the Japanese today perceive the region.

I. The Concept of Southeast Asia in the West

"It is only since the Second World War that the term South-east Asia has been generally accepted as a collective name for the series of peninsulas and islands which lie to the east of India and Pakistan and to the south of China. Nor is it altogether surprising that the West should have been slow to recognize the need for some such common term for this area, which today comprises the several territories of Burma, Thailand, Cambodia, Laos, Vietnam, Malaya, British Borneo, Indonesia and the Philippines. For, apart from the fact that all of these, with the solitary exception of Thailand, had long formed parts of different imperial groupings, British, French, Dutch or American, the inherent geographical unity of South-east

---

[8] Keizaburō Maruyama, *Bunka no fetishizumu* [Cultural fetishism] (Tokyo: Keisō Shobō, 1984), p. 121. Maruyama also discusses Saussurist linguistics in *Soshuuru no shisō* [Saussure's thought] (Tokyo: Iwanami Shoten, 1981) and *Soshuuru o yomu* [Reading Saussure] (Tokyo: Iwanami Shoten, 1983).

[9] Maruyama, *Bunka no fetishizumu*, p. 197.

[10] Kimitada Miwa, *Nihon: 1945 nen no shiten* [Japan: The View in 1945] (Tokyo: Tokyo Daigaku Shuppankai, 1986), p. 24.

Asia has always seemed somewhat negative in character."[11] With these words the distinguished British scholar of political geography Charles Fisher began his *South-east Asia: A Social, Economic and Political Geography*. Most other Western scholars of Southeast Asia have also entertained considerable doubt as to whether Southeast Asia actually constituted a region.

The prevailing view that the term itself as a designation of the region dates to the Allies' establishment of the South East Asia Command during World War II and entered general use after the war is probably correct. Before that, there seems to have been no appropriate name for the region as a whole aside from the old term "East Indies," which also included India.[12] The British journalist Dorothy Woodman, writing in 1948 after visiting India and Southeast Asia, put it succinctly: "This [Southeast Asia] includes the wide area stretching from the mountains of Arakan to the jungles of Indo-China, from the Chin Hills to the Outer Islands of Indonesia, all of which came under the control of South East Asia Command during the war. To thousands of men in this country today these names were so seldom heard here before the Japanese invasions of 1942."[13]

My search through the voluminous subject indexes of the British Library (formerly the library of the British Museum), which list books published since the sixteenth century, for titles including the words "Southeast Asia" or variants thereof (table 1) corroborates the view that the term originated during World War II. Its first appearance in a title was in the 1942 work *Government and Nationalism in Southeast Asia,* by Rupert Emerson, Lennox A. Mills, and Virginia Thompson.[14] Before this term became general, the region was classified as part of such regional concepts as "the East Indies," "Further India," "Monsoon Asia," "Tropical Asia," "the Far East," and "East Asia." From the 1920s onward, Southeast Asia was most often classified as part of the Far East or East Asia. This changed only after the establishment of the South East Asia Command.

I found only one title in the subject indexes including a term similar to "Southeast Asia"—"Southeastern Asia"—published before 1880.[15] "Southeastern Asia" appears to have been used occasionally in the nineteenth century. Howard Malcom's famous *Travels in South Eastern Asia* was published in 1840.[16] Dispatches from US consuls in Bangkok in the second half of the nineteenth century also contained scattered references to "South Eastern Asia."[17] Malcom's concept of the

---

[11] Charles A. Fisher, *South-east Asia: A Social, Economic and Political Geography* (London: Methuen, 1966), p. 3.

[12] Hikaru Watanabe, *Sekai chiri 3: Tōnan Ajia* [World Geography 3: Southeast Asia] (Tokyo: Asakura Shoten, 1980), p. 3.

[13] Dorothy Woodman, "Light on South East Asia," *Current Affairs,* no. 16 (August 1948): 2. In this and subsequent quotations, the italics are mine.

[14] Rupert Emerson, Lennox A. Mills, and Virginia Thompson, *Government and Nationalism in Southeast Asia* (New York: Institute of Pacific Relations, 1942).

[15] W. Bingley, *Travels in Southeastern Asia* (n.p., 1824).

[16] For more on this point, see Tōru Yano, ed., *Tōnan Ajia gaku e no shōtai* [An invitation to Southeast Asian studies] (Tokyo: Nippon Hōsō Shuppan Kyōkai, 1983), vol. 1, p. 18; vol. 2, p. 24.

[17] Department of State, *Despatches from United States Consuls in Bangkok, 1856–1880,* microfilm.

(*kokujoku*)." They thus started to move for the eradication of that occupation category, i.e., abolition of licensed Japanese prostitution (*haisho*).[24]

In the Dutch Indies, Japanese prostitution was "abolished" in 1912, two years after the consulate opened in Batavia. In Manila and Davao, it ended in 1920. But the major battles were fought in British Malaya, especially in Singapore, where the largest community of prostitutes was located. In 1914, the Japanese consul put strong pressure on the Straits Settlements government to deport as many Japanese pimps as possible. Under this pressure the British authorities arrested and deported some 70 Japanese pimps. But these steps proved insufficient. In 1919, 70 Japanese-owned brothels with 380 prostitutes still existed in Singapore alone, and there were some 1,500 Japanese prostitutes in British Malaya. In 1920, then, the deputy consul general in Singapore summoned some thirty representatives from the Japanese communities in British Malaya, who voluntarily decided to "abolish" Japanese prostitution "with no one speaking out against the decision at the meeting."[25] This decision broke the backbone of the Japanese prostitution business in British Malaya. Brothel owners shut down their brothels, at least officially, and opened "respectable" shops, even though these sometimes functioned as a cover for continuing their old trade. Prostitutes either returned home to Japan, continued their trade as unlicensed prostitutes, or married natives. In any event, Japanese prostitution officially disappeared, unlicensed pimps and prostitutes were seen as a national disgrace by respectable Japanese as well as by Japanese consulates, and those who married natives disappeared from the Japanese community and from official Japanese eyes to be assimilated into native society.[26]

Here it is important to emphasize the reasons why the Japanese consulates were successful in "abolishing" Japanese prostitution and why the Japanese representatives summoned to Singapore voluntarily decided to shut down their brothels without anyone openly opposing the decision, even though they were running very prosperous businesses and making good money as brothel owners. Undoubtedly, one important reason was that other and more respectable jobs were available to brothel owners and that many of them had, in fact, been moving in that direction even before the official abolition of Japanese prostitution. (It was an entirely different story for the prostitutes who were victims of this move.) The other, and for our present purpose more important, reason is that they were conscious of being "first-class" nationals (Ikkyu Kokumin or Itto Kokumin), and they could not lightly disregard the fact that the label, "national dishonor," thrown at them by the Japanese state, and the campaign for the abolition of Japanese prostitution placed them in an increasingly dubious outcast position in the Japanese community. They were no longer local bosses but simply pimps, shunned and despised by other Japanese who were proud of their own first-class national status. Japanese consulates shrewdly exploited the sense in the Japanese community of being first-class nationals, thus generating strong community pressures against brothel owners.

---

[24] *Koku'eki* means both national and state interests.

[25] Yano, "*Nanshin*" *no Keifu*, pp. 43–44.

[26] It was these former prostitutes, assimilated into native society, who stayed on in colonial Southeast Asia regardless of the state of relations between Japan and the European and American colonial powers, and who "welcomed" advancing Dai Nippon soldiers at the start of World War II. Those who lament the shallowness of the Southeast Asian Japanese community in the prewar era often conveniently forget their enduring presence.

The successful campaign for the abolition of Japanese prostitution clearly marked the opening of a new era of respectable Japanese in colonial Southeast Asia, now neatly classified into respectable occupation categories in the sight of the Japanese state. These Japanese expressed their sense of being first-class nationals in many different ways. Japanese peddlers dressed like Europeans, with "kaizer-style mustaches," white helmets, and tight collared five-buttoned jackets. They traveled around the countryside by bus, sitting in a front seat along with Europeans and Eurasians and attended by a native servant carrying their possessions. Their more prosperous fellows lived in Western-style houses, "different in style from those who lived in Korea, Taiwan, and Manchuria," with one understandable modification: the bath was Japanese-style.

Grocers preferred to establish fixed prices rather than bargain with native customers. If natives wanted to buy at the prices they set, all right, but no bargains, that was the principle. In explaining their attitude they said they wanted to show native customers that they did not cheat "as the Chinese did" and they were too busy to serve and bargain with each customer who came to their stores. Perhaps. But there was a certain arrogance in the way they dealt with "natives [domin]." It was, we suspect, also because bargaining with them would have placed these Japanese on equal terms with the natives, thus downgrading them from first-class nationals to third-class natives.

Ishihara Hiroichiro even went further in his pride as a first-class national. Simply because he supplied iron ore for the Japanese steel industry, he could happily believe that he was working for Japan at the same time as making a huge fortune. He saw himself as an exemplary patriot and made it an unspoken and unwritten company principle that "a company employee may sleep with a Malay woman, but may not live with her. Once he is married to a Malay woman, his way of thinking would also become Malayanized and sexual desire-first-ist [seiyoku daiichi shugi]."[27] Ishihara was not exceptional. Though not as explicit as his unspoken and unwritten company principle, there was a strong notion that Southeast Asian Japanese were somewhat slow because of the tropical climate and their contacts with the natives. Large Japanese companies thus rotated their branch office staff every three or four years before their slowness became too serious. And the Singaporean Japanese schoolmaster pronounced his judgement about his students in 1926 thus:

> When I first taught children here, I was surprised that they lacked enthusiasm, flexibility and guts. Compared with the children in the metropolis [naichi], they are not as smart.[28]

Larger Japanese merchants in major urban centers, whose customers were not natives but respectable Japanese and Europeans, ran their shops as their fellow merchants did in Japan. "Like any good *gofuku-sho* [draper] in Japan," the largest draper's store in Singapore, Takahashi Chuhei's Echigo-ya, recruited clerks from his hometown of Kashiwabara, Echigo (now Niigata); trained them to command "good" English, keep the store always clean and neat, and serve customers in a

---

[27] It would be interesting to know what he would have to say if he had seen his offspring go on sex tours to Southeast Asia.

[28] Yano, *"Nanshin" no Keifu*, p. 134.

polite and respectful manner; and he strictly supervised the way they dressed and spent their own money.[29]

For his hometown Takahashi also built a public hall at a cost of 170,000 yen as well as a luxurious house. This was a way of saying to his countrymen that he had been successful. Tsutsumibayashi Kazue, the head of the most successful *toko Jepang* chain in Java, also frequently returned to his hometown of Shinjo, Yamagata, gave lectures at Shinjo Junior High School, recruited its graduates for his stores, and patronized Yamagata products.

The new sense of respectability local Japanese expressed in these various ways—trying to be like Europeans, despising Chinese and natives, and showing off their success and riches to their countrymen—was in turn manipulated and mobilized by the Japanese consulates to control and guide Southeast Asian Japanese and their communities. The successful campaign the consulates organized to abolish Japanese prostitution was a good example. But more generally Japanese associations (*Nipponjin-kai*) and Japanese schools provided the most useful instruments for the consulates.

Japanese associations were established in Singapore in 1915, a year after the consulate seriously started its campaign for the abolition of Japanese prostitution; in Batavia in 1913, three years after the consulate opened there; in Davao in 1918 at the suggestion of the Japanese consulate in Manila; and in Surabaya in 1921, two years after the consulate opened there, and in many other places. The purpose of the associations was "mutual friendship and exchange of information" among resident Japanese. The managing board was typically composed of local bosses (successful merchants, planters, wholesale dealers, and so forth) and company and bank representatives, and it worked, usually in close cooperation and consultation with the consulate, in organizing Japanese clubs and youth associations, lectures and sports meetings, of which the most important was an annually held *Undo-kai* (sports meeting). Such games as baseball, tennis, badminton, sumo, and even *kendo* (Japanese fencing) were also frequently organized, though *kendo* was not popular because putting on armor was unbearably hot. In major urban centers, Japanese associations also purchased land for a Japanese cemetery, and in due course invited Buddhist priests to tend the dead.[30]

The most important role Japanese associations played was, however, in establishing and managing Japanese schools. If the Japanese association had organized only recreational activities, many of the local Japanese would have stayed away and the association would have become a club for the local bosses, elite company and bank representatives, and consulate officials. Once they settled down with their families, however, the major concern of local Japanese was the education of their children. By the early 1920s, many of them, including those who settled down in the countryside as petty shopkeepers, had been re-integrated into Japanese trading networks. Besides, they were *singkeh*, seeing Japan as their homeland and hoping some day to retire with a small fortune to their hometown. They were in Southeast Asia to earn their livelihood, but they hoped their children would make their way back to Japan and become more respectable than their parents. They saw the key to their children's success in education. The Japanese school was to respond to their needs.

---

[29] Ibid., p. 100.

[30] Ibid., pp. 129–32.

The first schools were established in Singapore in 1911, in Davao in 1924, in Surabaya in 1925, and in Batavia in 1928. The schools provided dormitories for those coming from the countryside. Other than those who could afford to send their children back to Japan for education, most Japanese had no choice but to send them to these local Japanese schools if they did not want to educate them in "foreign" schools. What they wanted for their children, however, was not general schooling, but an education in the standardized Japanese school system. The Japanese school, therefore, had to be recognized as such by the Japanese Ministry of Education, the curriculum had to be the same as those in Japan, the licenced school teachers had to come from Japan to teach, and the diploma had to have the same validity as one issued by a school in Japan, so that graduates could get jobs worthy of their diploma or could continue their high school studies in Japan. Besides, the Japanese government made subsidies available for establishing and managing Japanese schools. The Japanese consul had the authority to decide whether a school was recognized as official and given government subsidies. The consulate and the managing board of the Japanese association thus worked closely together in establishing and running the Japanese school, which provided the consulate with strong leverage in controlling and guiding the local Japanese community under its jurisdiction.[31]

*****

In the late 1910s and 1920s, Southeast Asian Japanese thus became respectable in their census categories, in their social and economic positions, and in their behavior, and they came increasingly within the orbit of the Japanese state. The linkage between the Japanese state and local Japanese was now firmly established. But the logic had been developing since the turn of the twentieth century, for those Japanese dependent on prostitution either directly or indirectly were also aware of being Japanese nationals and would happily have become respectable if they could afford to. But in the earlier years this had been impossible, and though they were Japanese, i.e., born in Japan, speaking Japanese as their mother tongue, and aware of being Japanese, they tended to disappear from sight in official Japanese eyes. They were loose and free-floating on the margin of Japanese society. With their re-integration into Japanese trading networks, their re-entry into the field of vision of official Japan through consular head counting, and their organization into Japanese associations and Japanese schools, they officially reemerged as Japanese nationals with stakes of their own and of their children firmly embedded in the fate of the Japanese state and economy. Now shopkeepers, traders, planters, company and bank officials could not only live respectable lives, hope their children would become more respectable through their education in the Japanese school system, and have realistic dreams of retiring to their hometowns as successful Japanese, but they would also become aware that all these expectations eventually depended on "Japan" as embodied by the Japanese state. In this sense, Ishihara was indeed an exemplary Southeast Asian Japanese, for he achieved what others only dreamt of: working for his country while making a fortune. To live like Europeans as first-class nationals, to despise natives and non-native Asiatics, and to behave as the Japanese government wished were their ways of expressing their Japaneseness.

---

[31] For more about Japanese schools in Davao, see chapter 7 in this volume.

We may understand this point more clearly if we briefly compare them with their fellow foreign orientals—the Chinese. Certainly the overseas Chinese were far more numerous than the Southeast Asian Japanese, their economic positions were far stronger and more deeply rooted in the local economies, and their history in the region was far longer than that of the Japanese. But we do not need to dwell on these aspects. More interesting for our discussion is the fact that they did not obtain first-class national status in colonial Southeast Asia. The reasons for this are not difficult to find. They lay in the fact that the Chinese state, both the Ch'ing dynastic state and the Republic of China, remained weak throughout the period, and became not an imperialist power but a prized prey for East Asian imperialist power games. The Chinese in Southeast Asia could not expect protection and improvement for their positions from the Chinese state. They had to protect their interests by themselves, and they could not realistically bet their and their children's future on that of the Chinese state. They thus formed their community organizations on their own initiative, quite independently of the Chinese state and often with the Chinese Chamber of Commerce as their center. It was community organizations, above all the Chinese Chamber of Commerce, that negotiated with the colonial authorities in behalf of the community's interests, established Chinese schools and invited teachers from China, and in the Ch'ing period managed consular affairs. In the 1910s and 1920s, Chinese consulates were established in colonial Southeast Asia, but even then the consulate remained a mere arm of the Chinese state, far less influential than the Chinese Chamber of Commerce and the larger speech group associations. If Japanese community leaders were respectable in the eyes of both the colonial authorities and the Japanese state, their Chinese counterparts were respectable in the eyes of the colonial state but not necessarily of the Chinese state. And Chinese nationalist leaders were not respectable at all, but troublemakers for the local authorities.

This difference in respectability alone already suggests how differently Japanese and Chinese expressed their sense of nationality. While Japanese saw living like Europeans, despising natives, and behaving as the Japanese consulate wanted as ways of saying "we are Japanese, first-class nationals," Southeast Asian Chinese expressed their Chineseness in campaigns to improve their positions, in their educational reform movement, in anti-Japanese boycotts, and in their contributions to the Chinese national salvation movement. Their nationalism was popular nationalism largely divorced from the Chinese state, while Japanese nationalism was patently official with the linkage, both imagined and real, between the Japanese state and the Japanese nationals firmly and intimately established.[32]

The above excursion will perhaps serve to clarify the foundations on which the linkage between the Japanese state and the Japanese nationals in Southeast Asia was established. It was official and conscious manipulation and mobilization of the sense of Japaneseness held and expressed in many different ways by Southeast Asian Japanese that established the linkage. And it was this linkage that gave a final ironic touch to the fate of Japanese toward the end of the 1930s and 1940s.

Toward the end of the 1920s, both Japanese and Southeast Asian economies were hit hard by the onset of the World Depression. Japanese companies dumped their products in Southeast Asian markets, resulting in serious trade disputes

---

[32] For popular and official nationalism, see Benedict Anderson, *Imagined Communities* (London: Verso, 1983).

between Japan and the Southeast Asian colonial powers. The colonial authorities took legal measures to curb Japanese imports and restrict Japanese commercial activities in their colonies. The Depression also hit Southeast Asian Japanese economic activities directly. Many small shopkeepers and traders went bankrupt and many large companies were forced to shut down branch offices. Then the Japanese army invaded and occupied Manchuria, starting its long and disastrous war with China. In response, Southeast Asian Chinese began their national salvation movement and anti-Japanese boycotts. Japanese children on their way to school got stoned; Chinese friendly with Japanese were boycotted by anti-Japanese groups; clients of Japanese stores were harassed; and filth and tar were thrown into Japanese shops. With the beginning of the Japanese policy of Southward Expansion, the colonial authorities started to impose ever tougher restrictions on local Japanese economic activities and to place their movements under surveillance. In the Dutch Indies, Japanese immigration was severely restricted in 1936. Most of the large firms could no longer do business. Shopkeepers began to send their families to Japan. And in early 1941 the Indies government finally froze Japanese assets in the colony. It was the linkage between the Japanese state and the Japanese nationals in the Indies that invited this disaster, though those who returned briefly to the Indies during the war as *orang Dai Nippon* might have thought otherwise for a while. Virtually all the Southeast Asian Japanese thus ended up by returning to Japan, not because they were not "real" Southeast Asian Japanese deeply rooted in the colonial societies, but because their fate was inseparably intertwined with that of the Japanese state.

2

SOUTHEAST ASIA AS A REGIONAL CONCEPT IN MODERN JAPAN: AN ANALYSIS OF GEOGRAPHY TEXTBOOKS

Hajime Shimizu

INTRODUCTION

The indictment against the Japanese defendants in the International Military Tribunal for the Far East, convened in 1946, opened with a declaration that the minds of the Japanese people had been systematically poisoned by Japan's pernicious ideology of racial superiority over other peoples, not only in Asia but in the entire world.[1] This expressed the basic mind-set underlying the Allied occupation authorities' suspension, following Japan's defeat in World War II, of the teaching of geography, along with Japanese history and morals (*shūshin*), in Japanese elementary and middle schools. The teaching of geography was reinstated in 1947 as part of social studies. It was several more years, however, before any mention of Southeast Asia was seen in textbooks.

The Japanese term "Tōnan Ajia," or "Southeast Asia," first appeared in a middle school textbook in 1955;[2] but it was only ten years later, in 1965, that it was seen in an elementary school textbook.[3] Behind the postwar emergence of this term in the context of compulsory education lay Japan's rising interest in Southeast Asia in the early 1950s and the first postwar enunciation of a Southeast Asia policy in Prime Minister Shigeru Yoshida's administrative policy speech in the lower house of the National Diet in June 1953, following the inauguration of his fifth cabinet.[4]

---

[1] Preamble to the indictment, International Military Tribunal for the Far East; quoted in Masami Yamazumi, *Nihon kyōiku shōshi* [A short history of Japanese education] (Tokyo: Iwanami Shoten, 1987), p. 2.

[2] *Chūgakusei no shakai: Tochi to seikatsu* [Social studies for middle school students: Land and life], vol. 2 (Tokyo: Nihon Shoseki, June 1955), ch. 6. This was a textbook for first-year middle school students.

[3] *Shōgaku shakai* [Elementary school social studies], vol. 2 (Tokyo: Nihon Shoseki, January 1965), p. 33.

[4] Nobuyuki Hagiwara, "Sengo Nihon to Tōnan Ajia no ichizuke: Haisen kara 10 nen no kiseki" [Postwar Japan and the meaning of Southeast Asia: The first ten years after the defeat], in Ken'ichirō Shōda, ed., *Kindai Nihon no Tōnan Ajia kan* [The view of Southeast Asia in early modern Japan] (Tokyo: Ajia Keizai Kenkyūsho [Institute of Developing Economies], 1978), pp. 131–35; Tōru Yano, *"Nanshin" no keifu* [The lineage of southern expansion] (Tokyo: Chūō Kōronsha, 1975), pp. 179–80.

The succession of policy concepts regarding Southeast Asia formulated by the government in the early 1950s was inextricably linked with the change in occupation policy toward Japan—part of the United States' global strategy—occasioned by the intensification of the Cold War. And so it was with the Japanese "Tōnan Ajia" which was in fact a translation of the English "Southeast Asia."

As we will see in the following section, in the West, too, the term "Southeast Asia" first came into general use only after World War II. Before that, there had been no appropriate name for the region as a whole, nor had any been needed, since it had sufficed for the Western nations that had colonized the region to devise names for their own territories. It is generally accepted that the English term came into use after the Allied Powers established the South East Asia Command in Colombo, Ceylon, in 1943 because of the need to deal with the region as a whole for reasons of military strategy in order to liberate the territories occupied by the Japanese military during the war.

In addition to its appearance in the context of compulsory education, "Tōnan Ajia" as a translation of "Southeast Asia" gradually came into general use in the 1950s; and in the 1960s, with Japan's increasing economic involvement with Southeast Asia, it rapidly became the established name for the region. Most Japanese regard "Tōnan Ajia" as a new term that became current in the postwar period. It is important to realize, however, that, aside from children educated after the war, it was not actually a new term to most Japanese (even if many had forgotten that fact). From around the end of World War I until the beginning of World War II, the term was used consistently in the teaching of elementary school geography, which means that all Japanese educated in the interwar period should have remembered encountering the term at least once. This leads to the conclusion that the Japanese, unlike people in Western countries, had formed some kind of regional concept of Southeast Asia as early as the post–World War I period.

Before discussing this regional concept, however, we should define what we mean by "region." Actually, it is not as easy as one might think to formulate a definition that is both objective and workable. That is because the concept of region is itself somewhat arbitrary. Thinking of regions in terms of two fairly commonsensical concepts—"real regions," or areas classified by type of natural environment, cultural pattern, stage of social and economic development, and so on, as is done in the study of geography, and "nominal regions," areas determined by national borders and other artificial boundaries[5]—does nothing to solve this problem, since regions in these senses do not actually exist as clearly demarcated areas, much less as inherently unified organic wholes.[6] Although scholarship naturally requires defining regions in as theoretically consistent and rigorous a manner as possible, the fact remains that regions can be demarcated in any way that suits one's specific criteria and purpose. For example, formal political territories, whose nominal borders have been defined for convenience' sake or have been contrived, such as those of most countries of the world, have no basis for reference except as historical realities.[7]

---

[5] For a discussion of "real regions" and "nominal regions," see Osamu Nishikawa, *Jimbun chirigaku nyūmon: Shisōteki kōsatsu* [An Introduction to descriptive geography: A philosophical approach] (Tokyo: Tokyo Daigaku Shuppankai, 1985), pp. 128–32.

[6] Ibid., p. 125.

[7] Ibid., p. 129.

Table 1. References to Southeast Asia in Titles in British Library Subject Indexes

Unit: No. titles

	Asia	Orient	Central Asia	Far East	SEA[a]	Country name	Other[b]	EA, WA, SA, NA, SWA[c]
–1880	35	3	16	2	1	2	0	5
1881–1900	29	4	22	0	0	5	1	2
1901–1905	17	0	4	0	0	1	0	0
1906–1910	5	3	4	0	0	8	0	0
1911–1915	7	1	4	0	0	2	1	2
1916–1920	10	14	5	2	0	0	2	3
1921–1925	22	17	7	7	0	3	1	6
1926–1930	21	34	6	11	0	11	1	9
1931–1935	57	39	10	17	0	11	3	3
1936–1940	36	50	3	40	2	15	2	4
1941–1945	7	10	0	16	3	2	2	4
1946–1950	35	34	2	28	11	11	1	11

[a] "SEA" includes South East Asia, Southeast Asia, Southeastern Asia, Südostasien.

[b] "Other" includes Vorderasien, Morgenland, Moslem Asia, the Tropics, Monsoon Asia, East Indies, Vorderen Orient, Equatorial, Tropical Far East, Pacific, etc.

[c] EA: East Asia; WA: West Asia; SA: South Asia; NA: North Asia; SWA: South West Asia.

Sources: R. A. Peddie, *Subject Index of Books Published before 1880* (London: Grafton, 1933, 1935, 1939, 1948); British Museum, *Subject Index of Modern Books Acquired* (London: The Trustee of the British Museum, 1961); G. K. Fortescue, *Subject Index of the Modern Works Added to the Library of the British Museum* (London: H. Pordes, 1965, 1968).

region included some of the continental areas of present-day Southeast Asia: Burma, Assam, Cambodia, and Cochinchina.[18]

In the mid-1930s, the German economist C. J. Pelzer used the term "Südostasien."[19] His concept of the region, which included India, Ceylon, Burma, Malaya, Sumatra, Java, and Guangdong and Fujian in southern China, was much broader than today's.[20] It has also been pointed out that the ethnologist Robert Heine-Geldern used this term in 1923 and the geographer Alfred Hettner used it in *Die Geographie, Ihre Geschichte, Ihr Wesen, und Ihre Methoden* in 1926.[21]

Use of the term "Southeast Asia" increased rapidly in the 1946–1950 period. The British Library subject index for the 1951–1955 period added "South East Asia" to the subcategories under "Asia" (the others were "Near East & Middle East," "Central Asia," and "Far East"), an indication that it had become an established term.[22] This subcategory has been retained down to the present.

[18] Yano, ed., *Tōnan Ajia gaku*, vol. 2, p. 24.

[19] C. J. Pelzer, *Die Arbeiterwanderungen in Südostasien: Ein wirtschafts- und bevölkerungs geographische Untersuchung* (Hamburg: Friederichsen, de Gruyter & Co., 1935).

[20] Ibid., p. 113.

[21] Watanabe, *Sekai chiri*, p. 4. It has also been pointed out (Yano, ed., *Tōnan Ajia gaku*, vol. 1, p. 29) that the English term "Southeast Asia" was used occasionally in research reports of the Institute of Pacific Relations in the latter half of the 1930s, but I have not been able to verify this.

[22] British Museum, *Subject Index of Modern Books Acquired* (London: The Trustee of the British Museum, 1961).

The following passages from the "Editorial Note" of *Government and Nationalism in Southeast Asia* make it clear that the term as used in that book referred to the territories under Japanese occupation: "This book was completed and in proof when Japan went to war against the United States and the British and Netherlands empires. Despite the changes which the Japanese offensive in Southeast Asia is inevitably bringing to the political and economic systems of that area, it has seemed best to publish the book immediately without attempting to revise it for the day-to-day changes produced by the war. . . . Whatever the initial success of the Japanese attempts it is almost certain that far-reaching readjustments in the colonies of Southeast Asia will be necessary after the war. . . . For that reason alone there is urgent need for careful study of the situation as it existed and was developing just before the Japanese attack."[23]

That this region was not conceptualized as Southeast Asia from the outset, however, can be seen from the fact that the original name chosen for what became the South East Asia Command was the East Asia Command. The first draft of the plan to set up the command, dated June 21, 1943, was titled "The Organization of Command in East Asia: Memorandum by the Prime Minister and Minister of Defence," reflecting the regional concept prevailing in Britain at the time.[24] In the first revised draft, dated July 1, only ten days later, the name was changed to one that would apply specifically to the Southeast Asian territories under Japanese occupation.[25] Although the third revised draft was adopted on August 31, with no change in name, the following annex to the first draft was retained unchanged:

Proposed Boundaries of East Asia Command
1. Eastern Boundary
From the point where the frontier between China and Indo-China reaches the Gulf of Tonkin, southwards along the coasts of Indo-China, Thailand and Malaya to Singapore; from Singapore south to the North coast of Sumatra; thence round the East coast of Sumatra (leaving the Sunda Strait to the Eastward of the line) to a point on the coast of Sumatra at longitude 104 degrees East; thence South to latitude 08 degrees South; thence South-Easterly towards Onslow, Australia, and, on reaching longitude 110 degrees East, due South along that meridian.
2. Northern Boundary
From the point where the frontier between China and Indo-China reaches the Gulf of Tonkin, westwards along the Chinese frontier to a point on the Assam/Tibet frontier to be settled between the Supreme Commander East Asia and Commander-in-Chief, India; thence to the coast of Bengal along the western boundary of a zone in Assam and Eastern Bengal which is to be mutually decided by the Supreme Commander and Commander-in-

---

[23] Emerson, Mills, and Thompson, *Government and Nationalism*, pp. xi–xii.

[24] "The Organization of Command in East Asia: Memorandum by the Prime Minister and Minister of Defence," CO 968/11/8 (21/June/1943 [W.P. 43-253]), Public Record Office.

[25] "The Organization of Command in South-East Asia: Memorandum by the Prime Minister and Minister of Defence," CO 968/11/8 (1/July/1943 [W.P. 43-253, Revised Draft]), Public Record Office. The second and third revised drafts, dated August 1 and August 31, respectively, retained this title.

Chief, India. Thence around the coasts of India and Persia to meridian 60 degrees East.

3. Western Boundary

Southward along meridian 60 degrees East to Albatross Island, thence South-Eastward to exclude Rodriguez Island and thence due southward.[26]

That this region was renamed "Southeast Asia" is understandable, in view of Western geographical attitudes. Both "Southeast Asia" and the nineteenth-century "Southeastern Asia" referred, naturally, to the southeastern part of Asia; and to Westerners, long accustomed to calling the region centered on Turkestan "Central Asia," Southeast Asia would clearly refer to the portion of Asia southeast of that region.[27]

The Allies' renaming the areas under Japanese occupation "Southeast Asia" is highly significant for another reason, however. As we will see in the next section, the Japanese had themselves called the same region "Southeast Asia" (*Tōnan Ajiya*) since late in the second decade of this century.

II. Formation of the Regional Concept of Southeast Asia During World War I

If the circumstances surrounding the adoption of the term "Southeast Asia" in the West were as outlined above, it may seem rather startling to state that *Tōnan Ajia*, which appears to be a literal translation of the English "Southeast Asia" and indeed looks similar to *Tōnan Ajiya*, was already established as a regional concept in prewar Japan. But that is the fact. What was the process by which this came about?

1. The Regional Concept of Nan'yō (the South Seas)

At first the region was known to the Japanese as *nan'yō*, or "South Seas." The origin of this term is not clear. There is no question that the word *nan'yō* itself is the Japanese reading of the Chinese *nanyang*, but even in China the use of *nanyang* was relatively recent in comparison with the use of such ancient terms as *hainan zhuguo* (literally, "countries south of the sea") and *nanman* (literally, "southern barbarians"), and is believed to date to around the middle of the Ming dynasty (1368–1644).[28] And of course its use to refer to the present-day region of Southeast Asia was a great deal more recent than that. Though some instances of *beiyang* (northern seas) in reference to the area of the Pacific north of the mouth of the Yangtze and *nanyang* in reference to the Pacific south of that boundary are seen in sources from

---

[26] Annex 1, "Proposed Boundaries of East Asia Command," CO 968/11/8 (21/June/1943 [W.P. 43-253]), Public Record Office.

[27] The British Library subject indexes have included the subcategory "Central Asia" since 1881.

[28] Hiroshi Kimura, "16 seiki izen, Chūgokujin no nankai chiiki ni kansuru chiikiteki chishiki: Chūgokujin no Tōnan Ajia ni taisuru shiken" [Chinese regional knowledge of the southern region before the sixteenth century: Chinese perceptions of Southeast Asia], in *Chiri no shisō* [The philosophy of geography], ed. Kyoto Daigaku Chirigaku Kyōshitsu [Kyoto University Geography Department] (Kyoto: Chijin Shobō, 1982), p. 116.

the Qing dynasty (1644–1912),[29] the latter term did not necessarily designate present-day Southeast Asia. From the Ming dynasty onward, the Chinese divided the sea route to southern Asia into two: the route east of Borneo, usually called *dongyang* (eastern seas), and that west of Borneo, usually called *xiyang* (western seas). Thus the Philippines belonged to the "eastern seas," whereas the "western seas" included the Indochinese Peninsula, Java and the other islands of the East Indies, the Malay Peninsula, and the area stretching from India to Arabia and Africa.[30] One example of this usage is the description of Cheng Ho's voyage as *xia xiyang* (going to the western seas) in Ming histories.

If we believe Li Zhangzhuan's statement, in his 1938 *Nanyangshi zheyao* [Outline of the history of the South Seas], that "in the last twenty years the name 'South Seas' has come into general use,"[31] we see that this term may even have been reimported to China from Japan. The reason "South Seas" became popular in Japan shortly after World War I is of course that that was the period when Japan first became fully engaged with the South Seas and, as I shall discuss below, when the regional concept of Southeast Asia was formed. It is also of interest that the same book refers to the Indochinese Peninsula, the Malay Peninsula, and the East Indies as the "rear South Seas" and to Australia, New Zealand, and the Pacific islands as the "outer South Seas," using the Japanese coinages *ura nan'yō* and *soto nan'yō*, respectively,[32] a fact that strengthens the supposition that the South Seas as a regional concept in modern China was a reimport from Japan.

The word *nan'yō* was already in use in Japan in the late Tokugawa period (1603–1868). Toshiaki Honda's *Seiiki monogatari* [Tales of the western regions], published in 1798, stated: "In former times Japanese ships, too, sailed from Zhejiang and Guangdong in China as far as *Annam, Cochinchina, Champa, and the islands of the South Seas* [*nan'yō*] to trade and serve the government, without having to wait for foreign ships to come to Japan."[33] The South Seas were mentioned parallel with the countries of Indochina. Elsewhere the same book referred to the East Indies as *tō tenjiku nan'yō* (East Indies South Seas).[34] In his 1801 *Chōkiron*, Honda wrote, discussing the sailor Magotarō, who had been stranded on Borneo after setting sail from Mindanao on the *Isemaru* in the Meiwa era (1764–1772): "Everyone knows the story of how the ship on which Magotarō, a sailor from Karadomariura in Chikuzen [modern Fukuoka Prefecture], was sailing . . . *drifted to the big port of Banjarmasin on Borneo, in the South Seas* [*nan'yō*] . . . , and how [he] was able to return to Nagasaki nine years later on the orders of the general of the Dutch House in the great port of Batavia, Java."[35] From this we can tell that

[29] Inazō Nitobe, "Nan'yō no keizaiteki kachi" [The economic value of the South Seas], in *Nitobe hakase shokumin seisaku kōgi oyobi rombun shū* [Lectures and papers on colonial policy by Dr. Nitobe], ed. Tadao Yanaihara (Tokyo: Iwanami Shoten, 1943), p. 278.

[30] Li Zhangzhuan, *Nan'yōshi nyūmon* [Introduction to the history of the South Seas], trans. and rev. Keiichi Imai (Tokyo: Ashikabi Shobō, 1942), p. 16.

[31] Ibid., p. 15.

[32] Ibid., p. 16.

[33] Akihiro Tsukatani and Seiji Kuranami, eds. *Honda Toshiaki, Kaiho Seiryō* [Toshiaki Honda and Seiryō Kaiho], vol. 44 of *Nihon shisō taikei* [Outline of Japanese Thought], ed. Saburō Ienaga et al. (Tokyo: Iwanami Shoten, 1970), p. 102.

[34] Ibid., p. 117.

[35] Ibid., pp. 197–98.

Honda's regional concept of the South Seas included at least the island territories of Southeast Asia, such as Borneo and Java.

The Japanese concept of the South Seas was rather amorphous, however, differing from person to person and period to period. At first the islands of the Pacific were the focus—as for Southeast Asia, only insular Southeast Asia was included—as we have seen in the above passage from Honda's writings. The distinction between continental and insular Southeast Asia was based on contemporary Western geographical knowledge, which classified the former as Asia and the latter as Oceania. That not only Honda but also other Japanese of the Tokugawa period had considerable knowledge of world geography can be seen easily from the spread of maps modeled on Matteo Ricci's "Mappa Mundi," which were first produced in Japan in 1645, and from the so-called Katsuragawa map, Hoshū Katsuragawa's 1794 reproduction and translation of a new map imported from Russia.

The concept of the South Seas that began to attract attention around the middle of the Meiji era (1868–1912), amid excitement over the idea of "southward advance," indicated the same region as that in the Tokugawa period. As far as I know, beginning with Jūgō Sugiura's use of the expression *nan'yō tatōhin* (the myriad isles and strands of the South Seas) in his 1886 *Hankai yume monogatari* [The fantastic tale of Fan Kuai], Shigetaka Shiga, Ukichi Taguchi, Teifū Suganuma, Tōru Hattori, Tsunenori Suzuki, and other contemporary advocates of southward advance generally meant by "South Seas" the oceanic region including the southwestern Pacific islands and insular Southeast Asia. Shiga in particular, through his 1887 work *Nan'yō jiji* [Current affairs in the South Seas], helped popularize the term "South Seas" and contributed significantly to establishing the concept of the South Seas as a distinctive region differing from both the West (*seiyō*, lit. West Seas) and the East (*tōyō*, lit. East Seas).[36]

The important point here is that, spearheaded by the Meiji-era advocates of southward advance, Japanese intellectuals who had been knowledgeable about world geography since Tokugawa times conceived of the South Seas as a region (Oceania) distinct from Asia and did not regard what we call Southeast Asia as a single region. They drew a firm line between today's three countries of Indochina, Thailand, Burma, and the rest of continental Southeast Asia on the one hand and the Philippines, Indonesia, and the rest of insular Southeast Asia on the other. The two were perceived as two discrete spatial areas.

Yukichi Fukuzawa's famous popular geography, the best-selling *Sekai kunizukushi* [The countries of the world], published in 1869, was no exception. Fukuzawa distinguished between Asia (*Ajia shū*) and Oceania (*taiyō shū*): "In southern Asia, the Indies, bordering the ocean, are divided into west and east; . . . well-known countries here are Siam, Annam, and Burma."[37] "[In] Oceania . . . , the islands of the Pacific Ocean are myriad in number; close to the coast of southern Asia are Sumatra, Borneo, Java, the Celebes, Luzon, the Spice Islands, and New Guinea."[38] In other words, the countries in continental Southeast Asia, such as Siam, Annam, and

---

[36] Kimitada Miwa, *Shiga Shigetaka: A Meiji Japanist's View of and Actions in International Relations* (Tokyo: Institute of International Relations, Sophia University, 1970), p. 31; Yano, "Nanshin" no keifu, p. 57.

[37] Masafumi Tomita and Shun'ichi Dobashi, eds., *Fukuzawa Yukichi senshū* [Selected works of Yukichi Fukuzawa] (Tokyo: Iwanami Shoten, 1981), vol. 2, pp. 114–15.

[38] Ibid., p. 168.

Burma, were thought to belong to Asia, whereas insular Southeast Asia, including Sumatra, Borneo, Java, the Celebes, and Luzon, was regarded as belonging to Oceania.

2. WORLD WAR I AND CHANGES IN THE REGIONAL CONCEPT OF THE SOUTH SEAS: THE INNER AND OUTER SOUTH SEAS

The regional concept of the South Seas began to change after the Russo-Japanese War (1904–1905). The first change was that territories of both continental and insular Southeast Asia, under such names as Indochina and the Malay archipelago (or the East Indies archipelago), respectively, began to be classified as parts of Asia.

The preface to Yosaburō Takekoshi's 1910 best seller *Nangokuki* [Chronicle of southern lands], for example, stated that he traveled "from the islands of the Dutch East Indies through French Indochina and also to Yunnan, in China, observing some of the southern lands."[39] The book was, then, a travelogue of both continental and insular Southeast Asia. Takekoshi purposely chose the term "southern lands" (*nangoku*) instead of the more familiar "South Seas," and also used such expressions as "southern Asia" (*nampō Ajia*)[40] and "southern lands of the Malays" (*nampō Mareejin no kuni*).[41] He defined the region as follows: "It begins with British Burma in the west, stretches south through Siam and the French Indies, and ends with Singapore, at the tip of the Malay Peninsula. Beginning again with Sumatra and Java, including the islands of the Dutch Indies and the American Philippines—though there is some racial mixture—it has an area of 1,680,000 square *ri* [1 *ri* equals approximately 3.9 kilometers], even more extensive than continental China's 1,532,400 square *ri*."[42] It is worth noting that this region, combining continental and island territories, corresponded to present-day Southeast Asia.

The greatest change, however, was occasioned by World War I, which marked a major turning point in Japan's relations with Southeast Asia and in the southward-advance concept, as I have pointed out elsewhere.[43] The major feature of this change was a marked rise in interest in Southeast Asia, which was seen as the next region for Japanese expansion. The rapid penetration by Japanese goods of Southeast Asian markets, where the war had created a vacuum, and Japan's de facto possession of a number of South Pacific islands that had formerly belonged to Germany, prompting the idea of using them as a base for southward advance, led rapidly to the perception of Southeast Asia as the target of further southward advance.[44]

---

[39] Yosaburō Takekoshi, *Nangokuki* [Chronicle of southern lands] (Tokyo: Niyūsha, 1910), preface, p. 1.

[40] Ibid., p. 269.

[41] Ibid., p. 2.

[42] Ibid., p. 3.

[43] Hajime Shimizu, "Taishō shoki ni okeru nanshinron no ichi kōsatsu: Sono Ajiashugiteki hen'yō o megutte" [A consideration of the ideology of southward advance in the early Taishō era: Its Asianist transformation], *Ajia kenkyū* [Asian studies] 30, no. 1 (April 1983); Hajime Shimizu, "Nanshin-ron: Its Turning Point in World War I," *Developing Economies* 25, no. 4 (December 1987).

[44] Sumio Hatano, "Nihon kaigun to 'nanshin': Sono seisaku to riron no shiteki tenkai" [The Japanese navy and "southward advance": The historical development of its policy and theory], in *Ryōtaisenkanki no Nihon Tōnan Ajia kankei no shosō* [Aspects of Japan's relations with South-

This was the viewpoint of the Japanese navy, which, citing the Anglo-Japanese Alliance, entered the war against Germany in the Pacific in September 1914. Seeking to gain the military advantage, between the end of September and the middle of October—a little over two weeks—the navy occupied Jaluit, Kusaie, Ponape, Truk, Yap, Palau, Angaur, Saipan, and other islands.[45] The navy's underlying consideration, however, was the importance of these islands as bases for future advance into Southeast Asia, New Guinea, and other parts of the "outer South Seas" (*soto nan'yō*). "The Future of the Newly Occupied South Seas Territories," a Navy Ministry war document, stated: "The occupied South Seas territories are also in the most important position *as bases linking Japan and the Philippines in the East Indies, New Guinea, and the Polynesian islands.* Even if they yield no direct profit, surely they must be carefully protected *as steppingstones to the treasure-trove of the South Seas.*"[46]

The navy's concept of the Pacific islands as bases for southward advance and its view of Southeast Asia as the next target of advance had a great impact on civilian advocates of southward advance, most of whom were influenced by it. Sohō Tokutomi, for example, wrote in the foreword to the book *South Seas,* edited by Sakuzo Yoshino and published at the end of 1915, the year "The Future of the Newly Occupied South Seas Territories" was issued by the Navy:

The German South Seas may not be large in area, but in terms of geographical position they constitute steppingstones linking America and Asia or America and Australia and are indeed the key to the Pacific. In terms of economic position, too, they should not be underestimated as sources of raw materials. . . . As a result of the great European conflict, these colonies have now become Japanese-occupied territories. *The foundation for future Japanese ventures in the South Seas has already been laid.*

In short, *economically speaking the South Seas are blessed with natural resources, and politically speaking they are an area of contention among the powers; not only the Netherlands, Britain, and Germany but also France, Spain, and America have moved in.* They are determined not to lose what land they already possess, be it a single island, and to gain possession of land they do not yet hold, even the tiniest island. This is the present situation. For Japan, given domestic circumstances in which the population is growing inordinately every year, and also given its geographical relationship, the South Seas are the ideal area for future expansion.[47]

---

east Asia in the interwar period] ed. Hajime Shimizu (Tokyo: Ajia Keizai Kenkyūsho [Institute of Developing Economies], 1986), p. 213.

[45] "Nan'yō senryō shotō shisei hōshin" [Administrative policy for the occupied South Seas islands], a navy document dated January 9, 1915, states that "the primary objective of all policy measures [is] military advantage." Navy Ministry, "Taishō sen'eki senji shorui" [War documents of the Taishō war], vol. 16, National Institute for Defense Studies. For a discussion of the sequence of events at that time, see Masaaki Gabe, "Nihon no Mikuroneshia senryō to 'nanshin'" [Japan's occupation of Micronesia and southward advance], *Hōgaku kenkyū* [Journal of law, politics and sociology] 55, no. 7 (July 1982); 55, no 8 (August 1982).

[46] Navy Ministry, "Taishō sen'eki," vol. 18.

[47] Sakuzō Yoshino, ed., *Nan'yō* [The South Seas] (Tokyo: Min'yūsha, 1915), foreword by Sohō Tokutomi, pp. 3–5.

These developments exerted a decisive influence on the regional concept of the South Seas, as well. The former German islands of Micronesia (the Mariana, Caroline, and Marshall islands) occupied by Japan were declared C-category mandated territories by the League of Nations after the war. Whether the Japanese attitude of *uchi* (inside) and *soto* (outside) had anything to do with the matter is not clear, but these Pacific island groups, which had become de facto Japanese territories, came to be called "the inner South Seas" (*uchi nan'yō*) or "the rear South Seas" (*ura nan'yō*), whereas the rest of Southeast Asia was known as "the outer South Seas" (*soto nan'yō*) or "the frontal South Seas" (*omote nan'yō*) and was regarded as the target of advance and expansion in the near future.

The outer (or frontal) South Seas were defined as follows:

> Frontal South Seas, briefly, is the name for the myriad islands large and small and the portion of the continent within the tropical zone *of the southeastern part of Asia*. Specifically, it includes the Philippine Islands; the Dutch East Indies—that includes Java, West Borneo, the Celebes, Sumatra, the Lesser Sundas, the Moluccas, New Guinea; British Borneo; the Malay Peninsula; Siam; and French Indochina. It is the overall name for a region with an area of 3.8 million square kilometers and a population of more than 100 million.[48]

The formation of the regional concept of the outer (frontal) South Seas, more or less equivalent to present-day Southeast Asia, is not the only important point. There is another little-known but extremely important fact: after World War I the term that Japanese elementary school geography textbooks began to use to refer to this region was not "South Seas" or "outer South Seas" or "frontal South Seas" but *Tōnan Ajiya* "Southeast Asia," the very same term used today. This new name for the outer (frontal) South Seas made its first appearance in volume two, chapter eight, paragraph five, of the third-phase state geography textbook, *Jinjō shōgaku chirisho* [Elementary school geography], published in February 1919.[49]

The use of this term was motivated by the government's view of the region as most important for postwar Japan's economic expansion and external policy. It was after World War I that the region was first earmarked as important in terms of resource and market policies in connection with the development of Japan's heavy chemical industries; and since the primary objective of compulsory education was to create loyal imperial subjects and workers who would contribute to economic growth and modernization, it is not at all surprising that elementary school geography education should have been used to inform the populace of the government's policy intentions and to secure support for them.

---

[48] Kinsuke Matsumura, *Minami ni mo seimeisen ari* [The lifeline in the south] (Tokyo: Moriyama Shoten, 1933), p. 2. It has also been pointed out that use of the term "inner South Seas" in reference to Micronesia began around 1935. Hisao Hayashi, "Nan'yō guntō no gensei ni tsuite" [On present conditions in the South Sea islands] (Nampō Keizai Chōsakai [Southern Region Economic Survey Group], 1936), p. 5.

[49] The third-phase state geography textbook was published as part of the revision of all state textbooks carried out in the Taishō era (1912–1926). Volume one was published in March 1918.

3. Formation of the Regional Concept of Southeast Asia, *Tōnan Ajiya*

Since the beginning of the modern period geography education, reflecting a surge of nationalism, was strongly colored by foreign-policy considerations. There was a tendency for all aspects of the geography of other countries to be discussed from Japan's viewpoint alone.[50] Especially after World War I, however, a marked change in the focus of geography education occurred. There was a subtle deviation from the doctrine of free trade and external cooperation, the idea of mutual accommodation and complementarity of countries, that had been emphasized in geography textbooks until around the time of the Russo-Japanese War,[51] and a nationalistic and expansionist tinge became noticeable.

Of course "the great upheaval . . . in the world economy" and "the reorganization of the political map"[52] brought about by World War I required a change in geography education. The most pressing practical issue had to do with the Japanese overseas expansion. That the perception of geography education as a prime necessity for the sake of Japanese overseas expansion was the government's basic position at the time is demonstrated clearly by the following passage in a book by Heisuke Yamabe, a Ministry of Education textbook editorial supervisor, which was published not long after the war:

> Japan's fortunes have risen extremely rapidly. Before the war Japan was already one of the world's eight great powers, and because Germany, Austria, and Russia have fallen behind, it is now one of the world's five great

[50] For example, the first page of the preface to Chiri Kyōju Kenkyūkai [Geography Education Study Group], ed., *Chūtō shin chiri kyōkasho: Gaikoku no bu* [New intermediate geography textbook: Foreign countries], vol. 1 (Tokyo: Yoshikawa Kōbunkan, October 1903), states: "This book does not take the position that the scope of Japan's geography is strictly limited to Japan. *We consider the places where Japanese people are active to lie within the scope of Japanese geography. Foreign countries' geography, as well, is all discussed from the standpoint of Japan,* and we have made a special effort to describe the nature of Japanese people's overseas activities. Therefore, wherever there are Japanese people we have invariably noted their number, whether large or small, and have explained the major occupations in which they are engaged." The first page of the preface to Sanseidō Henshūjo, ed., *Saishin gaikoku chiri* [Recent foreign geography] (Tokyo: Sanseidō, January 1905) specifies the following three objectives of geography education: to "teach world geography, centered on Japan"; to "teach [other countries'] relationship to Japan"; and to "teach the world situation, including recent international relations."

[51] For example, the following passage is found in Sanseidō, ed., *Saishin gaikoku chiri*, pp. 1–2: "There are many countries in the world besides Japan; they have different natural environments, and their people's manners, customs, occupations, and products are different, as well. Country A's products are the raw materials of country B; eastern countries' goods fulfill the demand of western countries, so that [different countries] complement one another. For example, Japan's raw silk thread becomes silk in France; Indian cotton comes to Japan and becomes cotton thread. Japan's tea goes to America and becomes a beverage; Indochina's rice comes to Japan and becomes food. Japan's matches go to Oriental and South Seas countries, where they serve to light fires; America's oil comes to Japan and lights up the night.

"Not only products but also people come and go. Japanese catching salmon in America, Japanese gathering pearls in the South Seas, Japanese producing sugar in Hawaii: Japanese people engaged in various kinds of work are found here and there around the world. A considerable number of foreigners from various countries have also come to Japan and live here. The world is thus a common community, and Japan is part of it. Therefore if one hopes to understand Japan's true value and to raise Japan's status, one must study world geography."

[52] Heisuke Yamabe, *Taisengo ni okeru chiri kyōju no kakushin (Gaikoku no bu)* [The postwar reform of geography education: Foreign countries] (Tokyo: Meiji Tosho, 1921), pp. 1–2.

powers. As Japan's position in the world rises, it is necessary of course to improve the people's knowledge of geography. Moreover, needless to say peaceful overseas expansion is Japan's national policy. *It is hardly necessary to tediously lecture this growth-minded populace about the importance of a knowledge of geography.* It is our earnest hope that as soon as possible all the people will understand, assist, and support overseas expansion ventures, as they did the military during the war, and will await [the return of] those who have been successful overseas in the same way that they would the triumphal return of heroes.[53]

As this passage indicates, the prime objective of geography education and of textbook compilation, given imperial Japan's rapid development since the war, was to increase the Japanese public's understanding of the importance of overseas expansion and to motivate people to venture forth "to the South Seas, to South Africa."[54] One key region to which overseas expansion was encouraged was the South Seas, especially the so-called Malay archipelago, centered on the Dutch East Indies and the Philippines. This is clear from Yamabe's recommendation that textbooks include discussion of the way in which "Japan in recent years has begun focusing attention on the policy of expansion in the South Seas, and in regard to these islands [the Malay archipelago] . . . has opened up routes to the South Seas, . . . [and] therefore mutual trade has been improving."[55]

The demands of the period led to concern that geography textbooks devote special care to discussion of the outer South Seas, particularly the Malay archipelago. This is the context in which the term *Tōnan Ajiya*, "Southeast Asia," appeared in volume two of the third-phase state geography textbook, *Jinjō shōgaku chirisho*, which had been heavily revised because of changes both inside and outside Japan after World War I.

Many geography textbooks were published following the promulgation of the Education Order (Gakusei) of 1872, but the early texts, such as the 1874 *Bankoku chishiryaku* [Outline of world geography] and the 1880 *Shōgaku chishi* [Elementary school geography], like Honda's *Seiiki monogatari* and Fukuzawa's *Sekai kunizukushi*, basically relied on Western geography texts and generally divided present-day Southeast Asia into two parts, putting continental Southeast Asia into Asia and insular Southeast Asia into Oceania.[56]

---

[53] Ibid., p. 3.

[54] This is clear from the following passage in a middle school textbook published shortly after the war: "Since the war the Empire's prosperity has increased rapidly, and external relations have also grown closer and become extremely important. Whether it be the South Seas, South Africa, or China and Siberia in the East, there are more and more excellent educational materials to help foster growth-minded people. This is the second point we have borne in mind in compiling this book." Manjirō Yamagami, *Shinshiki sekai chiri* [New world geography], vol. 1 (Tokyo: Dai Nippon Tosho, February 1919), pp. 1–2.

[55] Yamabe, *Taisengo*, pp. 158–59.

[56] Japan's first elementary school textbook of world geography, *Bankoku chishiryaku*, relied on geography texts by the Americans W. Colton and S. A. Mitchell and the British Goldsmith and was compiled by Tokyo Normal School (teacher training school) and published by the Ministry of Education. The following passages describe Southeast Asia: "Asia . . . : Further India . . . includes Annam, Siam, Burma, British Burma, Laos, and the Malay Peninsula." Tokiomi Kaigo, ed., *Nihon kyōkasho taikei: Kindaihen, chiri ichi* [An outline of Japanese textbooks: The early modern period, geography 1], vol. 15 of *Nihon kyōkasho taikei*, ed. Tokiomi Kaigo (Tokyo:

This treatment was followed until around the time of the Sino-Japanese War (1894–1895). *Bankoku chiri shoho* [Beginning world geography], a textbook for upper elementary school use approved by the Ministry of Education and published in 1894, just before the outbreak of that war, included the following passages: "Asia . . . : Annam, Siam, etc. . . . : This is the overall name for Annam and its neighbors to the west, the countries of Siam, Burma, and so on, which Westerners call Further India."[57] "Oceania . . . : Oceania is the overall name for the continent of Australia and the nearby islands, which are located in the southeast seas of Asia. It is divided into three parts, Australasia, Malaysia, and Polynesia. . . . The islands near the Asian continent are called Malaysia or the East Indies. Luzon, Borneo, Sumatra, Java, and the Celebes belong to it."[58] As we see, continental Southeast Asia was still considered to belong to Asia and insular Southeast Asia to Oceania.

This began to change after the Elementary School Order of August 20, 1900, when all ordinary elementary schools were made four-year institutions. Volume three of *Shōgaku chiri* [Elementary school geography], published late that year, stated in the section "The world" [*Bankoku no bu*], chapter one, "Asia" [*Ajiya shū*]: "Indochina . . . : (1) French Indochina . . . (2) Siam . . . (3) Burma (British) . . . (4) the Malay Peninsula" and "East Indies . . . : (1) the Sunda Islands . . . (2) the Philippine Islands,"[59] thus placing both continental Southeast Asia, under the name Indochina, and insular Southeast Asia, under the name East Indies, in Asia. This classification was close to the one with which we are familiar today, but it must be noted that, although both continental and insular Southeast Asia were associated with Asia, the two parts were not considered to constitute a single region but were regarded as separate regional entities. No change in the handling of Southeast Asia was seen following the inauguration of the system of state textbooks (*kokutei kyōkasho*) in 1903. In both the first-phase state geography textbook, *Shōgaku chiri*, published in October 1903, and the second-phase state geography textbook, *Jinjō shōgaku chiri*, published in November 1910, Southeast Asia, divided into the Indochinese Peninsula and the Malay archipelago, was handled perfunctorily.[60]

Kōdansha, 1965), p. 227. "Oceania . . . is divided into three parts. One is called Malaysia (Luzon, the Celebes, Borneo, Java, and Sumatra). In other words, these are the East Indies. Another part is called Australia, and the other is called Polynesia." Ibid., p. 268. *Shōgaku chishi*, compiled by Tsunanori Namma and printed by the Ministry of Education in March 1880, contains the following passages: "Asia . . . : Its countries include Japan, China, Korea, Asiatic Russia, Asiatic Turkey, Arabia, Persia, Afghanistan, India, *Burma, Siam, Annam, and others.*" Ibid., p. 443. "Oceania . . . can be divided broadly into three parts, Malaysia, South Asia, and Polynesia. . . . Malaysia is divided into Borneo, Sumatra, Java, the Celebes, the Philippines, and so on. Because it is mostly below the equator, it is very hot." Ibid., p. 491.

[57] Tokiomi Kaigo, ed., *Nihon kyōkasho taikei: Kindaihen, chiri ni* [An outline of Japanese textbooks: The early modern period, geography two], vol. 16 of *Nihon kyōkasho taikei*, ed. Tokiomi Kaigo (Tokyo: Kōdansha, 1965), p. 129. In accordance with the Elementary School Order of 1886, the textbook authorization system was inaugurated the following year. *Bankoku chiri shoho*, edited by Gakkai Shishinsha and published in January 1894, was the first geography textbook for upper elementary school to be authorized by the Ministry of Education.

[58] Ibid., p. 158.

[59] Ibid., p. 242. Volume three of *Shōgaku chiri*, compiled by Fukyūsha Henshūjo and published by Fukyūsha in October 1900, is typical of the geography textbooks published during the later textbook-authorization period.

[60] For the relevant passages in the first-phase state geography textbook, see Ministry of Education, *Shōgaku chiri*, vol. 3 (Tokyo: Nihon Shoseki, November 1903), pp. 23–26. For the relevant

The first major revision was seen in volume two of the third-phase state geography textbook, *Jinjō shōgaku chirisho*. Not only were continental and insular Southeast Asia discussed together, under the heading "Asia" (*Ajiya shū*), but also, surprisingly, were even given the name Southeast Asia (*Tōnan Ajiya*).[61] This textbook was in use for seventeen years, longer than any other state geography textbook. The fourth-phase state geography textbook, published in February 1936, and the fifth-phase state geography textbook, published in March 1939, continued to use the term "Southeast Asia," and discussion of the region became more detailed over the years.[62]

The term "Southeast Asia" also began to appear in middle school geography textbooks during this period. Volume one of *Santei chirigaku kyōkasho: Gaikoku no bu* [Third revised geography textbook: Foreign countries], by Takuji Ogawa, published in October 1917, defined "southern Asia" as including "most of the region along the Indian Ocean and *the islands of Southeast Asia*," and explained that "included are the Indian and Indochinese peninsulas and the Malay archipelago."[63] The fourth edition of this textbook, published the same year as the third-phase state geography textbook, as well as later editions, retained the term "Southeast Asia."[64]

---

passages in the second-phase state geography textbook, see Kaigo, ed., *Nihon kyōkasho taikei*, vol. 16, p. 442.

[61] About 440 characters were devoted to the discussion of Southeast Asia in volume two of the third-phase state geography textbook. Kaigo, ed., *Nihon kyōkasho taikei*, vol. 16, pp. 472–73. The term began to appear in general books, magazines, and so forth, only in the 1930s. As far as I can ascertain, the earliest appearances were in Shizuo Nonami, *Tōnan Ajia shokoku* [The countries of Southeast Asia] (Tokyo: Heibonsha, 1933) and Nanshin Nan'yō Keizai Kenkyūkai [Study Group on Economies of South China and the South Seas], "Tōnan Ashia oyobi Mareeshia ni okeru nōgyō no hattatsu" [The development of agriculture in Southeast Asia and Malaysia], *Nanshi nan'yō kenkyū* [Studies on South China and the South Seas], no. 19 (April 1934), a journal published by the Taipei College of Commerce. I am indebted for this information to Akihiro Yoshihisa of the National Diet Library.

[62] The fourth-phase state geography textbook devoted 560 characters to discussion of Southeast Asia and included four illustrations. Kaigo, ed., *Nihon kyōkasho taikei*, vol. 16, pp. 554–55. The fifth-phase state geography textbook had 640 characters and four illustrations. Ibid., p. 646.

[63] Takuji Ogawa, *Santei chirigaku kyōkasho: Gaikoku no bu* [Third revised geography textbook: Foreign countries], vol. 1 (Tokyo: Fuzambō, October 1917), p. 100. Another middle school textbook published the same year stated: "The Malay archipelago, across the South China Sea, [is] a string of islands forming the outer rampart of *Southeast Asia*." Hisagorō Ōzeki, *Chūtō kyōiku chiri kyōkasho: Gaikokuhen* [Intermediate education geography textbook: Foreign countries], vol. 1 (Tokyo: Meguro Shoten, October 1917), p. 84.

[64] The first edition of this textbook was published in October 1913 under the title *Chirigaku kyōkasho: Gaikoku no bu* [Geography textbook: Foreign countries], vol. 1. In both this edition and the second edition, published in October 1915, the equivalent passage reads: "Southern Asia (most of the region along the Indian Ocean and the islands *in the Pacific Ocean*): Included are the Indian and Indochinese peninsulas and the Malay archipelago" (p. 21 in both editions). After its first appearance in the third edition, the term "Southeast Asia" was retained in the fourth edition (December 1919, p. 98), the fifth edition (January 1923, p. 98), the sixth edition (January 1925, p. 98), and the seventh edition (February 1928, p. 100). However, this was not necessarily the academically accepted term. Ogawa himself was aware that this textbook was written in a somewhat popular manner. To rectify this he wrote *Chūtō chirigaku: Gaikoku no bu* [Intermediate geography: Foreign countries] (Tokyo: Fuzambō, November 1921), a more rigorously theoretical textbook based on Western geographical research. In the preface to the fifth edition of *Chirigaku kyōkasho*, he explained why he had done so: "Recently, following the world war, international

The fact that Southeast Asia came to be perceived as a single regional bloc after World War I, just as it is today, is significant. What, then, was the regional concept of Southeast Asia, *Tōnan Ajiya*, presented in post–World War I geography textbooks?

III. FEATURES OF THE REGIONAL CONCEPT OF SOUTHEAST ASIA

As we have already seen, before World War II "Southeast Asia" was not yet an established term in the West. Therefore *Tōnan Ajiya*, the Japanese equivalent, could not have been a translation of the English term but was the expression of an original, autonomous Japanese concept. This is clear from the revision prospectus for the third-phase state geography textbook, which made the point that Southeast Asia was not an established, internationally recognized regional concept like North and South America or Central Asia but was a concept used in the textbook only for the sake of convenience: "Names of foreign countries written in *kana* [phonetic syllables] have been underlined with a double line, as before. In the case of place names written in a mixture of *kana* and *kanji* [ideographs], instead of only the *kana* portion being underlined, as before, the entire name has been underlined, as in 'Amerika gasshūkoku' [United States of America], 'Chū Ajiya' [Central Asia], 'Kita Amerika shū' [North America], and 'Minami Amerika shū' [South America]. However, in the case of the name 'Tōnan Ajiya,' because it is used only for the sake of geographical convenience, as before only 'Ajiya' has been underlined—'Tōnan Ajiya'—to distinguish it from such place names as Chū Ajiya and Minami Amerika."[65]

This proviso indicates, at the least, that "Southeast Asia" was not an established term in the Western geography texts that were the models for Japanese textbooks. But the fact that the term was officially sanctioned for use in the state textbook, which devoted a separate section to the region, underscores most eloquently that Southeast Asia was an original, autonomous regional concept of post–World War I Japan.

Why, then, did the Japanese name this region Southeast Asia? There are two questions to be considered: Why did the Japanese consolidate continental and insular Southeast Asia, which had formerly been treated as separate regions? And why did they give this consolidated region the name Southeast Asia?

Naturally, the regional concept of Southeast Asia combines the directional concept of southeast and the spatial concept of Asia, indicating a part of Asia de-

---

relations have gradually been growing closer. . . . The responsibility of middle school textbooks has become even heavier. That such geography textbooks have become more vulgar in tone goes against the trend of the times and is most deplorable. The reason I published *Chūtō chirigaku*, employing slightly more theoretical explanations, was that I wished to oppose this trend. However, given the nature of the schools and the circumstances of the provinces, it is also natural that some people desire a simple and popular work. That is why I have decided to issue this revised edition of *Chirigaku kyōkasho*" [pp. 2–3]. The term "Southeast Asia" does not appear in *Chūtō chirigaku*.

[65] "Jinjō shōgaku chirisho maki ni, jidō yō shūsei shuisho" [Revision prospectus for the second-volume elementary school geography book], in use from 1919 onward; quoted in Arata Naka, Tadahiko Inagaki, and Hideo Satō, eds., *Hensan shuisho I* [Collected prospectuses I], vol. 11 of *Kindai Nihon kyōkasho kyōjuhō shiryō shūsei* [Collected documents on textbook teaching methods in early modern Japan], ed. Arata Naka, Tadahiko Inagaki, and Hideo Satō (Tokyo: Tokyo Shoseki, 1982), p. 743.

fined directionally as southeast. First it was necessary to conceptualize the region as being part of Asia. As I have already noted, in the geographical perception of the Japanese formed in the Tokugawa period, under the influence of Western learning, only part of what we today consider Southeast Asia, that is, continental Southeast Asia, was included in Asia as the southeastern portion of the Asian continent centered on China and India. Insular Southeast Asia, together with the southwestern Pacific region, was called the South Seas. In fact, it was this traditional concept of the South Seas as an ocean region separate from Asia that enabled Shigetaka Shiga to formulate his idea of the South Seas as a region differing from both the East and the West.[66]

The trend toward including insular Southeast Asia in Asia began after the turn of the century, as we have seen from the elementary school textbooks cited earlier. Exerting a decisive impact on this trend was the turn taken by southward-advance ideology after World War I. The rhetoric of southward advance began to take on a stronger Asianist tinge—originally a relatively minor aspect—which perforce led to a change in the definition of the regional concept of the South Seas. Whereas earlier advocates of southward advance, especially in the mid–Meiji era, had thought of the South Seas as a region differing from the East, or Asia, the Asianists regarded it as part of a culturally and racially homogeneous East, or Asia.

In view of the fact that most of Micronesia, the main part of the South Seas in the traditional sense, had become de facto Japanese territory during World War I, it was perhaps inevitable that the idea arose of identifying insular Southeast Asia, which together with Micronesia had comprised Oceania, as part of Asia, to which Japan belonged. This trend was expressed clearly in one post–World War I middle school geography textbook. Its preface stated: "Since most of Micronesia has now become a Japanese mandate, *it is perhaps no longer unnatural to teach about Oceania as an extension of Japanese geography.*"[67] And the text declared: "Although Japan is situated at the eastern edge of Asia, *it can be said to be in a position in which it should represent all of Asia, lead all of Asia, and protect all of Asia.* This is a great responsibility but, surely, also something to rejoice in."[68] As we see, to the southward-advance advocates of the time the conceptual boundary between the East and the South Seas had become blurred. More important, the annexation of Korea and the establishment of vested interests in Manchuria had led to a general perception within Japan of the East as Japan's sphere of influence, which gave rise in turn to the tendency to regard the South Seas, part of the East, as also lying within the empire's sphere of interest.

In a 1915 book on the South Seas, Bunji Jimbo, a reserve infantry major, expressed a sentiment typical of such southward-advance advocates: "I declare categorically that the area for Japan's national development must be *the region from the Malay Peninsula east, which is the Empire's sphere of influence.*"[69] In connec-

---

[66] Miwa, *Shiga Shigetaka,* p. 31.

[67] Chiri Kyōju Dōshikai [Geography Education Study Group], *Sekai chiri* [World geography], vol. 1 (Tokyo: Teikoku Shoin, December 1922), p. 3.

[68] Ibid., p. 85.

[69] Bunji Jimbo, *Tōsa kenkyū: Nan'yō no hōko* [A field survey: The treasury of the South Seas] (Tokyo: Jitsugyō no Nihonsha, 1915), p. 27.

tion with the problem of Japanese immigrants to California, he wrote: "The Empire's sphere of influence does not extend to North America, which is why immigrants to California are in such an unfortunate position. If only California were in the East, the problem would never have arisen."[70]

Passages like this reveal clearly the perception of the East (Asia) as a sphere in which Japan was assured freedom of action. Could it be that the southward-advance advocates of the time considered it self-evident that the East (Asia) from the Malay Peninsula east was Japan's sphere of influence, as the above passage indicates? Japan had made colonies of Taiwan and Korea, had begun exploiting Manchuria, and was in the process of bringing part of the South Seas within its sphere of influence by virtue of possession of formerly German South Pacific islands. There is no doubt that national pride springing from these developments was at least partly responsible for inflating Japan's "imperial image" and for motivating it to expand its sphere of influence to include the East (Asia) as far as the Malay Peninsula.

Nevertheless, why did the Japanese call this region newly incorporated within the imperial image *Southeast* Asia? The process by which the region came to be defined directionally as southeast can be understood best by examining changes in middle school geography textbooks.

Although Takuji Ogawa's middle school textbook *Santei chirigaku kyōkasho* did use the expression "Southeast Asia," to my knowledge this was an exceptional case. Even after elementary school textbooks began using the term in the 1920s, middle school textbooks refrained from giving the region a comprehensive name, generally dividing it into two regions belonging to Asia: Indochina and the Malay archipelago. Probably this was because middle school textbooks reflected contemporary Western geographical concepts more accurately than did elementary school textbooks.

We must not forget, however, that even without using the term "Southeast Asia," middle school textbooks gradually came to identify the regions called Indochina and the Malay archipelago with Asia and to perceive them as being located in the southeastern part of Asia. Tables 2 and 3 trace this process. We see that although in the Meiji era occasional mentions of the region identified its location in reference to Japan or China, such as "Annam . . . is about 2,380 nautical miles *southwest of Japan*"[71] and "Indochina begins *southwest of China proper*,"[72] from shortly after the turn of the century through the mid-1920s the region was described, with few exceptions, as being located in the southeastern part of Asia. The geographer Naokata Yamazaki, for example, later known as an advocate of southward advance,[73] wrote in a geography textbook published in 1905: "The Indochinese

---

[70] Ibid., p. 10.

[71] Masanaga Yatsu, *Chūgaku bankoku chishi* [Middle school world geography], vol. 1 (Tokyo: Maruzen Shoten, March 1896), p. 113.

[72] Yūrin Imamura, *Chūgaku kyōtei shinsen gaikoku chiri* [A new foreign geography for the middle school curriculum], vol. 1 (Tokyo: Chūtō Gakka Kyōjuhō Kenkyūkai [Study Group on Teaching Methods for Middle School Courses], February 1899), p. 44.

[73] One work in which he expressed such views is *Seiyō mata nan'yō* [The West and the South Seas] (Tokyo: Kokon Shoin, 1927).

Table 2. Treatment of Southeast Asia in Middle School Geography Textbooks in the Meiji Era (1868–1912)

Publication date	Title	Author/editor	Publisher	Classification	Location	Remarks
Aug. 1888	Zōho bankoku chiri	Takayoshi Maebashi	Fuzambō	O		
Nov. 1888	Chūtō kyōiku Jo shi chiri kyōkasho	Takao Fujitani	Uchida Rōkakuho	△		Translation & adaptation
Sept. 1890	Bankoku chiri shōshū, vol. 1	Tōsaku Tanaka, Gō Matsushima, Takeshi Hashimoto	Fukyūsha	×		Translation & adaptation
Sept. 1895	Gaikoku chishi	Shirō Akiyama	Kyōeki Shōsha Shoten	O		
Nov. 1895	Shin chirigaku: Gaikoku no bu	Gō Matsushima	Shun'yōdō	O		
Mar. 1896	Chūgaku bankoku chishi, vol. 1	Masanaga Yatsu	Maruzen Shoten	O	× = southwest (*seinan*)	"Annam occupies the eastern part of the Further India Peninsula and is about 2,380 nautical miles southwest of Japan" (p. 113).
Oct. 1896	Chūtō chū chiri: Bankokushi	Goroku Nakamura	Bungakusha	O		French Indochina & Malaysia
Mar. 1898	Chūtō kyōiku chirigaku kyōkasho, vol. 2	Denzō Satō	Hakubunkan	×	<	Malay archipelago & Malaysia
Feb. 1899	Gaikoku chiri kyōkasho	Sanseidō Henshūjo	Sanseidō Shoten	O		Indochina & Malaysia
Feb. 1899	Chūgaku kyōtei shinsen gaikoku chiri, vol. 1	Yūrin Imamura	Chūtō Gakka Kyōjuhō Kenkyūkai	O	× = southwest (*nansei*)	
Feb. 1899	Shinpen chūgaku chiri gaikokushi, vol. 1	Masaji Tsunoda	Shūeidō	O		

Table 2 (continued)

Publica-tion date	Title	Author/editor	Publisher	Classifi cation	Location	Remarks
Feb. 1899	Chū chirigaku: Gaikokushi	Masanaga Yatsu	Maruzen Shoten	△		"This book aims to teach world geography centered on our Empire, guiding [students] to consider foreign countries in comparison with Japan" (preface, p. 2).
? 1899	Shinshiki bankoku chiri	Jūzō Iwasaki, Shikanosuke Ikeda	Uchida Rōkakuho	△	☆	"Cochin India is located in southeastern Asia, called Further India as a whole" (p. 124). "The [islands of the] Malay archipelago, also called the East Indies, are scattered between southeastern Cochin India and New Guinea, to the east" (p. 148). "Indochina [is] a large peninsula in southeastern Asia" (p. 138).
Mar. 1899	Gaikoku chiri, vol. 1	Shigetomo Kōda, Teikichi Kida	Kinkōdō Shoseki	△	<	"The Malay archipelago, also called the East Indies, is the general name for the islands scattered between the mouth of the Irawaddy, in southeastern Asia, and Taiwan" (pp. 149–50); adaptation
Jan. 1900	Chūtō kyōiku futsū chiri kyōkasho: Gaikoku no bu, vol. 1	Yasuoki Noguchi	Seibidō, Meguro Shobō	×		Not authorized by the Ministry of Education. Most of Southeast Asia is placed in Asia, but Malaysia, in Oceania, includes the Lesser Sundas, the Celebes, the Moluccas, etc.
Mar. 1900	Gaikoku chū chiri	Shigetomo Kōda	Kinkōdō Shoseki	△		
Oct. 1900	Chūtō shō chiri: Gaikoku no bu	Bungakusha Henshūjo	Bungakusha	△		Textbook for use in girls' high schools
Dec. 1901	Chūtō shin chiri: Gaikoku no bu	Masayoshi Ono, Kan Muraki	Rokumeikan	×	<	Flagged query by textbook inspector: "Why two names, Malay archipelago and Malaysia?"

Table 2 (continued)

Publica-tion date	Title	Author/editor	Publisher	Classification	Location	Remarks
Dec. 1901	Gaikoku chiri shōshi	Banji Shimpo	Kinkōdō Shoseki	O		Chapter 1, Asia: 4. Further India, or Indochina; Chapter 6, Oceania: 4. The islands north of Australia. "While numerous sources both Japanese and foreign have been consulted in the compilation of this book, the most valuable source for ordinary material was *A New Geography Comparative* [sic] by Prof. Meiklejohn" (preface, p. 4).
Oct. 1902	Chūtō kyōiku gaikoku chiri kyōkasho	Yoshi Ihara	Shun'yōdō	△		Indochina & East Indies
Dec. 1902	Chirigaku kyōkasho: Gaikoku no bu, vol. 1	Tanuma Shoten Henshūjo	Tanuma Shoten	△	☆	South Indies (India, Indochina, Malay archipelago)
Feb. 1903	Chūgaku gaikoku shin chiri, vol. 1	Yoshi Ihara	Yoshikawa Kōbunkan	△	∨	
Mar. 1903	Chūtō chiri kyōkasho, vol. 2	Tōzō Takimoto	Fukyūsha	△		
Oct. 1903	Chūtō shin chiri kyōkasho: Gaikoku no bu, vol. 1	Chiri Kyōju Kenkyūkai	Yoshikawa Kōbunkan	△	☆	
Dec. 1903	Chūtō saishin chiri kyōkasho: Gaikoku no bu, vol. 1	Chūzaburō Hagino, Shōzaburō Katō	Shūseidō	△		
Dec. 1903	Chiri kyōkasho: Gaikoku ichi	Tetsugorō Wakimizu	Kinkōdō Shoseki	△	∨	
Jan. 1904	Chiri kyōkasho: Gaikokuhen, vol. 1	Shigetaka Shiga	Fuzambō	△		Part 1, Asia: Chapter 2, The central plains: Section 4, Indochina; Chapter 5, The islands of Asia: Section 1, The Malay archipelago

Table 2 (continued)

Publication date	Title	Author/editor	Publisher	Classification	Location	Remarks
Jan. 1905	Saishin gaikoku chiri	Sanseidō Henshūjo	Sanseidō	△	˅	
May 1905	Futsū kyōiku chirigaku kyōkasho: Gaikokushi, vol. 1	Naokata Yamazaki	Kaiseikan	△	☆	"The Indochinese Peninsula . . . [is] a peninsula in the southeast of the Asian continent" (p. 70). "The Malay archipelago lies to the southeast of the Asian continent" (p. 77).
Nov. 1905	Gaikoku chiri kyōkasho, vol. 1	Futsū Kyōiku Kenkyūkai	Mizuno Shoten	△	˅	
Dec. 1905	Saikin tōgō gaikoku chiri, vol. 1	Manjirō Yamagami	Dai Nihon Tosho	△		
Dec. 1905	Gaikoku shin chiri, vol. 1	Rokumeikan Henshūjo	Rokumeikan	△	˄	
Dec. 1906	Chūtō gaikoku chiri, vol. 1	Shūzaburō Inoma	Keiseisha	△		
Dec. 1907	Saishin chirigaku: Gaikoku no bu, vol. 1	Sanseidō Henshūjo	Sanseidō	△	˅	
Dec. 1907	Shin Nippon chūtō chiri: Gaikoku no bu, vol. 1	Chiri Kyōju Kenkyūkai	Yoshikawa Kōbunkan	△		
Sept. 1908	Chūtō kyōka gaikoku chiri, vol. 1	Yasuoki Noguchi	Meguro Shoten, Seibidō Shoten	△	˅	
Nov. 1908	Saishin naigai ittō chiri: Gaikoku no bu, vol. 1	Hōbunkan Henshūjo	Hōbunkan	△	˅	
Nov. 1911	Saishin keitō chiri: Gaikoku no bu, vol. 1	Amio Moriya	Kōbunkan	△	☆	

Table 2 (continued)

Publication date	Title	Author/editor	Publisher	Classification	Location	Remarks
Dec. 1911	Saishin chiri kyōhon: Gaikokuhen	Chigaku Kenkyūkai	Keiseisha	△		
Dec. 1911	Shinpen sekai chiri kyōkasho, vol. 1	Satoru Nakame	Sanseidō	△		
Jan. 1912	Chūtō kyōka Meiji chiri: Gaikoku no bu, vol. 1	Rokumeikan Henshūjo	Rokumeikan	△	∨	
Mar. 1912	Chiri kyōkasho shintei gaikokuhen, vol. 1	Shigetaka Shiga	Fuzambō	△		
Mar. 1912	Kōyō sekai chiri, vol. 1	Masanaga Yatsu	Maruzen Shoten	△	☆	

Classification key: ○ = continental Southeast Asia classified as Asia (*Ajia shū*), insular Southeast Asia classified as Oceania (*taiyō shū*); △ = both continental and insular Southeast Asia classified as Asia; × = other classifications.

Location key: ☆ = both continental and insular Southeast Asia identified as southeast; ∧ = continental Southeast Asia identified as southeast; ∨ = insular Southeast Asia identified as southeast.

Source: Compiled by the author.

Table 3. Treatment of Southeast Asia in Middle School Geography Textbooks in the Taishō Era (1912–1926)

Publication date	Title	Author/editor	Publisher	Classification	Location	Remarks
Oct. 1912	Shinpen chūtō chiri: Gaikokuhen, vol. 1	Hisagorō Ozeki	Meguro Shoten	×		Eurasia (China, Indochina, Malay archipelago, India, Iran), Indochina (French Indochina, Straits Settlements, Federated Malay States, Siam)
Oct. 1912	Chūtō gaikoku chiri	Kiichirō Yoda	Dōbunkan	△	☆	
Oct. 1912	Saishin chiri kyōhon: Gaikokuhen	Chigaku Kenkyūkai	Keiseisha	△		"The Indochinese Peninsula, east of the Indian Peninsula"
Oct. 1913	Chirigaku kyōkasho: Gaikoku no bu, vol. 1	Takuji Ogawa	Fuzambō	△	∨	"Southern Asia (most of the region along the Indian Ocean and the islands in the Pacific Ocean): Included are the Indian and Indochinese peninsulas and the Malay archipelago" (p. 21).
Oct. 1913	Shin chiri: Gaikoku no bu, vol. 1	Chiri Kenkyūkai	Bungakusha	△	☆	
Oct. 1914	Shintei chūtō chirigaku kyōkasho	Shūzaburō Inoma	Keiseisha	△		
Oct. 1914	Futsū kyōiku sekai chiri kyōkasho	Naokata Yamazaki	Kaiseikan	△	☆	
Sept. 1915	Shin chiri: Gaikoku, vol. 1	Fusatarō Kobayashi	Bungakusha	△	☆	
Oct. 1915	Kaitei shinpen sekai chiri kyōkasho, vol. 1	Satoru Nakame	Sanseidō	△	South	"The Indochinese Peninsula [is] a large peninsula jutting out from southern Asia."
Oct. 1915	Shintei gaikoku chiri, vol. 1	Rokumeikan Henshūjo	Rokumeikan	△	☆	"Indochina . . . : This region has had close ties to Japan since ancient times, and in recent years has come to be seen as an area for Japanese expansion. The term "South Seas" usually includes this region, as well" (pp. 31–32). "The Malay archipelago is essential to Japan's southward advance; close to ten thousand Japanese have already settled there, and trade is also expected to expand" (p. 35).
Dec. 1916	Chūtō kyōka saikin sekai chiri, vol. 1	Sanseidō Henshūjo	Sanseidō	△	∨	

Table 3 (continued)

Publication date	Title	Author/editor	Publisher	Classification	Location	Remarks
Oct. 1917	Santei chirigaku kyōkasho: Gaikoku no bu, vol. 1	Takuji Ogawa	Fuzambō	∆	∨	Part 2: Chapter 10, general remarks: 4. "Southern Asia (most of the region along the Indian Ocean and the islands of Southeast Asia): Included are the Indian and Indochinese peninsulas and the Malay archipelago" (p. 100).
Oct. 1917	Chūtō kyōiku chiri kyōkasho: Gaikokuhen, vol. 1	Hisagorō Ōzeki	Meguro Shoten	∆	☆	"The Malay archipelago, across the South China Sea, [is] a string of islands forming the outer rampart of Southeast Asia" (p. 84).
Oct. 1917	Shintei chūtō gaikoku chiri, vol. 1	Keiseisha	Keiseisha	∆	∨	
Jan. 1918	Chūtō kyōka sekai shin chiri	Susumu Yamazaki	Keiseisha	∆	☆	
Dec. 1918	Shinshiki sekai chiri, vol. 1	Manjirō Yamagami	Dai Nihon Tosho	∆		
Dec. 1919	Yontei chirigaku kyōkasho: Gaikoku no bu, vol. 1	Takuji Ogawa	Fuzambō	∆	∨	"Southeast Asia" (p. 98)
Dec. 1919	Shin chiri: Gaikoku	Fusatarō Kobayashi	Bungeisha	∆	☆	
Dec. 1919	Futsū kyōiku sekai chiri kyōkasho, vol. 1	Naokata Yamazaki	Kaiseikan	∆	☆	
Jan. 1920	Sekai chiri, vol. 1	Chiri Kyōju Dōshikai	Teikoku Shoin	∆	☆	Indochina, East Indies
Nov. 1921	Chūtō chirigaku: Gaikoku no bu, vol. 1	Takuji Ogawa	Fuzambō	∆	∨	
Dec. 1922	Sekai chiri, vol. 1	Chiri Kyōju Dōshikai	Teikoku Shoin	∆	☆	
Dec. 1922	Shinshiki sekai chiri, vol. 1	Manjirō Yamagami	Dai Nihon Tosho	∆		

Table 3 (continued)

Publication date	Title	Author/editor	Publisher	Classification	Location	Remarks
Jan. 1923	Gotei chirigaku kyōkasho: Gaikoku no bu, vol. 1	Takuji Ogawa	Fuzambō	△	∨	"Southeast Asia" (p. 98)
Oct. 1924	Shinpen sekai chiri	Gorō Ishibashi	Fuzambō	△	☆	
Dec. 1924	Kōyō gaikoku chiri	Gorō Ishibashi	Fuzambō	△	☆	
Dec. 1924	Chiri taiyō: Gaikoku	Rokumeikan Henshūjo	Rokumeikan	△	∨	
Jan. 1925	Rokutei chirigaku kyōkasho: Gaikoku no bu, vol. 1	Takuji Ogawa	Fuzambō	△	∨	"Southeast Asia" (p. 100)
Oct. 1925	Sekai shin chiri	Chiri Kyōju Dōshikai	Teikoku Shoin	△	☆	Indochina, East Indies
Oct. 1926	Kōyō sekai chiri	Amio Moriya	Teikoku Shoin	△	∨	"Indochina [is] a large peninsula to the southwest of China proper" (p. 15).

The classification and location keys are the same as for table 2.

Source: Compiled by the author.

Peninsula . . . [is] a peninsula *in the southeast of the Asian continent*"[74] and "the Malay archipelago *lies to the southeast of the Asian continent.*"[75]

Once the region was perceived as being part of Asia and its location was generally accepted as southeast, the appearance of the term "Southeast Asia" in post–World War I elementary school state textbooks and in successive editions of Takuji Ogawa's *Chirigaku kyōkasho* followed naturally. Clearly, however, this region is not southeast but southwest of Japan. During the Pacific War the Japanese military quite correctly called it "the southwest region" (*nansei hōmen*). And as I have noted, some early middle school textbooks described it as lying southwest of Japan.

Viewing the region as southeast required accepting the image of the world, and of Asia, created by Westerners. It required seeing the world through Western eyes. The reason, as I have already stated, is that the direction of southeast has meaning only if the long-established European standard of Central Asia as the focal point of Asia is accepted. The Japanese concept of Southeast Asia was formed under the strong influence of Western geographical knowledge—which is hardly surprising, since so many of the middle school geography textbooks listed in tables 2 and 3, especially the early ones, were translations or adaptations of Western geographies[76] and thus were heavily colored by the Western geographical perspective.

This geographical perspective was not limited to middle school textbooks. Since the late Tokugawa period most Japanese had been accustomed to viewing the world through Western eyes, as can be seen in the line of educational geographies stretching from the 1789 *Seiiki monogatari* of Toshiaki Honda to the 1869 *Sekai kunizukushi* of Yukichi Fukuzawa and the 1870 *Yochishiryaku* [A short geography], written as a textbook for Daigaku Nankō by Masao Uchida, who had studied geography under Ridder Huijssen van Kattendijke at the Nagasaki Naval Academy toward the end of the Tokugawa period.[77] This is why the early modern Japanese were able so facilely to identify the region as being in "southeastern Asia."

The regional concept of Southeast Asia, being the direct result of this geographical perception, was a contradictory mental construct: on the one hand an original Japanese concept, and on the other hand a concept shaped by the Western geographical perspective. In other words, it had a dual nature, being an independent Japanese interest in the region expressed in terms of a Western yardstick.

Is it going too far to see in this dual nature a correspondence with the duality that characterized early modern Japanese attitudes toward the outside world, Traditionalism in the form of Asianism (*Ajia shugi*) and Modernism in the form of Westernization and the repudiation of Asia (*datsu-A shugi* [get-out-of-Asia-ism])?

---

[74] Naokata Yamazaki, *Futsū kyōiku chirigaku kyōkasho: Gaikokushi* [Ordinary education geography textbook: Foreign countries], vol. 1 (Tokyo: Kaiseikan, January 1905), p. 70.

[75] Ibid., p. 77.

[76] For example, Takao Fujitani, *Chūtō kyōiku Jo shi chiri kyōkasho* [Mr. J's intermediate education geography textbook] (Tokyo: Uchida Rōkakuho, November 1888); Tōsaku Tanaka, Gō Matsushima, and Takeshi Hashimoto, trans. and eds., *Bankoku chiri shōshū* [Orthodox world geography] (Tokyo: Fukyūsha, September 1890).

[77] Tsukatani and Kuranami, eds. *Honda Toshiaki, Kaiho Seiryō*; Tomita and Dobashi, eds., *Fukuzawa Yukichi senshū*, vol. 2. The introduction to *Yochishiryaku* stated: "This book is based on material translated from geographies by A. Mackay and Goldsmith (both in English) and by [a Dutch geographer] (in Dutch) but also includes material taken from a number of other works." Kaigo, ed., *Nihon kyōkasho taikei*, vol. 15, p. 63.

The prototypes of these two strands of thought were Tōkichi Tarui's *Daitō gappōron* (the idea that Japan and Korea should merge on an equal basis to form a single nation, which, with the addition of China, would join with other Asian nations in opposing the Western powers) and Yukichi Fukuzawa's *datsu-A ron* (the argument that Japan should "remove from Asia"), respectively. Both concepts emerged in the early Meiji era. But the ideology vis-à-vis the external world that exerted the strongest influence on Japan's subsequent course was neither the "Asian solidarity" advocated by the former nor the "modern imperialism" or "international (Western) cooperationism" implicit in the latter, but a composite "subspecies," the so-called *tōyō meishuron* (the idea of a coalition of Asian nations, led by Japan, that would oppose the Western powers and ensure peace in Asia).

If Tarui's *Daitō gappō ron* and Fukuzawa's *datsu-A ron* represented ideal types at either end of the ideological spectrum, the composite ideology was a "traditionalist imperialism" or "moralistic imperialism" combining Asianism and modern imperialism.[78] One type of this composite ideology was expounded in an essay written in 1918, the year of the third-phase state textbook revision, by the young Fumimaro Konoe, later to be prime minister, who would establish the ideology of the Greater East Asia Co-Prosperity Sphere. The essay, "Ei Bei hon'i no heiwa-

---

[78] I have devised a model, presented in diagram form below, of early modern Japanese ideologies concerning the outside world to enable this phenomenon to be more easily understood. The East-West axis in the diagram indicates the degree of racial, cultural, religious, and geographical proximity, while the civilization, modernization–tradition axis indicates the degree of modernization and Westernization. The *datsu-A ron*, abandoning East and West as cultural and regional concepts and unequivocally endorsing Western civilization and modernization, is located in the upper right quadrant. The *Daitō gappōron* and other ideologies advocating Asian solidarity, which repudiated modernization and proposed dealing with the West by forging an Asian alliance based on the concept of cultural and racial homogeneity, is located in the lower left quadrant. The relative positions of both types of ideologies are consistent with their tenets. But the position of composite ideologies of the *tōyō meishuron* type, which combined the contradictory elements of modernization and the East, is defined by vectors that diverge from the directionality of the model's two axes. These composite ideologies, which accepted the duality of contradictory vectors while attempting to reconcile the contradiction, were peculiar to early modern Japan. The subsequent course of modern Japanese history down to the establishment of the Greater East Asia Co-Prosperity Sphere was the process through which most ideologies having to do with the external world converged on this dimension. The ideologies of Asian solidarity and those of cooperation with the West premised on the repudiation of an Asian identity were no exception. The former, through the medium of the *tōyō meishuron*, became the advocacy of a Greater Asia. The latter shifted toward the concept of a Greater Japan based on righteous rule and of a "moralistic imperialism." In both cases, the period from the Russo-Japanese War through World War I provided the catalyst for this shift. The concept of southward advance could not avoid such a shift, either, as I have explained elsewhere (see note 43).

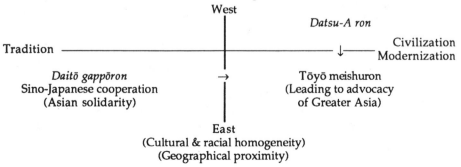

West | Datsu-A ron

Tradition ———————————————— ↓——— Civilization / Modernization

Daitō gappōron   →   Tōyō meishuron
Sino-Japanese cooperation   (Leading to advocacy
(Asian solidarity)   of Greater Asia)

East
(Cultural & racial homogeneity)
(Geographical proximity)

shugi o haisu" [A condemnation of pacifism centered on the interests of England and America], argued that a just international order centered on Japan's interests should take the place of "international cooperationism."[79]

This way of thinking clarifies the meaning of the duality inherent in the term "Southeast Asia" as used in post–World War I Japan. Use of the term cannot be separated from Japan's ideology toward the outside world at the time, especially the ideology of southward advance. I do not think it is not going too far to say that this new term already possessed ideological overtones of "traditionalist (moralistic) imperialism." Heisuke Yamabe, explaining the significance of the radical reform of geography education after World War I, repeatedly stressed that Japanese imperialism differed in nature from that of Western countries and therefore possessed the attribute of justice. For example:

> Such terms as "systematic aggression" and "evil war" exist, but what do they mean? . . . The sensibility of the Japanese warrior, forged over long years by a parklike natural environment and the noble cause of loyalty and filial piety, cannot possibly be imagined by the warriors of northern Europe. *How much less can Western science fathom divine grace. . . . Scrutinize Japan's unbroken history. Where is there a trace of unjustified or aggressive war? Not only will you realize that Japan is a just and chivalrous nation, but also you will discover therein the light of divine grace. . . .* Let us say to those [Westerners who regard Japan as aggressive]: If Japan had not taken it upon itself to ensure peace in the East, where would China be now? Is there a chance that it would be torn apart by internal political warfare? . . . In short, the opening of Japan immediately released the strength built up over long years, and the nation prospered; in less than fifty years it has become the leading nation of Asia's almost five hundred million people and is on a par with the world's powers. . . . If so, we must do our best to apprise the world of the unique qualities of the Japanese people. . . . It is not necessary to repeat that world peace is achieved by actuating noble thought.[80]

How was the regional concept of Southeast Asia, symbolic as it was of early modern Japan's ideology vis-à-vis the rest of the world, perceived? Specifically, how was the region described in textbooks and what were pupils taught about it in the classroom? I will elucidate this by examining contemporary textbooks and teaching manuals. First, however, let me make one important point: geography education of this period had stressed all the major arguments for southward advance that would be offered in the second and third decades of this century. It is easy to imagine that it served to popularize that ideology.

The first characteristic of the regional concept of Southeast Asia that should be noted is that the region was perceived first and foremost as a market for Japanese goods and as a supplier of raw materials. Eloquent proof is the fact that the

---

[79] Takeshi Itō, ed., *Konoe Fumimaro kō seidanroku* [The words of Prince Fumimaro Konoe] (Tokyo: Chikura Shobō, 1937), pp. 234–41; Miwa, *Nihon*, pp. 104–6.

[80] Yamabe, *Taisengo*, pp. 575–77.

brief—about 440 characters—description of the region in the third-phase state geography textbook was devoted entirely to resources and trade with Japan. After noting that Indochina produced rice, the Malay Peninsula rubber, Java sugar, Borneo and Sumatra oil, and the Philippines Manila hemp, this textbook continued: "The number of people going to the Malay archipelago from Japan has finally begun to grow, and in recent years Japanese steamships have opened routes. Meanwhile, trade has also begun gradually to expand."[81]

The view of Southeast Asia as primarily a market and a supplier of raw materials was inextricably linked to post–World War I Japan's categorical imperative of building up its heavy chemical industries. It was essential for Japanese capitalism, technologically inferior to that of the Western powers, to develop its heavy chemical industries by securing cheap raw materials from the geographically close region of Southeast Asia.[82] The resource and market policy of seeking raw materials not only in continental China, as before, but also in Southeast Asia appeared fairly early in this period, as indicated by such policy proposals as the Economic Survey Group's suggestion that "it is probably best to rely on sources in the relatively nearby East and South Seas, such as Siberia, China, French Indochina, Burma, and Australia, to augment the supply of raw ore [for smelting]"[83] and the Steel Industry Survey Group's proposal that "as a means of [securing] supplies, sites with iron mines in the East, the South Seas, and Australia [be] surveyed."[84]

This point of view was expressed still more clearly in the teaching manual for the third-phase state geography textbook, which enumerated four objectives of education on Southeast Asia:

1. To teach the geographical features, industries, and trade of the Indochinese Peninsula, where agriculture flourishes, and of the Malay archipelago, where pioneering development has recently been progressing, and especially to elucidate this region's relationship to Japan.
2. In regard to industry, to teach especially the state of development of rice and rubber cultivation on the Indochinese Peninsula and their special relationship to Japan.
3. To explain in detail the cultivation of sweet potatoes, Manila hemp, and coconuts as products of the Malay archipelago.

---

[81] *Jinjō shōgaku chirisho*, vol. 2, p. 75.

[82] Akio Kawakita, "Shigen mondai to shokumin seisaku no tenkai" [The problem of resources and the development of colonial policy], in Ryūzō Yamazaki, ed., *Ryōtaisenkanki no Nihon shihonshugi* [Japanese capitalism in the interwar period] (Tokyo: Otsuki Shoten, 1978), vol. 2, p. 75.

[83] Keizai Chōsakai [Economic Survey Group], "Sangyō dai ni gō teianchū kōgyō ni kansuru ketsugi" [Resolution on mining in the second set of recommendations on industry], in Ministry of International Trade and Industry, ed., *Jūyō chōsakai* [Major survey groups], vol. 4 of *Shōkō seisakushi* [A history of commercial and industrial policy], ed. Ministry of International Trade and Industry (Tokyo: Ministry of International Trade and Industry, 1961), p. 210.

[84] Shōkō Gyōseishi Kankōkai [Association for the Publication of a History of Government Administration of Commerce and Industry], ed., *Shōkō gyōseishi* [A history of government administration of commerce and industry] (Tokyo: Shōkō Gyōseishi Kankōkai, 1955), vol. 2, p. 65.

4. To teach that these regions have long had very close relations with Japan and that they are regions with which Japan has and should continue to have political, economic, and cultural ties.[85]

The teaching manual, reflecting the content of the textbook itself, concentrated on the industries and resources of Southeast Asia. Because these were discussed solely in terms of Japan's interests, it was natural that the relationship between Southeast Asia and Japan was the major educational aim of the textbook, as indicated by the fourth objective.

We must note that the teaching manual also directed teachers to emphasize the historical ties and the cultural and racial affinity that had existed between Japan and Southeast Asia before the seclusionist Tokugawa period and to give the impression that the people of Southeast Asia actually welcomed the influx of Japanese:

[Japan's] historical relationship with this region is also quite deep, as indicated by the fact that in the time of Hideyoshi Toyotomi [1536–1598] there was a plan to subjugate it. . . . What makes the Japanese especially happy is that the Malays living on Sumatra and Borneo feel *friendly* toward Japanese people. Malays resemble Japanese so closely as to suggest *a common ancestor*. First, their way of sitting is the same as that of the Japanese; they sit cross-legged, and the women also sit in Japanese fashion. The way they build their houses is similar, too, and they thatch their roofs in exactly the same way. Malays like Japanese food, and there are even some who say they would like to escape the Dutch government's oppression and *wish to receive Japan's support*.[86]

To trumpet the inevitability of Japanese involvement in the region on the grounds of historical ties and of cultural and racial affinity—"a common ancestor"—was a typical ploy of contemporary proponents of southward advance. The use of such phrases as "the liberation of Southeast Asia from the white clique," "Japan, preserver of peace in the Orient," "state concept," "loyalty to the Imperial Family," and "Japan as a first-class nation" in the manual's "Commentary on Teaching Materials" also reveals the strong stamp of this ideology.[87]

In addition to emphasizing maritime expansion, geography education advocated systematic training to adapt to both tropical and arctic regions, a fact that coincides interestingly with post–World War I southward-advance ideology.[88]

---

[85] Eisaku Nakayama and Katsunosuke Kikuchi, *Kaitei jinjō shōgaku chiri kyōjusho: Dai roku gakunen yō* [Teaching manual for the revised elementary school geography textbook: Sixth year] (Tokyo: Hōbunkan, 1926), p. 368.

[86] Ibid., pp. 375–76.

[87] Ibid., pp. 503–4.

[88] Yamabe, for example, wrote: "As well as receiving tropical and arctic training, we should acquire the ability to adapt to various climates. It is because the Dutch live in a country of water from childhood, are trained to cope with a cold and humid climate, and are knowledgeable about flood control that they were able to enjoy such great success when they came to hot, humid Java and made their main base of operations Batavia, known as 'the white man's grave.' In the future, the rise and fall of the world's nations will be determined by their expansion in both tropical and arctic regions. In addition to attempting to expand in tropical regions, we must al-

Elsewhere I have discussed at some length the idea of southward advance as part of a simultaneous drive to both north and south,[89] so I will say no more on the subject here except to note that this was one of the major features of southward-advance ideology at the time.

Next we should examine the view of Southeast Asia espoused by the third-phase state geography textbook, that is, the image that formed the basis of the regional concept of Southeast Asia at that time. The first two items in the manual's "Notes on Teaching" are as follows:

> 1. Have [the pupils] think about why it is that despite the great fertility of the soil of this region its countries are so stagnant.
> 2. Natural riches and cultural development are not directly proportionate. Teach that too many natural blessings have the contrary effect of making people lazy.[90]

These words quite clearly convey the image of Southeast Asians as lazy, and of their countries as backward and undeveloped as a consequence. Implicit is encouragement of the contrasting values emphasized in morals and other textbooks: Japan's nationalism, supported by the diligence of its people.

It has been pointed out that it was in this period that the image of the South Seas as lazy, undeveloped, inferior, and unhygienic was popularized and fixed in the public mind.[91] There can be little doubt that these "Notes on Teaching" both reflected and amplified this trend. For example, the following passage in a book published in 1920, the year after volume two of the third-phase state geography textbook was published, closely echoed this teaching policy: "Their idleness and indolence are the result of their natural environment and therefore must be conidered only natural. Congenitally lazy people who dislike work are fit only to flee to Java and lead a subhuman life."[92]

The attention focused on the natural fertility of the region, which was believed to be underdeveloped as a result of its people's inherent indolence, was a manifestation of the expansionism of southward-advance ideology, as expressed in the third item in the "Notes on Teaching": "In addition to explaining the past and present expansion of Japanese people in this region, *you should try to stimulate the pupils to aspire to venture overseas in the future.*"[93] More important, however, is the fact that the key region targeted for Japan's southward advance was the so-called Malay archipelago, in other words, insular Southeast Asia, and that efforts

---

ways bear in mind both arctic and tropical regions. Building specialized schools in both arctic and tropical regions and acquiring the ability to conquer both kinds of climates is one suggestion, but fostering people who will spread culture, not [securing] a supply of cheap labor, should always be our priority." Yamabe, *Taisengo*, p. 583.

[89] Shimizu, "Taishō shoki ni okeru nanshinron," p. 39.

[90] Nakayama and Kikuchi, *Kaitei jinjō shōgaku chiri kyōjusho*, p. 379.

[91] Tōru Yano, "Taishōki 'nanshinron' no tokushitsu" [The characteristics of the ideology of southward advance in the Taishō era], *Tōnan Ajia kenkyū* [Southeast Asian studies] 16, no. 1 (June 1978): 19.

[92] Reisui Fukami, *Nan'yō hōkōki* [Travels in the South Seas] (Tokyo: Kairiku Un'yu Jihōsha, 1920), p. 79; Yano, "Taishōki 'nanshinron,'" p. 20.

[93] Nakayama and Kikuchi, *Kaitei jinjō shōgaku chiri kyōjusho*, p. 379.

were made to teach that expansion into this region would have a decisive impact on Japan's future fortunes. Items six and seven of the "Notes on Teaching" stated:

> 6. Teach that whether Japan's star rises or falls depends on gaining actual power in the Pacific, and *devote attention to Japan's control of the Pacific and the position of the Malay archipelago.*
> 7. Teach *the historical facts of Japanese activities since ancient times, as well as their present activities in the Malay archipelago and use this to motivate pupils to venture overseas.*[94]

Actually, the Western powers were already apprehensive over Japan's southward advance, which targeted the Malay archipelago as the key region. Japanese penetration of British North Borneo, for example, an area extolled by southward-advance enthusiasts as ideally suited to Japanese expansion, was eyed with rapidly mounting suspicion. Secret telegrams flew between North Borneo and London warning that the Japanese ships that docked regularly at Jesselton were engaged in espionage and predicting the imminent collapse of the Anglo-Japanese Alliance. Most Englishmen in North Borneo were convinced that Japan's advance into the area was motivated not by economic concerns but by political and territorial ambitions.[95]

In 1921, when the four-power treaty on the Pacific signed by Britain, France, Japan, and the United States in effect superseded the Anglo-Japanese Alliance, the British government approved a resolution to strengthen Singapore's defenses, spurred by fear of a Japanese southward advance.[96] Contemporary Japanese geography education, which, ever mindful of the British presence, was encouraging maritime expansion,[97] naturally evinced a keen interest in international relations in the Pacific, especially the issue of the Singapore naval base. The fifth item in the above-mentioned manual's "Notes on Teaching" stated: "Inform pupils of the vitally important military and industrial position of the Straits Settlements and have them understand *the problem of the expansion of the Singapore naval base.*"[98] Later, when Japan invaded Southeast Asia, events rapidly made this teaching policy a practical necessity.

As we have seen, the regional concept of Southeast Asia that took form in post–World War I elementary school geography textbooks reflected Japan's strong stake in the region and its expansionist ideology. Geography education at that time, and indeed compulsory education in general, can hardly be said to have been based on the "Taishō democracy" and internationalism that are commonly held to have

---

[94] Ibid.

[95] See, for example, "Jesselton to The British North Borneo Co., London," February 21, 1917 (CO 874/873), and "The North Borneo Chamber of Commerce, Sandakan to Jesselton," October 7, 1917 (CO 874/873), Public Record Office.

[96] For discussion of this point, see Arvid Balk, *Singapur* (n.p., 1936). A Japanese translation by Akira Yamauchi was published as *Tōyō heiwa no kagi: Shingapōru daikonkyochi* [The key to peace in the East: The great base at Singapore] (Tokyo: Nippon Tanken Kyōkai [Japan Exploration Society], 1938).

[97] Yamabe, *Taisengo*, p. 581.

[98] Nakayama and Kikuchi, *Kaitei jinjō shōgaku chiri kyōjusho*, p. 379.

characterized the period.[99] On the contrary, it seems to me that the way in which geography education paved the way for the militarism of the 1930s and 1940s should be considered much more significant. The term "Southeast Asia," which made its first appearance in the third-phase state geography textbook, was retained in the fourth- and fifth-phase textbooks. And volume two of the sixth-phase textbook, *Shotōka chiri* [Beginning geography], published in May 1943, during the "Greater East Asia" War, devoted about twelve thousand characters to the region.[100]

Unfortunately Japan's pre–World War II regional concept of Southeast Asia, springing from a narrow interest in the region's markets and resources, was destined never to mature further, as the following excerpts from the sixth-phase textbook indicate:

> Japan is a noble, divine nation created by the gods. . . . In the ancient past, needless to say, and recently through the Sino-Japanese and Russo-Japanese wars, the radiance of Japan's national prestige has shone overseas. Further, the Manchurian and China incidents and now the Greater East Asia War have finally enabled Japan to apprise the entire world of its mighty power. . . . Since the [start of the] Greater East Asia War the islands of the Philippines and the East Indies, centered on Shōnan Island [Singapore], have become strong participants in the building of Greater East Asia. The alignment of these islands is similar to that of Japan. Moreover, rich in tropical products and minerals, they are the veritable treasury of Greater East Asia. Because of the self-serving and arbitrary behavior of the United States, Britain, the Netherlands, and other countries, the people were secretly awaiting Japan's help. . . . The regions of Greater East Asia, through Japan's strength and guidance, have risen up or are on the verge of doing so. It is Japan's mission to revitalize all the people of these regions as Greater East Asians and enable each one to gain his own place.[101]

---

[99] The prevailing view among scholars of education is that compulsory education in the Taishō era, under the influence of "Taishō democracy," was "liberal" and "democratic" in nature. This point of view is typified by Tomitarō Karasawa, "Changes in Japanese Education as Revealed in Textbooks," *Japan Quarterly* 2, no. 3 (July–September 1955). Some scholars, however, do regard the third-phase state textbooks as a crucial link between the second-phase revision carried out at the end of the Meiji era and the fourth-phase revision that began in 1933. See, for example, Harry Wray, "The Lesson of the Textbooks," in *Japan Examined: Perspectives on Modern Japanese History*, ed. Harry Wray and Hilary Conroy (Honolulu: University of Hawaii Press, 1983). Moreover, as pointed out in Hiroshi Konakawa, *Kokutei kyōkasho* [State textbooks] (Tokyo: Shinchōsha, 1985), pp. 131–39, the nationalistic subject matter of contemporary national-language (*kokugo*) textbooks belies the prevailing view. To give just one example, the section titled "Greater Japan" in volume five, part one, of the national-language state textbook contained the following passage: "Greater Japan has never been defeated by enemies in all the time since the Age of the Gods, and with the passage of time the nation's light shines ever brighter."

[100] Tokiomi Kaigo, ed., *Nihon kyōkasho taikei: Kindaihen, chiri san* [An outline of Japanese textbooks: The early modern period, geography three], vol. 17 of *Nihon kyōkasho taikei*, ed. Tokiomi Kaigo (Tokyo: Kōdansha, 1966), pp. 58–66, 80–85. The first volume of the sixth-phase state geography textbook was published in February 1943, the second volume in May 1943. The second volume, in addition to about twelve thousand characters of text on Southeast Asia, included forty illustrations.

[101] Ibid., pp. 55–58.

CONCLUSION

It is an odd coincidence that Japan formed its own regional concept of Southeast
Asia following World War I and that the term "Southeast Asia" took form in the
West upon the establishment of the South East Asia Command, set up by the
Allied Forces during World War II to liberate this region from Japanese occupation.
As can be seen from the preceding discussion, however, the regional concept of
Southeast Asia in early modern Japan was constricted by policy considerations and
interests and was redolent of the ideology of imperial Japan. Clearly, insufficient
attention was paid to the major factors that must be examined sincerely when trying to define a regional concept: the "uniformity and consistency" as well as
"dissimilarity" of "topography, climate, vegetation, and other natural patterns,"
of "population, language, religion, lifestyle, and other cultural patterns," and of
"the stage of social and economic development."[102] This is why, despite its independent formulation of a regional concept, Japan was unable to develop this into a
mature perception of the region before being defeated in World War II and entering
the postwar period.

　　Moreover, the education reform undertaken by the Allied occupation authorities began with the erasure of this regional concept. The Civil Information and
Education Section (CIE), set up by General Douglas MacArthur's General Headquarters on September 22, 1945, to oversee education, issued four directives on education that aimed to eradicate militarism and ultranationalism from Japanese
education and instill the philosophy and principles of democracy.[103] The fourth
directive (on the suspension of the teaching of morals, Japanese history, and geography), conveyed to the Japanese government on December 31, 1945, suspended
geography education on the grounds that it "reflected the map of international
relations." The directive ordered the Ministry of Education to suspend immediately all courses in morals, Japanese history, and geography and not to resume classes
until receiving permission from GHQ.[104] The occupation authorities also ordered
that all textbooks and teaching manuals be withdrawn and pulped.[105] With this
the very words "Southeast Asia," which had long adorned the prewar state textbooks, were literally scrapped.

　　The suspension of geography was lifted in April 1947, when the new elementary school system was inaugurated, with the addition to the curriculum of social
studies, which incorporated the former subjects of history and geography. The basic
policy of social studies education at the time, however, followed the lines of the
democratic education reform suggested by the US educational mission that had vis-

---

[102] Nishikawa, *Jimbun chirigaku nyūmon*, pp. 130, 212.

[103] Yoshizō Kubo, *Tai Nichi senryō seisaku to sengo kyōiku kaikaku* [Occupation policy toward
Japan and postwar education reform] (Tokyo: Sanseidō, 1984), pp. 197–204.

[104] Tokiomi Kaigo, *Kyōiku kaikaku: Sengo Nihon no kyōiku kaikaku* [Education reform: Postwar
Japan's education reform] (Tokyo: Tokyo Daigaku Shuppankai, 1975), p. 59. There was no reference to the suspension of geography classes in the document on education policy toward
Japan drafted by the Department of State before the end of the war (PWC 287); it was first mentioned in the December 1945 directive ordering the suspension of three subjects. Apparently
geography was added to the list after the CIE's careful analysis of prewar state textbooks. For
a discussion of this point, see Sōji Katagami, "Teishi saserareta shūshin, Nihon rekishi, chiri"
[The suspension of morals, Japanese history, and geography], *Kyōiku kagaku: Shakaika kyōiku*
[Education science: Social studies education], June 1987, pp. 129–30.

[105] Kaigo, *Kyōiku kaikaku*, p. 60.

ited Japan the previous spring. The draft teaching guidelines for social studies drawn up by the Ministry of Education in 1947 stated: "Since the aim of education, especially social studies, henceforth is to nurture adults fit to build a democratic society, teachers must not only have a good grasp of the special features of Japanese traditions and life but also fully understand the meaning of democratic society, that is, the principles underlying democratic society."[106]

A total of eight elementary school social studies textbooks reflecting this policy were issued in 1947 and 1948, beginning with *Tochi to ningen* [Land and people], published on August 25, 1947.[107] Geography was covered predominantly in the second-year textbook, *Masao no tabi* [Masao's trip], and in the fifth- and sixth-year textbooks, which had the general title *Watashitachi no seikatsu* [Our daily life]. (The volume titles of the two fifth-year texts were *Mura no kodomo* [Village children] and *Toshi no hitotachi* [City people]; those of the two sixth-year texts were *Tochi to ningen* [Land and people] and *Kikō to seikatsu* [Climate and life].)[108] It is clear that one of the CIE's major educational objectives was that pupils be given a better understanding of the interdependent nature of the world, and especially that they be taught how dependent Japan was on the democratic countries of the world.[109]

Despite this declared aim, the new social studies textbooks' method of presenting material was very different from that of the old geography textbooks, and the new textbooks' immediate educational objective was to teach pupils how to solve problems arising in daily life. Thus, "even in textbooks that concentrate on geography, absolutely no systematic geographical discussion of Japan or foreign countries is to be found."[110] This peculiar state of affairs was the outcome of compliance with repudiation of ultranationalism, one of the criteria of textbook censorship adopted at a staff meeting of the Education Division of the CIE on February 4, 1946. All educational material reflecting the ideology of the Greater East Asia Co-Prosperity Sphere and all other ideologies aimed at territorial aggrandizement was to be ex-

---

[106] "Gakushū shidō yōryō: Shakaikahen" [Teaching guidelines: Social studies], fiscal 1947, in Kokuritsu Kyōiku Kenkyūjo [National Institute for Educational Research], Sengo Kyōiku Kaikaku Shiryō Kenkyūkai [Study Group on Materials on Postwar Education Reform], ed., *Mombushō gakushū shidō yōryō 4: Shakaikahen* [Ministry of Education teaching guidelines 4: Social studies] (Tokyo: Nihon Tosho Sentaa, 1955), p. 4.

[107] Yamazumi, *Nihon kyōiku shōshi*, chronology, p. 48.

[108] Kaigo, ed., *Nihon kyōkasho taikei*, vol. 17, p. 629.

[109] In connection with the second-year textbook, *Masao no tabi*, the CIE censors issued a list of eighteen points they considered it especially important that pupils be made to understand. These having been incorporated, printing was approved on November 10, 1947, and the book was published on February 20, 1948. The first point was "People in the world depend on each other for obtaining necessary things they use." The third point was "The world will become a more comfortable place to live in, as the people work for its progress." "Grade II, Masao's Trip," File 38, Box 5513, National Record Center, Washington, D.C. The CIE's "Plans for Fiscal 1951–52" included guidelines for educating children to understand the world. These stated, in effect, that Japan was now dependent on other regions of the world to a degree unprecedented in the nation's history and was facing both the absolute necessity to become a fully participating member of the community of democratic nations and the ideal opportunity to do so; it was most important that middle schools concentrate on providing education to foster citizens of the world. Secondary Education Branch, Education Division, CIE Section, to Chief of Education Division, CIE Section, "Plans for Fiscal Year 1951–52," dated March 26, 1951, p. 27, Joseph C. Trainor Collection, Hoover Institution on War, Revolution and Peace, Stanford.

[110] Kaigo, ed., *Nihon kyōkasho taikei*, vol. 17, p. 629.

punged, which led to the elimination not only of phrases suggesting national expansion, such as *hakkō ichiu* (eight corners of the world under one roof), *kōkoku no michi* (the Imperial Way), *tengyō kaikō* (propagation of the divine mission), *chōkoku no seishin* (nation-building spirit), *kokui no hatsuyō* (enhancement of national prestige), and *yakushin Nippon* (Japan, leaping forward), but also of comparative statistics and graphs on the distribution of world population, world resources, and world trade.[111] Of course the phrase *nanshin Nippon* (southward-advancing Japan) was also removed.[112]

In the circumstances, there could be no substantive discussion of Southeast Asia. *Kikō to seikatsu* contained one line, referring to the region as the South Seas: "On the islands of the South Seas, daily squalls temporarily soak the earth."[113] The textbook *Shōgakusei no shakai: Sekai o tsunagu mono* [Social studies for elementary school pupils: Things that link the world], published in May 1950, did not touch on either Southeast Asian countries or the region as a whole. The first discussion of the region, under the heading "The Indochinese Peninsula and the Southern Islands," appeared in *Shōgakusei no shakai: Nihon to sekai* [Social studies for elementary school pupils: Japan and the world], published in December 1954.[114]

Chūgakkō no shakai: Sekai no ishokujū [Middle school social studies: Clothing, food, and shelter around the world], published in June 1953, was the first middle school textbook to discuss the region, under the heading "Tropical Asia: (1) The Indochinese Peninsula, (2) The Malay archipelago."[115] As I noted at the beginning of this paper, the term "Southeast Asia" reappeared in middle school textbooks in 1955, and in elementary school textbooks in 1965 (table 4).

There can be no doubt that this development took place in the context of the shift in occupation policy toward Japan that accompanied the change in the United States' global strategy occasioned by the Cold War. As the Cold War spread in Asia, the view of Japan as the "workshop of Asia," which would act as an "anticommunist bulwark," rapidly gained ground in the United States.[116] The establishment of the People's Republic of China in October 1949 prompted the United States to move toward opening the markets of Southeast Asia to Japan once again.

The Japanese government's interest in the region was already apparent in the white paper on trade issued on August 15, 1949. A number of policy statements followed: Minister of Finance Hayato Ikeda's proposal of "joint U.S.-Japan development of Southeast Asia" in the lower house of the Diet on May 15, 1952; Bank of Japan Governor Hisato Ichimada's remarks advocating "triangular trade among

---

[111] Yoshizō Kubo, "Senryōgun no kyōkasho ken'etsu to kentei seido" [The occupation forces' textbook censorship and authorization system], *Gendai no esupuri: Senryōka no kyōiku kaikaku* [Modern spirit: Education reform under the occupation], no. 209 (December 1984), pp. 106–7.

[112] Ibid., p. 107.

[113] Ministry of Education, *Kikō to seikatsu* [Climate and life] (Tokyo: Tokyo Shoseki, March 1948); Kaigo, ed., *Nihon kyōkasho taikei*, vol. 17, p. 428.

[114] Yoshishige Abe, ed., *Shōgakusei no shakai: Nihon to sekai* [Social studies for elementary school pupils: Japan and the world] (Tokyo: Nihon Shoseki, December 1954), pp. 57–61. This was the textbook for the second half of the sixth year of elementary school.

[115] Yoshishige Abe, ed., *Chūgakkō no shakai: Sekai no ishokujū* [Middle school social studies: Clothing, food, and shelter around the world] (Tokyo: Nihon Shoseki, June 1953), p. 52. This was the textbook for the first year of middle school.

[116] Hagiwara, "Sengo Nihon to Tōnan Ajia," p. 117.

Table 4. Southeast Asia in Postwar Social Studies Textbooks

Title	Publisher	Publication date	Remarks
Elementary school (2d half of 6th year)			
Kikō to seikatsu	Tokyo Shoseki	Mar. 1948	East Indies, South Seas
Shōgakusei no shakai: Sekai o tsunagu mono	Nihon Shoseki	May 1950	No mention of countries or region
Shōgakusei no shakai: Nihon to sekai	Nihon Shoseki	Dec. 1954	Indochinese Peninsula, southern islands
Shimpan shōgakusei no shakai: Nihon to sekai	Nihon Shoseki	May 1956	Indochinese Peninsula, southern islands
Shōgaku shakai	Nihon Shoseki	Jan. 1962	Indochinese Peninsula, countries in the southern islands
Shōgaku shakai	Nihon Shoseki	Jan. 1965	The countries of Asia: 4. The countries of Southeast Asia[a]
Shōgaku shakai	Osaka Shoseki	Mar. 1965	Map of "Southeast Asian countries" (p. 45)
Shimpan shōgaku shakai	Nihon Shoseki	May 1968	The countries of Asia and Africa: 2. Southeast Asia
Shimpan shōgaku shakai	Osaka Shoseki	May 1968	The countries of Asia and Africa: 2. Southeast Asia[b]
Shōgaku shakai	Osaka Shoseki	May 1971	The countries of Asia and Africa: 2. Southeast Asia[b]
Shōgaku shakai	Osaka Shoseki	May 1974	The countries of Asia and Africa: 2. Southeast Asia[b]
Shōgaku shakai	Osaka Shoseki	May 1977	The countries of Asia and Africa: 2. Southeast Asia[b]
Middle school (1st year)			
Chūgakkō no shakai: Sekai no ishokujū	Nihon Shoseki	Jun. 1953	Tropical Asia: (1) The Indochinese Peninsula, (2) The Malay archipelago; overseas Chinese in the South Seas
Chūgakusei no shakai: Tochi to seikatsu, vol. 2	Nihon Shoseki	Jun. 1955	Chapter 6: Southeast Asia
Shimpan chūgakusei no shakai: Tochi to seikatsu, vol. 2	Nihon Shoseki	Jan. 1959	Asia: Southeast Asia (section 2)
Chūgaku shakai: Chiriteki bun'ya	Nihon Shoseki	Jan. 1962	Asia: Southeast Asia (section 2)
Chūgaku shakai: Chiriteki bun'ya	Nihon Shoseki	Jan. 1966	Asia: Southeast Asia (section 2)
Chūgaku shakai: Chiriteki bun'ya	Nihon Shoseki	Jan. 1969	Asia: Southeast Asia (section 2)
Chūgaku shakai: Chiriteki bun'ya	Nihon Shoseki	Jan. 1972	Southeast Asia Aims for Economic Independence (section 3)
Chūgaku shakai: Chiriteki bun'ya	Nihon Shoseki	Jan. 1975	Southeast Asia Aims for Economic Independence (section 3)
Chūgaku shakai: Chiriteki bun'ya	Nihon Shoseki	Jan. 1978	Southeast Asia Aims for Economic Independence (section 3)

[a] "The Indochinese Peninsula and the Malay Peninsula, stretching south of China, and the islands around them are called Southeast Asia" (p. 33).

[b] "The Indochinese Peninsula, between China and India, and the surrounding islands of the Philippines and Indonesia are called Southeast Asia" (p. 40).

Source: Compiled by the author.

Japan, the United States, and Southeast Asia" at a meeting of the Bankers Association of Japan on June 16 that year;[117] and finally Prime Minister Shigeru Yoshida's administrative policy speech in the lower house on June 16, 1953, in which he stated: "Today, when little can be expected of the Chinese economy, *the importance of Southeast Asia* goes without saying. The government will not hesitate to cooperate in every way to further the prosperity of Southeast Asian countries, providing capital, technology, and services, in the hope of further deepening *mutually beneficial relations.*"[118]

These developments provided the climate for the popularization of the term "Southeast Asia" (Tōnan Ajia) in postwar Japan, but the regional concept it embodied differed from the concept that had developed independently in prewar Japan; the postwar image of Southeast Asia was, as it were, projected on the screen of US policy toward Asia, Southeast Asia, and Japan, which was part of the United States' global strategy. The very words "Southeast Asia" (Tōnan Ajiya) had been physically eradicated when geography education was prohibited as part of occupation policy, and the regional concept was reintroduced as something totally new conveyed to the postwar Japanese by the United States.

Symbolic of this was the region's reappearance in postwar elementary and middle school geography textbooks. The basic principle of the United States' education policy toward postwar Japan was expressed in a document by a staff member of the Southeast Asian Affairs Division of the Department of State named Turner, which was approved on July 14, 1944, by a State Department regional committee. This document recommended that the guiding principle applied to administering the education system under military occupation be to bring education into line with the general US policy for creating a world in which we can live in peace.[119] This principle acted as a tacit constraint on Japan's education policy not only during the occupation but also in the period following the restoration of independence.

The Japanese people's linguistic space, which was thoroughly controlled during the occupation, when regulation of culture, speech, and education left no room for freedom to criticize the Allies in any way, remained the same after the occupation ended, limiting the Japanese people's perceptions.[120] The term "Southeast Asia," "Tōnan Ajiya," had first to be erased from elementary and middle school textbooks during the occupation leaving not a trace of the regional concept created by the prewar Japanese. Then "Tōnan Ajia" was newly introduced to postwar Japan as a translation of the English term "South East Asia" and a concept compatible with the United States' global strategy.

The prewar regional concept of Southeast Asia had been based entirely on Japan's own interests, and almost no attempt had been made to understand the region on its own terms. This had rendered it impossible to develop a mature concept that could demonstrate Southeast Asia's regional cohesiveness in terms of natural and cultural patterns and stage of social and economic development. But because the new regional concept of Southeast Asia that emerged after the war was never rigorously tested against the prewar concept but was merely accepted expediently, just

---

[117] Ibid., pp. 119, 133–34.

[118] Yano, *"Nanshin" no keifu*, pp. 179–80.

[119] Kubo, *Tai Nichi senryō seisaku*, p. 33.

[120] Jun Etō, *Wasureta koto to wasuresaserareta koto* [What we forgot and what we were made to forget] (Tokyo: Bungei Shunjūsha, 1976), p. 72.

as it had been received from the United States, it too was destined to remain in a half-baked state that resisted development into a mature concept.

This paper was originally published under the title "Kindai Nihon ni okeru 'Tōnan Ajiya' chiiki gainen no seiritsu: Shō, chūgakkō chiri kyōkasho ni miru" [The regional concept of Southeast Asia in early modern Japan as seen in elementary and middle school geography textbooks] in *Ajia keizai* [Developing economies] 28, no. 6 (June 1987): 2–15; 28, no. 7 (July 1987): 22–38. It was written in conjunction with a series of lectures in fiscal 1985 titled "Nihon, Tōnan Ajia kankei no shiteki kōsatsu" [Historical perspectives on Japanese–Southeast Asian relations]. I would like to thank the Tōsho Bunko Library of Tokyo Shoseki Kabushiki Kaisha for permitting me to study prewar elementary and middle school textbooks and other valuable documents in its collection and Professor Shirō Takahashi of Meisei University's Research Center on Educational History of the Occupation for facilitating my study of occupation-period documents.

3

THE PATTERN OF JAPANESE ECONOMIC PENETRATION OF PREWAR SINGAPORE AND MALAYA

Hajime Shimizu

This analysis of the pattern of Japanese economic penetration of prewar Singapore and Malaya is based primarily on data from the "Consular Population Survey of Expatriate Japanese by Occupation," in the Diplomatic History Archives of the Ministry of Foreign Affairs. In this paper, however, I will not discuss the content of the consular population survey itself or its character as a historical source, since I have done so elsewhere.[1]

I. OVERALL JAPANESE POPULATION TRENDS IN SINGAPORE AND MALAYA

Prewar Singapore and Malaya included the Straits Settlements, the Federated Malay States, the Unfederated Malay States, British North Borneo, Sarawak, and Brunei. Figure 1 shows the fluctuations in the Japanese population within this region between 1907 and 1936. As can be seen, there were several rises and declines in the Japanese population, which peaked in 1919, bottomed out in 1923, peaked again in 1929, and bottomed out once more in 1933.

These fluctuations clearly reflected international events. The first peak coincided with the boom in Japanese trade with Southeast Asia that was triggered by World War I. The decline that began in 1920 and bottomed out in 1923 reflected the postwar recession in the world economy. The second rise paralleled the recovering world economy as the price of rubber in international markets, for example, began to stabilize. The second decline in the number of Japanese in Singapore and Malaya was, of course, caused by the Great Depression of 1929–1933. The rapid rise thereafter, triggered by the sudden decline in the exchange value of the yen following the prohibition on gold exports from Japan that went into effect on December 13, 1931, helped accelerate the entry of Japanese products into Southeast Asian markets.

The cyclical rise and fall in Japanese population was, of course, affected by the difference between the number of Japanese entering the region and the number returning to Japan or leaving for other regions. The pattern of the flow of Japanese

---

[1] Hajime Shimizu, "Gaimushō 'Kaigai zairyū hompōjin shokugyōbetsu jinkō chōsa ikken' no shiryōteki seikaku" [The character of the "Consular population survey of expatriate Japanese by occupation" of the Ministry of Foreign Affairs as a historical source], *Ajia keizai* [Developing economies] 26, no. 3 (March 1985).

Figure 1. Trends in the Japanese Population of Singapore,
Malaya, and North Borneo, 1907–1936

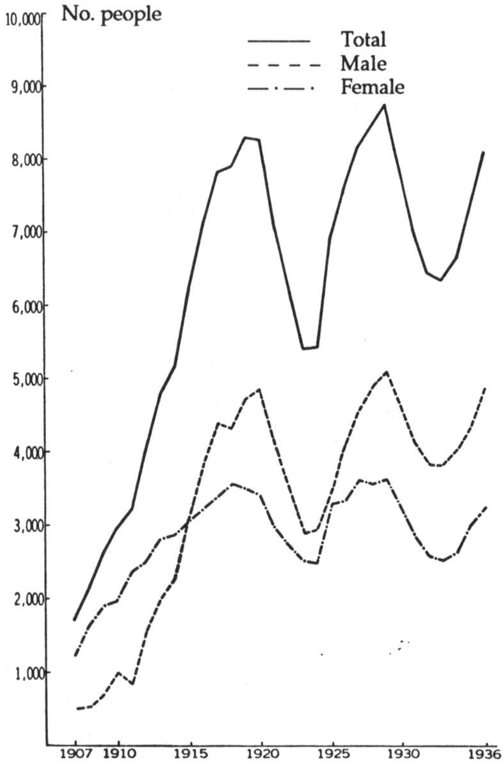

Source: "Kaigai zairyū hompōjin shokubyōbetsu jinkō chōsa ikken" [Consular population survey of expatriate Japanese by occupation], Diplomatic History Archives, Ministry of Foreign Affairs.

population to and from Singapore and Malaya during the prewar era can be traced through analysis of Japanese government statistics on the number of passports issued and number of Japanese citizens emigrating, the number of Japanese traveling or residing abroad, and the number of Japanese citizens granted travel or emigration permits.[2] The number of Japanese entrants to British Malaya and the Straits Settlements each year from 1907 through 1940 is shown in figure 2, whose curve is essentially the same as that of figure 1.

---

[2] Ministry of Foreign Affairs, Consular and Emigration Affairs Department, ed., *Waga kokumin no kaigai hatten: Ijū hyaku nen no ayumi* [Japanese nationals overseas: One hundred years of migration] (Tokyo: Ministry of Foreign Affairs, 1971), "References table III-3, pp. 142–43. The flow of Japanese overseas and back to Japan can also be followed to some extent through study of the statistics regarding the number of passports issued and returned listed in *Nippon teikoku tōkei nenkan* [Statistical yearbook of the Empire of Japan], compiled by the Bureau of Statistics. The figures provided by this source are extremely low, however, and cannot be said to reflect accurately the actual movements of Japanese citizens overseas. Furthermore, the statistics for returned passports are restricted to the very early period, prior to 1907, the year that consular population surveys got well under way. These data, therefore, are not really applicable in charting the flow of Japanese overseas.

Figure 2. Trends in the Number of Japanese Entrants to British
Malaya and the Straits Settlements, 1907–1940

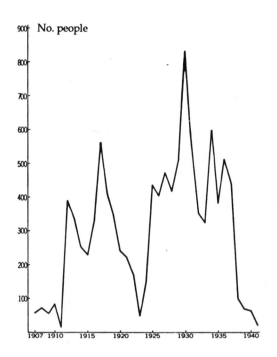

Source: Ministry of Foreign Affairs, Consular and Emigration Affairs Department, *Waga
kokumin no kaigai hatten: Ijū hyaku nen no ayumi* [Japanese nationals overseas: One hundred
years of migration] (Toyko: Ministry of Foreign Affairs, 1971), "References," Table III-3, pp.
142–43.

What do the fluctuations shown in figure 1 indicate about the flow of Japanese
population into and out of the region? Between 1915 and 1919, for example, the
stock statistics (fig. 1) record a net rise of 2,038 Japanese in Singapore and Malaya.
The flow statistics for the same period (fig. 2) indicate a total influx of 1,884 Japanese. The reliability of these flow statistics has not been adequately examined, but
for the time being let us assume that they are trustworthy. Taken at face value,
they suggest that the increase in the Japanese population for the 1915–1919 period
can be attributed directly to the inflow of new Japanese entrants to the region, including some immigrants from other regions. In other words, the rise in population
(paralleling an upswing in business conditions) was due largely to the influx of new
entrants, very few Japanese already in the region leaving for Japan or other regions.

In the 1919–1923 period, by contrast, the Japanese population declined by 2,738.
The flow statistics indicate a drop in the number of Japanese entrants (in 1923, the
lowest point, only 57 Japanese entered the region, one-tenth the number who entered at the time of the peak). But while there were fewer entrants, there were
still some, which means, obviously, that the decline in the Japanese population
must have been due to more people leaving than entering.

The conclusion, then, is that the fluctuations in the Japanese population of
Singapore and Malaya can be attributed simply to the gross inflow and outflow of
people rather than to the net inflow and outflow. In sum, the figures tell us that

when economic conditions were good, there was a corresponding increase in the flow of Japanese to Singapore and Malaya and that when economic conditions were poor there were both a sharp decline in the number of Japanese entrants to the region and a greater outflow than inflow. The statistics indicate the existence of an economic mechanism sensitive to business conditions and quick to respond to change.

II. THE EARLY JAPANESE COMMUNITY IN SINGAPORE AND MALAYA

As figure 1 illustrates, the pattern of fluctuations in the Japanese population of Singapore and Malaya diflered somewhat for men and for women, especially in the early period (up to 1920). For one thing, there were more Japanese women than men in the region until 1915. Furthermore, the female Japanese population peaked in 1918, a year before the Japanese population as a whole reached its first peak. The number of women remained relatively stable until 1920, when it began to drop rapidly. Thus, in the early years the Japanese population in Singapore and Malaya was characterized by the large number of women and by the fact that for a long time women outnumbered men.

Between 1907 and 1915 more than half the Japanese population in the region comprised women: in 1908 women accounted for a phenomenal 77.8 percent of the total. Similarly high percentages of women characterized the contemporary Japanese populations of Burma and French Indochina, but in those regions the total Japanese populations were very small. (In 1911 there were only 291 Japanese in Burma and 154 in French Indochina.) Women also outnumbered men in the Netherlands East Indies up to 1913, but there women accounted for 50 to 60 percent of the total Japanese population, a somewhat lower percentage than in Singapore and Malaya, and their number was never more than one-third the number in Singapore and Malaya.

Why were there so many Japanese women in Singapore and Malaya, and what were they doing there? Most were prostitutes, the so-called *karayuki-san* who were found in much of Asia in the years between the Meiji Restoration of 1868 and the end of World War II in 1945. Their numbers in Singapore and Malaya between 1907 and 1923 are shown in table 1.[3] The fact that prostitution was legal in the British colonies of Asia helps to explain their large numbers.[4] In 1920, however, the Singapore government prohibited prostitution throughout the Malay Peninsula.[5] The sharp decline thereafter in the female Japanese population of the region

---

[3] Japanese prostitutes working overseas were classified in consular population surveys as "entertainers, prostitutes, serving women," a category that first appeared in 1911. Prior to that they were most often included under "miscellaneous occupations." Yet even after the category "entertainers, prostitutes, serving women" was created, Japanese prostitutes working overseas were classified sometimes in this new category, sometimes in some other category, such as "miscellaneous occupations." Not only was the consulate unclear in its classifications, but there is evidence that classifications were often arbitrarily changed by the Foreign Ministry, as well. In some records the category "prostitute" has been crossed out in red ink and the notation "Move to 'miscellaneous occupations'" added. This reluctance to call a spade a spade is indicative of the Foreign Ministry's struggle to wipe out what was perceived as a shameful stain upon the honor of a "first-class nation."

[4] Tōru Yano, *"Nanshin" no keifu* [The lineage of southern expansion] (Tokyo: Chūō Kōronsha, 1975), pp. 40–41.

[5] Ibid., pp. 43–44. See also Tamio Takemura, *Haishō undō* [The antiprostitution movement] (Tokyo: Chūō Kōronsha, 1982), pp. 90–91.

Table 1. The Japanese Community in Singapore and Malaya, by Occupation, 1907–1923

Unit: No. people

	Prosti- tutes, etc. (female)	Rooms for rent, clubs & restaurants (male)	Inns & boarding houses (male)	Barbers & hair- dressers (male)	General merchants (male)	Clothing & dry goods merchants (male)	Medicine vendors (male)	Company & bank employees (male)
1907	752	266	83	35	100	8	24	—
1908	1,078	194	107	35	83	50	30	—
1909	1,489	(91)	83	53	92	63	46	—
1910	1,628	82	95	44	133	—	57	—
1911	1,646	94	111	60	95	67	57	18
1912	1,626	106	118	76	176	—	77	20
1913	1,679	97	119	91	121	77	77	36
1914	1,681	(30)	170	102	138	78	83	45
1915	1,781	144	159	136	194	62	82	106
1916	1,745	165	185	149	279	69	97	144
1917	1,912	135	132	127	299	63	44	172
1918	1,693	123	147	144	399	13	51	220
1919	1,580	132	99	116	350	56	40	136
1920	1,136	41	42	60	138	17	30	1,136
1921	86	39	65	101	154	21	29	1,478
1922	209	119	81	101	147	9	19	526
1923	276	20	91	87	121	3	19	865

"Company & bank employees" includes clerks and shop employees.

Source: Same as figure 1.

was the result of efforts by the Japanese consulate in Singapore and by members of the local Japanese community to put a stop to the traffic in *karayuki-san*.

What became of all those women? After the ban on prostitution went into effect, they had four choices: return to Japan, move to neighboring regions, marry indigenous men or members of the local Japanese community, or strike out on their own and continue to work clandestinely as prostitutes. Many chose the last option, as vividly described by the poet, essayist, and novelist Mitsuharu Kaneko (1895–1975): "Their arrival throws the people of this remote region into ecstasy. Men flock to savor the exotic flesh of the foreign women. There are native Malays, Japanese, and migrant laborers speaking unknown tongues. They pay a dollar each; the women make twenty to thirty dollars a night. And the next day they move on, pushing farther into the interior, continuing their harsh journey. They scatter in all directions, these women, with no idea of where they are or where they are going. They carry one or two thousand silver coins wrapped around their bodies, hard against their skin, and wander in no man's land."[6]

Reports from the Japanese consulate in Singapore make it clear that many Japanese prostitutes continued their profession despite the ban. The Japanese government could not condone this, of course, and over the next few years there were repeated communications between the Japanese consulate in Singapore and the Foreign Ministry in Tokyo regarding the issue, such as the March 1924 "Memorandum Regarding the Resurgence of Japanese Prostitutes" and the August 1927

[6] Mitsuharu Kaneko, *Marē Ran'in kikō* [Malaya–Netherlands East Indies Travelogue] (Tokyo: Chūō Kōronsha, 1978; first published 1940), pp. 114–15.

"Chinese Protectorate Plan to Prosecute Operators of Japanese Brothels and Eradicate Independent Japanese Prostitutes." The latter stated: "Since prostitution was prohibited a few years ago a number of [Japanese] prostitutes have established 'sly' [unlicensed] brothels in a certain quarter of the city and, under the guise of [operating] ice shops, continue to engage in prostitution. This has given rise to no end of undesirable talk."[7]

The same report estimated that there were more than thirty such brothels in Singapore and a total of 126 independent Japanese prostitutes.[8] Yet the consular population survey of Japanese residents for the same year recorded only 67 women working as "entertainers, prostitutes, [and] serving women." Note, however, the number of women classified as "domestic employees." In the period from 1907 to 1919, none were recorded, except in 1917 when 18 female "domestic employees" were recorded. In 1920, however, suddenly there were 146, and thereafter the number ranged between 60 and 280. I believe these figures provide a clue to what happened to many Japanese prostitutes after the ban went into effect. There is no reason the same consulate that had counted 126 independent prostitutes in August 1927 would fail to include this number in its population survey for that year. The apparent discrepancy is explained, however, if one accepts that prostitutes were included in the category of "domestic employees."

Between 1924 and 1925 the number of "domestic employees" jumped from 65 to 281, yet between 1926 and 1927 the number dropped from 203 to 101. This great fluctuation in numbers can probably be attributed to the fact that 1924–1927 were the years in which the Japanese government was trying to suppress a resurgence in Japanese prostitution in Singapore. A Japanese government directive to the Japanese consul in Singapore dated March 11, 1924, reveals how intent the government was on eradicating prostitution: "It is highly regrettable that prostitution should be reviving after we have gone to so much trouble to abolish it. It is our policy to do away with all prostitution by Japanese women, and we ask that you convey this to the local authorities. You are furthermore directed to devise measures to ensure that there will be no further prostitution by Japanese women."[9]

Around that time the Chinese Protectorate of the Straits Settlements government was pursuing its own plans to shut down the Japanese brothels. This plan was put into effect on August 9, 1927, when the head of the Chinese Protectorate, Goodman, charged eleven proprietors of Japanese brothels with violating Article 19 of the Law to Protect Women and Girls. On August 18 the Singapore police court gave the brothel owners thirty days to close down their establishments.[10] The records state that there were forty-six prostitutes working in these brothels. Roughly half the Japanese prostitutes who had been working in Singapore are said to have left

---

[7] "Tōchi kamin hogokyoku no hōjin shishō eigyōshu kiso to hōjin shishō sōmetsu kikaku ni kansuru ken" [Chinese Protectorate plan to prosecute operators of Japanese brothels and eradicate independent Japanese prostitutes], Singapore consulate secret message 247, August 22, 1927, in "Zaigai hompō baishōfu torishimari narabini sōkan kankei zakken" [Miscellaneous documents concerning the control of Japanese prostitutes overseas and their repatriation], 1927–1938, Diplomatic History Archives, Ministry of Foreign Affairs.

[8] Ibid.

[9] "Hōjin shōfu fukkatsu mondai ni kansuru ken" [Memorandum concerning the resurgence of Japanese prostitution], Ministry of Foreign Affairs message 1, March 11, 1924, in "Zaigai hompō baishōfu."

[10] "Tōchi kamin hogokyoku no hōjin shisho," in "Zaigai hompō baishōfu."

after this incident.[11] The remaining prostitutes were urged by the Japanese Society of Singapore and the Chinese Protectorate to return to Japan on a voluntary basis or undertake honest employment if they intended to stay in Singapore. Azuma Moriya (1884–1975) of the Women's Christian Temperance union of Japan did persuade five of the more than fifty remaining prostitutes to return with her to Japan, but the majority opted to stay in Singapore, supposedly undertaking different occupations.

In its October 21, 1927, "Memorandum Concerning Resident Japanese Prostitutes," the Japanese consulate in Singapore noted that these women would probably resume their former trade: "While five of the prostitutes have returned to Japan, the majority say they prefer to remain in Singapore and vow that they will apply themselves to more suitable occupations. The brothels have closed. But there are a number of dubious inns and massage parlors in which these women are probably carrying on their former trade in secret."[12] The consulate's guess was probably correct. Nevertheless, most of the remaining prostitutes had gone to Singapore before prostitution was outlawed in 1920 and were now in their forties. They would be the last of the Singapore *karayuki-san*.

The ban on prostitution was obviously not as immediately effective as the figures in table 1 suggest. Still, the 1920 ban did eventually help change the demography of the Japanese population in Singapore and Malaya. As the *karayuki-san* disappeared, so did the men who had been involved in businesses connected with prostitution: rooms for rent, clubs, inns, boardinghouses, barbers and hairdressers, kimono and dry goods merchants, and medicine vendors.

Even as these occupations were waning, the region saw a rapid increase in the number of Japanese men who were salaried office and bank employees, clerks, and shop employees. As table 1 shows, the number of men in these occupations began to grow during World War I. At the end of June 1914, just before the outbreak of the war, there were only 45 men listed in this category, yet at the end of June 1915, less than a year into the war, the number had more than doubled, to 106. It continued to grow until in 1920 there were 1,136 men in this category, and in 1921 there were 1,478. These figures, coupled with the 1920 ban on prostitution, indicate the radical change that was taking place in the composition of the local Japanese population.

Another characteristic of this period was the appearance of the category of "trading companies." The consular population survey first included a category for the owners, managers, and executives of "trading companies" in 1917. In the early 1920s the number of people in this category hovered around 10. The employees of such companies were generally included in the category of "company and bank employees."[13] The 1924 consular population survey listed 13 traders, while the

---

[11] "Zairyū hōjin shishō ni kansuru ken" [Memorandum concerning resident Japanese prostitutes], Singapore consulate secret message 289, October 21, 1927.

[12] Ibid.

[13] The category of "trader" first appeared in 1917, when 24 people were classified under this heading. There is no record for 1918, but the number of traders for the years 1919 through 1922 were 203, 39, 11, and 19, respectively. Throughout the 1920s there were more than 10 people in this category. The number of traders, both large and small, grew rapidly during World War I, but during the postwar recession small trading operations were gradually consolidated into fewer and larger enterprises. This does not sufficiently explain the unexpectedly large number of 203 for 1919, however. Most probably the number was inflated by inclusion of the employees as well as the owners of Japanese trading companies. According to the December 1919 "Zaigai hompō jitsugyōsha shirabe" [Survey of expatriate Japanese businessmen] of the Foreign Ministry's Bureau of Commercial Affairs, there were 20 business owners involved in import-

Foreign Ministry's Bureau of Commercial Affairs recorded fourteen trading companies in its "Survey of Expatriate Japanese Businessmen." The slight discrepancy can be explained by the fact that the consular survey was made at the end of June and the Foreign Ministry survey was made at the end of December.

The fourteen companies were Mitsul & Co. (Singapore Branch), Senda Shōkai, Mitsubishi Trading Co. (Singapore Branch), Kawahara Shōten, Suzuki Shōten (Singapore Branch Office), Nichiran Bōeki, Nunoi Shōten, Ikeda Shōten (Singapore Branch), Katō Shōkai (Singapore Branch), Shimoda Kōōshi, Ebata Yōkō, Tōin Bōeki Shōkai, Otomune Shōten, and Santei Shōōkai. These companies employed a total of 78 people, and when the employees of the Singapore branches of the Yokohama Specie Bank, Bank of Taiwan, and China and South Bank, of the Nippon Yūsen, Osaka Shōsen, and Yamashita Kisen shipping companies, and of the Nan'yō Sōko warehousing company are added, the number of employees rises to 193. In this year the total number of company and bank employees was 297. Therefore, as these figures indicate, a large proportion of the people classified as company and bank employees were working for relatively large corporations.

Another index of the major changes taking place in the early Japanese community in Singapore and Malaya was the ratio of commodity merchants to those working as employees of companies and banks.[14] Table 2 shows that between 1915 and 1920 there was a rapid drop in the number of merchants and a correspondingly rapid rise in the number of employees, especially those working for trading companies, banks, shipping companies, and warehousing companies, in both Singapore and Malaya (including North Borneo).

Thus we see that World War I was a transitional period in the Japanese community in Singapore and Malaya, during which there was a shift from a community economy based on prostitution to one that was primarily business oriented. The end of the war and the banning of prostitution in 1920 can be seen as triggering the decline of the original Japanese community and its replacement by a new community grounded in Japanese capitalism.[15] This, in essence, is the historical reason for the reversal in the numbers of men and women in the Japanese community that began to be evident in 1915.

---

export trade, employing a total of 182 workers. These two figures add up to 202, which is very close to the consulate's 203.

[14] "Commodity merchants" excluded company employees, bank employees, sales and clerical staff, and such service categories as inns and boardinghouses, barbers and hairdressers, and restaurants. Specifically, in 1910, "commodity merchants" included people selling the following categories of goods: general merchandise; art objects and antiques; sewing machines and other small machines; ceramic wares; metalware; guns and explosives; medicines; dry goods; yarn, cotton, and bedding; clocks and watches; books; paper and stationery; notions; shoes and other footwear; secondhand goods; tobacco; miso and soy sauce; oils and fertilizers; coal and charcoal; grains; fruit and vegetables; fish, bird, and animal meat; groceries; beverages; and tea.

[15] Yano describes a shift in the pattern of Japanese migration to Singapore from "lower town" to "*gudane* [godown] people," after the popular name for Raffles Place, the center of commercial activity in Singapore (Yano, "*Nanshin*" *no keifu*, pp. 124–27). The basis for this model is to be found in such interwar sources as Nan'yō oyobi Nihonjinsha, ed., *Nan'yō no gojū nen* [Fifty years in the South Seas] (Tokyo: Shōkasha, 1938). As illustrated by table 2, the pattern of Japanese migration to the Netherlands East Indies and the Philippines resembled the Singapore pattern, though on a smaller scale.

Table 2. Proportions of Japanese Commodity Merchants, Company and Bank Employees, and Dependents, by Region, 1910–1940

Unit: %

	1910	1915	1920	1925	1930	1935	1940
Singapore							
Commodity merchants in commercial population	44.1	57.6	10.1	14.1	14.0	7.6	—
Company & bank employees in commercial population	—	11.3	73.3	46.7	53.0	60.0	—
Dependents of working males	—	—	31.3	54.1	67.0	78.1	—
Malaya & Borneo							
Commodity merchants in commercial population	38.5	33.5	20.3	13.9	18.7	19.8	—
Company & bank employees in commercial population	—	5.5	51.5	76.2	56.5	53.2	—
Dependents of working males	—	—	46.2	83.5	96.1	103.8	—
Netherlands East Indies							
Commodity merchants in commercial population	—	43.4	34.4	32.9	32.0	28.7	27.3
Company & bank employees in commercial population	—	36.8	38.4	42.9	55.7	60.5	58.6
Dependents of working males	—	—	36.3	68.0	72.4	79.1	93.5
Philippines							
Commodity merchants in commercial population	59.6	37.2	27.8	36.4	22.0	22.2	19.5
Company & bank employees in commercial population	3.2	9.6	33.8	42.1	61.5	70.7	68.3
Dependents of working males	—	—	16.1	34.0	58.9	87.3	110.4

"Company & bank employees" includes clerks and shop employees.

Source: Same as figure 1.

III. ANALYSIS OF THE JAPANESE COMMUNITY BY OCCUPATION

One of the first things to strike one's attention when studying the figures for the prewar Japanese population in Singapore and Malaya by occupation is the predominance of people listed in the categories for commerce and agriculture. At the time of the first population peak, in 1919, people involved in commerce and agriculture accounted for 48.7 percent and 23.5 percent of the total Japanese population, respectively. Breaking this down by locality, we see that the proportion of the Singapore population engaged in commerce was extremely high (43.0 percent of the total Japanese population, excluding prostitutes), while the proportion of the Malaya population involved in agriculture was high (36.4 percent of the total). Obviously, most of the Japanese who went to Singapore were engaged in commercial occupations, whereas most of those who went to Malaya were engaged in agricultural occupations.

To analyze the significance of these trends, it is necessary first to make some adjustments to the Japanese consular population survey figures. As I have noted elsewhere,[16] the subtle distinction between industry and occupation was not always clearly differentiated, a fact that caused some confusing overlap. This lack of

---

[16] Shimizu, "Gaimushō."

Figure 3. Trends in the Japanese Commercial Population
of Singapore and Malaya, 1907–1938

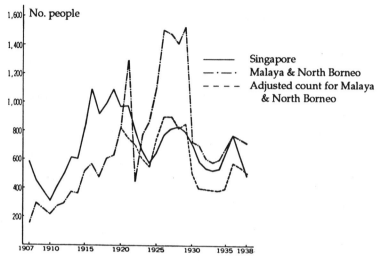

Source: Same as figure 1.

Figure 4. Trends in the Japanese Agricultural Population
of Singapore and Malaya, 1907–1938

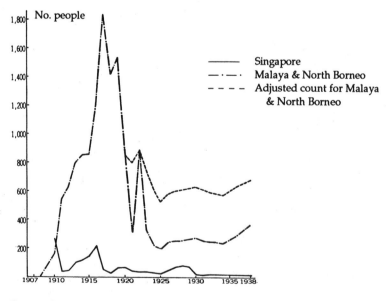

Source: Same as figure 1.

differentiation is especially evident in the category of "company and bank employees," which accounted for the largest proportion of the working Japanese populations of Singapore and Malaya in the interwar period. The problem is that many of these people were rubber-plantation employees. Unless we exclude them from our count, we cannot gain an accurate picture of the flow of commercial people to Singapore and of agricultural people to Malaya.

The question is how to make the necessary distinction. Fortunately, we have the Foreign Ministry's "Survey of Expatriate Japanese Businessmen," which provides data on the number of employees of overseas Japanese companies with sales or production of ¥10,000 or more. By adding up the annual employment figures for the rubber plantations and transferring these numbers from the commercial category of "company and bank employees" to the agricultural category of "rubber production," we can obtain more accurate population counts for the industrial classifications of commerce and agriculture. The dashed lines in figures 3 and 4 indicate the adjusted counts for the commercial and agricultural populations of Malaya and North Borneo.[17] The following analysis is based on these two figures.

1. THE JAPANESE COMMERCIAL POPULATION OF SINGAPORE

As figure 3 shows, the Japanese commercial populations of Singapore and Malaya followed similar trends. Both saw their first peak at the end of the second decade of this century and their first decline in the mid-1920s. They peaked again in the latter half of the 1920s and dropped once more in the early 1930s. This cyclical movement paralleled changes in economic conditions. Moreover, the cycles in the Japanese commercial populations of Singapore and Malaya also tended to reflect the ebb and flow in the Straits Settlements' trade with Japan (fig. 5), though there was a time lag of one or two years between trade and population trends. It hardly needs to be pointed out that the trade figures with Japan were an index of the economic stability of the local economies, which were heavily export oriented (for one thing, exports dictated the amount of foreign currency available to spend on imports). Taking into consideration the fact that the majority of the people involved in trade with Japan were Japanese, we can see that trade figures are also a good index of the Japanese population in the region. Changes in the price of rubber (fig. 6) were the major determinant of economic conditions in Singapore and Malaya, and from World War I to around 1930 rubber prices closely approximated fluctuations in the region's trade with Japan. The conclusion is that the Japanese commercial populations of Singapore and Malaya followed a cycle of growth and decline dictated primarily by trends in trade with Japan and in rubber prices.

Let us look at the types of employment that were the most sensitive to the changes in economic trends, as shown in the occupational subclassifications in the consular population survey for Singapore, where a majority of Japanese residents were involved in commerce. The top five occupations among Japanese commercial residents in Singapore in 1919, the year of the first population peak, were as follows (in descending order): entertainers, prostitutes, serving women, etc. (257); traders (203); general merchants (160); company and bank employees (124); and

---

[17] Unfortunately, since not all the annual data from the Foreign Ministry's "Zaigai hompō jitsugyōsha shirabe" and "Kaigai Nippon jitsugyōsha no chōsa" through 1918 have yet been collected, these adjustments can only be provisional. The figures for Singapore have not been adjusted because the number of rubber-plantation employees was so small as to be insignificant.

Figure 5. Trends in the Straits Settlements' Trade with Japan, 1900–1933

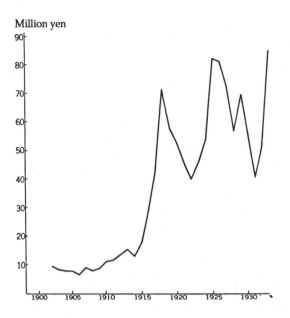

Source: Tōyō Keizai Shimpōsha, ed., *Nihon bōeki seiran* [Data on Japanese trade], reprint with supplementary material (Tokyo: Tōyō Keizai Shimpōsha, 1975).

Figure 6. Trends in Rubber Prices, 1915–1931

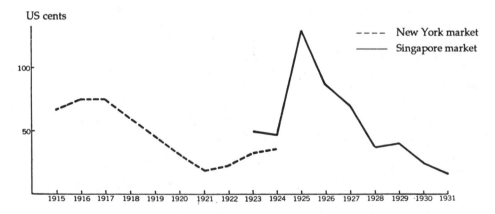

Values indicate average price per pound of ribbed smoked sheet.

Sources: Nan'yō oyobi Nihonjinsha, ed., *Nan'yō, no gojū nen* [Fifty years in the South Seas] (Tokyo: Shōkasha, 1938); Nan'yō Kyōkai [South Seas Association], trans. and ed., *Nan'yō no gomu saibai jigyō* [Rubber cultivation in the South Seas] (Tokyo: Nan'yō Kyōkai, 1932). The latter work is a translation of selected chapters of David M. Figart, *The Plantation Rubber Industry in the Middle East* (Washington, DC: Department of Commerce, 1926).

restaurant and bar proprietors (122). At the time of the second peak, in 1928, the ranking was company and bank employees (524); merchants (81); barbers, hair-dressers, and bathhouse proprietors (69); entertainers, prostitutes, serving women, etc. (60); and inn, restaurant, rooms-for-rent, and entertainment-business proprietors (53). Only 12 people were listed as traders, the second largest classification in 1919. This seems too drastic a drop over only nine years and is extremely suspect, given the history of the region after World War I.

The source of this anomaly is probably the number of traders counted in 1919. The traders in the consular population survey included the owners, managers, and directors of offices involved in the import-export business. It is hard to believe that there were as many as 203 such owners, managers, and directors in 1919. The Foreign Ministry's "Survey of Expatriate Japanese Businessmen" listed twenty companies, including the branch offices of Mitsui & Co. and Mitsubishi Trading Co., in its category for import-export trade, with 20 representatives and 176 employees, for a total of 196 people in this category. What this tells us is that the 1919 consular population survey probably included the trading companies' employees in the "trader" category instead of the category of "company and bank employees."

Who were the company and bank employees listed in the 1919 survey? Looking again at the Foreign Ministry's "Survey of Expatriate Japanese Businessmen," we find a total of 103 people working for the Yokohama Specie Bank, Bank of Taiwan, and China and South Bank and for the Nippon Yūsen, Osaka Shōsen, and Yamashita Kisen shipping companies. We know from this that the 1919 consular survey figure for company and bank employees was based primarily on these people and did not include employees of trading companies.

To compare the 1919 figures with those for 1928, it is necessary to shift the trading-company employees from the consular survey's "trader" category to its category of "company and bank employees." The 1919 figures resulting from this adjustment are 20 traders and 307 company and bank employees. Table 3 compares the revised figures for the three main categories—commodity merchants, company and bank employees, and people in service occupations in the peak years of 1919 and 1928 in terms of the percentages of the Japanese commercial population in Singapore represented by these categories. The service sector remained stable, at 14.6 percent, but there was a drastic fluctuation in the other two categories: a drop from 38.5 percent to 9.7 percent for commodity merchants and a rise from 28.0 percent to 62.9 percent for company and bank employees. Over the decade between the end of World War I and the early years of the Japanese Shōwa era, which began in 1926, the majority of Japanese entrants to Singapore gradually shifted to people connected with major Japanese companies. It naturally follows, therefore, that the

Table 3. Proportions of Commodity Merchants, Company and Bank Employees, and People in Service Occupations in Japanese Commercial Population, 1919 and 1928

Unit: %

	Commodity merchants	Company & bank employees	Service occupations
1919	38.5	28.0	14.6
1928	9.7	62.9	14.6

"Company & bank employees" includes clerks and shop employees.

Source: Same as figure 1.

balance of the local Japanese commercial population after World War I shifted to an increase in the number of company and bank employees.

The number of company and bank employees in each year from 1913 to 1934 is shown in the left-hand column of table 4. This category peaked for the first time in 1920, dropped to its first low in 1924, peaked again in 1928, and bottomed out once more in 1932. Basically, this was the same cyclical rhythm as that of the Japanese commercial population as a whole. Since the fluctuations in the commercial population reflected changes in business conditions, it can be concluded that the population of company and bank employees was equally sensitive to business trends.

Table 4. Trends in the Japanese Population of Company and Bank Employees, 1913–1934

Unit: No. people

	Company & bank employees[a]	Employees of branches of 8 largest Japanese companies[b]
1913	41	14
1916	129	37[c]
1917	176	
1918	212	126
1919	124	158
1920	712	
1921	689	117
1922	447	
1923	372	
1924	297	90
1925	307	
1926	446	
1927	497	
1928	524	
1929	516	
1930	377	
1931	305	
1932	274	
1933	288	
1934	323	

[a] "Company & bank employees" includes clerks and shop employees.

[b] The eight largest companies are Mitsui & Co., Mitsubishi Trading Co., Yokohama Specie Bank, Bank of Taiwan, China and South Bank, Nippon Yūsen, Osaka Shōsen, and Yamashita Kisen.

[c] This is the figure for 1915.

Sources: "Kaigai zairyū hompōjin shokugyōbetsu jinkō chōsa ikken," Diplomatic History Archives, Ministry of Foreign Affairs; Ministry of Foreign Affairs, Bureau of Commercial Affairs, "Kaigai Nippon jitsugyōsha no chōsa" (Survey of expatriate Japanese businessmen], 1913, 1916, 1918; Ministry of Foreign Affairs, Bureau of Commercial Affairs, "Zaigai hompō jitsugyōsha shirabe" [Survey of expatriate Japanese businessmen], 1919, 1921, 1924.

To permit a more detailed analysis, the employment figures for the eight leading Japanese companies in Singapore are shown in the right-hand column of table 4. These include the total number of employees working at the branch offices of the above-mentioned two trading companies, three banks, and three shipping companies. Unfortunately, no figures are available for the first peak year, 1920, but it is clear that the numbers were increasing up to 1919 and later decreased sharply. There was a 43 percent drop (a decrease of 68 employees) between 1919 and 1924.

Obviously, these companies' Japanese staffs reflected, albeit with a one- or two-year lag, fluctuations in the region's trade with Japan and in rubber prices. The large Japanese companies in Singapore, sensitive to business trends, apparently sought to maximize profits and minimize costs under short-term management policies of laying off or adding employees as circumstances dictated.

The employee cuts in the early 1920s reflected the pessimistic outlook for the future of the major Japanese companies. In October 1922 the Japanese consulate in Singapore conducted a survey "for internal use only" of local Japanese companies, "Survey of Companies Managed by Japanese," to collect information needed to respond to "inquiries by the colonial authorities on the income tax of Japanese residents," to requests "from Japanese or foreigners for credit checks," and to "requests for corroboration of bona fides."[18] Overall, the companies surveyed were quite pessimistic in their responses to question twelve of the survey, which asked about their current business conditions and outlook for the future.

Mitsui & Co.: "Business is slack."

Mitsubishi Trading Co.: "Transactions have been slack due to the general economic slump, and we have suffered unexpected losses as a result of bankruptcies among our trading partners."

Nan'yo Soko: "Business is not good. General merchants do not make much use of our kind of warehousing facilities, and the decrease in imports and exports has had a depressing effect on the warehousing business in general."

Osaka Shosen: "The shipping industry as a whole is suffering a slump this year. Now that Alllerican shipping has joined the European Line Conference, transport costs for pelagic shipping are rising."

China and South Bank: "Both trading and financial businesses are finding the going hard in this market. Our own operations are closely tied to fluctuations in the incomes of rubber-plantation owners, which in turn are affected by changes in the world price of rubber. Our survival depends heavily on the price of rubber. (Unless we see an upturn in rubber prices that will secure our income derived from the interest on loans made to rubber plantations, there is no telling what the future holds.)"[19]

---

[18] "Hompōjin keiei kigyō chōsa," in "Kakkoku keizai zakken: Kaikyō shokuminchi no bu (Taisho 9 nen 1 gatsu–)" [Miscellaneous documents concerning the economies of various countries: The Straits Settlements (January 1920–)], Diplomatic History Archives, Ministry of Foreign Affairs. The files also contain various documents concerning the effects of World War I on Japanese trade, such as "Ōshū sensō no keizai bōeki ni oyobosu eikyō hōkoku zakken" [Miscellaneous reports concerning the impact of the European war on the economy and trade].

[19] It is noteworthy that whereas large companies complained of poor business and depressed markets, individually owned small companies were relatively optimistic about their prospects, as the following examples indicate. Yamanaka Shoten (rattan and timber export and sale): "Rattan exports are doing extremely well. We are currently making adjustments in timber exports." Hara Shōten (rattan export and sale): "We are doing well, and the outlook is good." Sugimura Tokusaburō Shōten (cotton fabrics and sundries): "Fiscal 1921 was especially hard, given the economic confusion that followed the end of the war. Business will probably continue to be difficult in the future as we suffer the after effects of the recession. Still, we plan to remain in business." Tamoto Shōten (Japanese and Western alcoholic beverages): "Economic conditions are not good, but business is going well. The outlook is not clear." Fukuya (Japanese and Western alcoholic beverages): "Sales are $40,000 lower than in fiscal 1920, but we do not consider this threatening." Hanaya Shōkai (car rental, books, and exercise and weight-control equipment): "We just began book sales in January this year, so it is difficult to forecast for this category. If all goes as hoped, however, the prospects should be good, and we see no reason to

There was no comment from the Yokohama Specie Bank or the Bank of Taiwan.

Next let us examine what segnients of the local Japanese population were most sensitive to changes in business conditions. Figures available for the 1921—1926 period show which categories of people increased or decreased as a result of the economic slump (table 5). Company and bank employees and their dependents gradually decreased in number during this period. Close study of the figures reveals that the rate of decrease was greater among the employees themselves than among their dependents and much greater than among Japanese residents engaged in other occupations. In contrast, the number of dependents of company and bank employees and of people in other occupations remained relatively stable throughout the 1921–1926 period, an indication that the people most directly affected by business conditions were company and bank employees who were either unmarried or unaccompanied by their families.

Table 5. Trends in the Japanese Population of Company and Bank Employees, People Engaged in Other Occupations, and Their Dependents, 1921–1926

	1921	1922	1923	1924	1925	1926
Company & bank employees						
Working population (index no.)	100	64.9	54.0	43.1	44.6	64.7
Dependents (index no.)	100	90.5	84.2	91.6	72.6	186.8
Dependents (%)	27.6	38.5	43.0	58.6	45.0	79.6
Other occupations						
Working population (index no.)	100	100.1	82.4	77.8	113.6	112.0
Dependents (index no.)	100	124.2	117.3	113.3	94.2	76.7
Dependents (%)	46.2	57.3	65.8	67.3	38.3	31.6

"Company & bank employees" includes clerks and shop employees.

Source: Same as figure 1.

We can conclude from this that in post-World War I Singapore, company and bank employees who were either unmarried or unaccompanied by their families were a key factor in fluctuations in the local Japanese population. The inflow and outflow of these people was especially responsive to changes in the price of rubber and in trade with Japan. It is probably safe to say that most people in this category

give up any of our other business lines." Frank Shōkai (wholesale and retail sale of Japanese sundries): "We expect to go into the red this year, but the outlook is promising." Robin Shōkai (general merchandise): "Present conditions are not very good, but business is so-so, and the outlook is hopeful." Takeshita Shōten (general merchandise): "We cannot be overly optimistic, but neither is there cause for pessimism." Hashizume Shōten (clothing, sundries, and groceries): "Our business record is good. There is ample opportunity for growth." Matsuo Shōkai (clothing, sundries, and automobiles): "Our business record is good. We plan to expand into ceramic wares, glassware, and cotton fabrics wholesale." Haraguchi Shōten (clothing and sundries): "The outlook is good." Of all the small-business owners surveyed, only two were unequivocally pessimistic about the future. Shingapōru Kutsu Seizōsho (shoe production and sale): "No prospects." Tō Indo Bōeki Shōkai (export of South Seas products): "Right now business is good, but the collection and distribution of South Seas products in Singapore Harbor is not going as smoothly as before. Many products are being directly exported from their place of production, making it difficult for us to purchase the same products here. We hope to transfer our base of operations to Surabaya, Java." I believe that one key to the relative stability of the Japanese commercial population in the Netherlands East Indies during the recession of the 1920s is to be found in the contrast between the optimistic stance of small retail and wholesale businesses and the personnel cuts made by large companies.

were attracted to Singapore and Malaya by the profits that could be made from the local market and the region's rubber resources.

2. THE SUDDEN INCREASE IN THE JAPANESE FISHERY-INDUSTRY POPULATION IN THE LATE 1920s

The percentage of the local Japanese population made up of dependents grew steadily during the 1921–1926 period. Interestingly, as table 5 shows, the number of dependents of Japanese engaged in occupations other than company or bank employee dropped dramatically in 1925 and 1926. This was because in those two years there was a correspondingly rapid increase in the number of Japanese fishery workers, a category marked by its lack of accompanying dependents. In 1926, for example, only 4.3 percent of such workers in Singapore were accompanied by dependents.[20]

Beginning in the latter half of the 1920s, there was a marked increase in the number of Japanese involved in the fishery industry throughout Southeast Asia, with the sole exception of the Netherlands East Indies after 1933 (fig. 7). As is well known, around the time of World War I the Japanese fishery industry began developing overseas markets (with canned products and the like) that required fishing outside Japanese waters. The growth of Japanese fishing concerns in Southeast Asia was part of this expansion.

Figure 7. Trends in the Japanese Fishery Population of Southeast Asia, 1907–1938

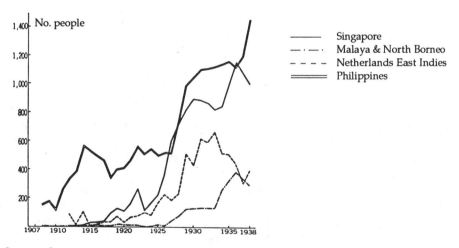

Source: Same as figure 1.

In the first half of the 1920s only 100 to 200 Japanese in Singapore—mainly fishermen—were employed in the fishery industry, but their number increased rapidly from 1925 onward, quadrupling in just four years: in 1929 there were 825 Japanese involved in the fishery industry, outnumbering the 800 people engaged in commerce and constituting the largest occupational category of Singapore's Japanese population. Thereafter this group remained at the top, its numbers decreasing

---

[20] If fishermen are excluded, the proportion of people in the fishery industry accompanied by dependents was 41.3 percent in 1925 and 39.3 percent in 1926.

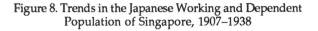

Figure 8. Trends in the Japanese Working and Dependent
Population of Singapore, 1907–1938

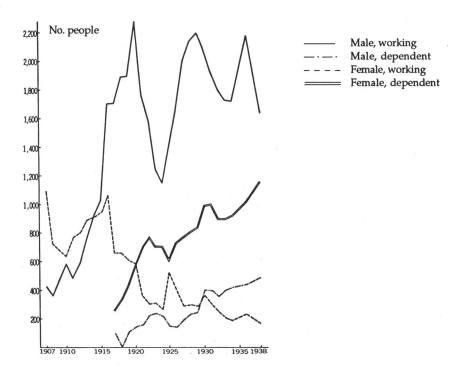

Source: Same as figure 1.

only with the outbreak of the Pacific War. Figure 8 shows the fluctuations in the number of Japanese in Singapore between 1907 and 1938. The narrowing in the range of fluctuation among working Japanese men from the latter half of the 1920s onward was due to the influx of workers in the fishery industry.

A Ministry of Finance report commented as follows on the activities of Japanese fishermen in Singapore in this period: "Japanese fishermen based in Singapore went beyond the Balimun Sea and the Riau Islands and across the equator to the coastal waters of Sumatra and the Bangka Strait. Their activities covered a wide expanse of ocean: eastward, from the South China Sea along the east coast of the Malay Peninsula to French Indochina, 600—700 miles from the Gulf of Siam; westward, through the Strait of Malacca and into the Indian Ocean. In particular, *supplied about half the fish for the Singapore market.*"[21]

---

[21] Ministry of Finance, Administration Bureau, "Nipponjin no kaigai katsudō ni kansuru rekishiteki chōsa" [A historical survey of Japanese overseas activities], no. 32, "Malaya," p. 72. For Japanese South Seas fishing activities based in prewar Singapore, see also Chikashi Kataoka, "Senzenki Shingapōru o chūshin to shita Nihonjin gyogyō: Nan'yō gyogyō no ichi ruikei" [Japanese fishery in and around Singapore before World War II: A representative type of fishery in Southeast Asia], in *Gyogyō keizai kenkyū* [Journal of fisheries economy] 27, no. 3 (December 1982); 28, nos. 1, 2 (June 1983).

Records for 1938 listed the ethnic distribution of the fishing population in Singapore as 5,874 Malays, 4,356 Chinese, and 1,083 Japanese.[22] Thus, the Japanese fishing population was only about one-fifth the size of either the Malay or the Chinese fishing population and less than one-tenth the size of the other two combined. Yet according to the Ministry of Finance report, Japanese fishermen were supplying roughly half the Singapore fish market with only one-tenth the labor, an indication of the superior productivity made possible by the use of motorized fishing craft, refrigeration equipment, and such sophisticated fishing teclmiques as the Okinawan method of driving large schools of fish into nets. Not to be overlooked is the fact such superior equipment and techniques could be utilized because Japanese fishing was organized on a corporate basis.

The first Japanese fishery company established in Singapore was Taisei Gyogyō Kōshi, founded at the end of 1917 by Tora Eifuku, a trainee of the pelagic-fishing training program of the Ministry of Agriculture and Commerce. During the postwar recession of the early 1920s a number of other Japanese fishery companies were established, among them Ishizu Gyogyō Kōshi (founded by Tōjirō Ishizu, a native of Nagasaki Prefecture) and Nammei Kōshi, both established in 1921; Taisei Gyogyō Kabushiki Kaisha, a company that shifted over from the rubber industry; and Daishō Kōshi, founded in 1922 by Tora Eifuku after leaving Taisei Gyogyō Kōshi. As economic conditions improved and the industry began to stabilize around 1923, Ishizu Gyogyō Kōshi, Daisho Hoshi, and other local Japanese fishery companies began to expand their activities, including the use of drive-in nets, in other areas of Southeast Asia, including the Netherlands East Indies, Penang, the Gulf of Siam, and the Mergui Islands of Burma.

The rapid rate at which the Japanese fishery population in Singapore increased in the latter half of the 1920s can be attributed to the growth of these companies and their employment of more and more Japanese workers. According to the "Survey of Expatriate Japanese Businessmen," at the end of December 1924, not long after Ishizu Gyogyō Kōshi and Daishō Kōshi were founded, the total number of workers employed by these two companies and Taisei Gyogyō Kōshi was 171, which tallies with the consular population survey figure of 170 for the same year. In other words *all* the Japanese involved in the fishery industry in Singapore in 1924 were employees of these three companies. It was even rarer in the fishery industry than in commercial occupations to find Japanese who were independent migrants. That almost all Japanese fishermen were employed workers and that very few were accompanied by their family reveals the same pattern of migration by employees without dependents.

3. The Japanese Agricultural Population of Malaya

The majority of Japanese in Malaya were involved in agriculture. As we see from figure 4, the agricultural population rose steadily from 1909 to 1917, after which it fell, remaining fairly stable from 1925 onward. A look at the classification of the local Japanese population by occupation shows how closely the fluctuations in the agricultural population were related to the fortunes of the rubber industry. For example, when the agricultural population peaked in 1917 at 1,831, there were 1,776 Japanese working on rubber plantations and only 55 cultivating other crops. In

---

[22] Ministry of Finance, Administration Bureau, "Nipponjin no kaigai katsudō," no. 32, "Malaya," p. 136.

Table 6. Changes in the Number of Rubber Plantations in British Malaya Owned by Japanese Companies and in the Number of Their Japanese Employees

	1921	1924	1937	1939
Johor				
No. plantations	23	28	18	8
No. employees	362	286	148	91
Negeri Sembilan				
No. plantations	7	2	1	1
No. employees	63	33	23	21
Selangor				
No. plantations	5	1	—	—
No. employees	16	3	—	—
Perak				
No. plantations	8	3	—	—
No. employees	14	2	—	—
British Borneo				
No. plantations	1	1	—	—
No. employees	47	50	—	—
Sarawak				
No. plantations	2	3	—	—
No. employees	19	15	—	—
Total				
No. plantations	46	39	19	9
No. employees	521	389	171	112

Source: Ministry of Roreign Affairs, Bureau of Commercial Affairs, "Zaigai hompō jitsugyōsha shirabe," 1921, 1924, 1937, 1939.

other words, 97 percent of the Japanese involved in agricultural activities in Malaya were engaged in rubber cultivation. It is no exaggeration to say that the Japanese population of Malaya fluctuated in direct relation to the fortunes of people engaged in the rubber industry.

Rubber was a commodity whose price was affected by supply and demand in world markets as determined by international economic conditions. Thus the Japanese population working in the rubber industry in Malaya ebbed and flowed with the fluctuations in the price of rubber on international markets. This can be readily seen when figure 4 is compared with figure 6, which shows price fluctuations for a pound of ribbed smoked sheet in New York and in Singapore from 1915 to 1931. Up to the mid-1920s, the two curves were roughly parallel. Thereafter, however, the number of Japanese agricultural workers in Malaya remained steady at between 500 and 600 regardless of fluctuations in rubber prices.

The most noteworthy development in the second half of the 1920s was a decline in the number of rubber plantations operated by individual owners or small companies and a decrease in the number of employees of company-owned plantations.

This becomes evident when we look again at the "Survey of Expatriate Japanese Businessmen." Table 6 compares survey figures for the number of company plantations and Japanese employees in the early 1920s and the late 1930s. As already mentioned, the survey was limited to relatively large plantations with sales or production of ¥10,000 or more. For comparison, table 7 shows changes in the number of small individually owned rubber plantation from 1911 to 1937. As these tables clearly indicate, from the 1920s to the 1930s there was a sharp decrease in

Table 7. Changes in the Number of Rubber Plantations in British Malaya Owned by Japanese Individuals, 1911–1937

	1911	1917	1920	1930	1932–1934	1937
Johor	47	60	38	56	47	33
Selangor	23	32	42	22	22	14
Negeri Sembilan	15	39	35	9	8	4
Perak	12	39	58	20	10	5
Pahang	5	28	33	19	15	16
Penang & Kedah	2	16	9	5	4	1
Other	2	7	11	2	1	0
Total	106	221	226	133	107	73

Source: Fujio Hara, *Eiryō Maraya no Nihonjin* [The Japanese in British Malaya] (Tokyo: Ajia Keizai Kenkyūsho [Institute of Developing Economies], 1986), Appendix, table 4, p. 222.

both individual and company plantations, with employees of company plantations cut to as little as one-third to one-fourth their former numbers.

In Johor, where most Japanese plantations were concentrated, of the twenty-three plantations owned by Japanese companies in 1921 only five survived in 1937, among them Sango Kōshi, Nettai Sangyō, and Nan'yō Gomu.[23] The same trend was evident among individually owned rubber plantations. Of the sixty such plantations in Johor in 1917, only eighteen remained in 1937.[24] What these figures tell us is that the Japanese-owned rubber plantations that were able to survive the slump in the rubber market that lasted from the latter half of the second decade of the century into the 1920s (the market revived slightly in the middle of this period) were the large plantations with a relatively solid capital base and stable management. The small individually owned plantations found it very hard going.

The Industry Promotion Bureau of the Taiwan government general reported on conditions in Malaya in 1917 as follows: "The rubber plantations of this region (the Straits Settlements and the Malay Peninsula) . . . both large and small number as many as ninety-one. While it is not possible to investigate each and every one, it is apparent that except for those with large capital, such as Sango Kōshi, Morimura, Mitsui, Ōkura, Fujita, and Suzuki, most of the plantations are struggling. This is especially the case with the plantations owned and operated by residents of Singapore who have invested in the rubber business what little they could save from operating inns or shops or from prostitution. Unfortunately, many have run into trouble because of lack of experience. Some have even fallen so low as to cover their operational costs with high-interest loans from mutual financing associations and *chettyars* (native Singapore moneylenders)."[25]

---

[23] Fujio Hara, "Taiheiyō sensōzen ni okeru Maraya e no shihon shinshutsu: Gomuen keiei o chūshin to shite" [Capital investment in Malaya before the Pacific War, with emphasis on rubber plantations], in *Ouchi Tsutomu kanreki kinen rombunshū* [Papers in Commemoration of Tsutomu ouchi's Sixtieth Birthday], ed. Ōuchi Tsutomu kanreki kinen rombunshū kankokai (Tokyo: Tokyo Daigaku Shuppankai, 1977), p. 258.

[24] Ibid., p. 262. The number of individually owned rubber plantation in Johor in 1937, including those established after 1917, was thirty-three.

[25] Taiwan Government General, Industry Promotion Bureau, Commerce and Industry Division, "Nan'yō ni okeru hōjin no kigyō" [Japanese businesses in the South Seas], South China and South Seas Survey 16, December 1917, pp. 55–56. Despite the parenthetical explanation in this document, *chettyars* were actually Indian, not "native Singapore," loan sharks.

Conditions were especially bad during the slump in the rubber market in the early 1920s, triggered by the recession following World War I. On July 21, 1922, the Federation of South Seas Planters, a federation of Japanese rubber planters headed by Nettai Sangyō, Nan'a Kōshi, Nan'yō Gomu, and Marai Gomu Kōshi, submitted a petition to Minister for Foreign Affairs Kosai Uchida requesting financing to cover operating costs: "Affected by the postwar recession, market prices have been gradually falling since the autumn of 1920 and there is no respite in sight. Because of this, we have been suffering heavy losses and now do not even have enough money to cover our operating expenses. Can this state of affairs continue? Much of the more than ¥40 million of Japanese money invested in the rubber industry has disappeared like so much foam, and the very foundations of Japanese enterprise in this region are being threatened. This is a deplorable situation for both our own interests and those of national policy. We therefore request that the Government institute measures to protect our industry with long-term, low-interest loans."[26]

Two years later, on August 30, 1924, representatives of the Finance, Agriculture and Commerce, and Foreign ministries held a hearing at the Industrial Club, in Tokyo, in response to another petition, this one submitted jointly by the Federation of South Seas Planters and the League of South Seas Traders, requesting the creation of "a special financial institution for South Seas trade and rubber cultivation," but no such financial institution was ever set up.[27] These petitions indicate the long and difficult period that followed the end of World War I. The temporary rise in rubber prices in 1925 was unable to revitalize the struggling Japanese rubber plantations. The only advantage of the brief boom was the opportunity it provided to sell off operations at a profit to eager American and British capitalists.[28] In Southeast Asia as a whole, 70,437 acres of rubber-plantation land—30,180 planted acres and 40,257 uncultivated acres—were sold for a total of $20,287,500 (about ¥25 million).

---

[26] "Gomu saibai jigyō kyūsai ni kansuru chinjōsho" [Petition concerning relief for rubber-cultivation enterprises], July 21, 1922, in "Zai nan'yō hompōjin keiei kigyō chōsa ikken" [Survey of companies managed by Japanese in the South Seas], Diplomatic History Archives, Ministry of Foreign Affairs.

[27] "Nan'yō Saibai Rengōkai narabini Nan'yō Bōeki Dōmeikai kyōdō seigan chōshu yōryō" [Gist of the hearing on the joint petition submitted by the Federation of South Seas Planters and the League of South Seas Traders], August 30, 1924, in "Zai nan'yō hompōjin keiei kigyō chōsa ikken." At this hearing Makoto Okada, head of the Special Banking Division, Banking Bureau, Ministry of Finance, pointed out that the major barrier to establishing a special financial institution was not lack of funds but the difficulty of securing appropriate guarantees. He stated: "At this point no financial measures taken for the colonies have succeeded, and yet there is nothing to keep the Government from providing the requested funding. However, one major barrier is the difficulty of securing appropriate guarantees. This was a problem when funding was made available to Manchurian financial circles, and it is likely to be a problem in funding South Seas enterprises. Unless the petitioning companies can satisfy the banks' security requirements, there is no way they can be financed, no matter what kind of special financial institution is created."

[28] In this connection, the following exchange between representatives of the government and of the Federation of South Seas Planters at the August 30, 1924, hearing is of particular interest:

"*Government:* The Chinese plantation owners appear to be sustaining operations over a substantial area [of land] despite the recession. How are they being financed?

"*Federation:* There are no special low-interest financing opportunities for the Chinese. But they treat their plantations like commodities, readily selling their property if the market price and their own circumstances are right. Hence no problem with low-interest funding. A drop in the price of rubber plantations has the same effect as a capital decrease. In this respect [the Chinese] are very different from the Japanese, who persist in maintaining their business."

At the end of 1925 Japanese-owned rubber plantations occupied 135,328 planted acres, which means that as much as 22.3 percent of this land was sold.

The above circumstances are the major reason that fluctuations in the Japanese agricultural population in Malaya from 1924 onward were unrelated to conditions in the rubber market. In addition, certain institutional factors had a bearing on the reduction in the Japanese agricultural population after World War I. One was the Rubber Lands Restriction Enactment, promulgated by the British colonial government in July 1917 in the Federated Malay States and the following month in the Straits Settlements and Johor. Under the provisions of the enactment, no more than 50 acres of rubber-plantation land could be sold except to British subjects, the subjects of the sultans of Malay states under British protection, and individuals or corporations with special permits.[29] The enactment was, of course, a severe blow to Japanese rubber-plantation owners. It was briefly revoked in December 1918, at the end of World War I, but the British colonial government soon reinstated it because of food and labor shortages. In any case, with the exception of a very few small-scale transactions, the government did not permit any sales of land even when the enactment was not in force.

As a result, many Japanese rubber-plantation owners on the Malay Peninsula moved to Sumatra and the Riau Islands, where they established new plantations.[30] This migration was reflected in the fluctuations in the Japanese agricultural populations of the Netherlands East Indies and of Malaya and North Borneo, shown in figure 9. The enactment of 1917 marked the beginning of the decline in the Japanese agricultural population of Malaya. As this decline continued (to around 1923–1924), there was a corresponding rise in the Japanese agricultural population of the Netherlands East Indies, a rise that can only be explained by the movement of Japanese rubber-plantation owners from Malaya to Sumatra.

Another institutional factor contributing to the decline in the Japanese agricultural population of Malaya in the 1920s was the Stevenson Rubber Restriction Scheme, issued in the British colonies on November 1, 1922. This scheme was intended to prop up declining rubber prices. It was withdrawn in October 1928 and was followed in April 1934 by the first International Rubber Regulation Agreement (1934–1943). The Stevenson Scheme proved a total failure. Because it applied only in British colonial territories, it was ineffective in reviving the depressed rubber market and also severely handicapped rubber-plantation owners in British territories who were in competition with their counterparts in the Netherlands East Indies. The Japanese rubber-plantation owners on the Malay Peninsula were just as much the victims of this scheme as everyone else, and many were forced to abandon their operations on the peninsula altogether.

---

[29] "Kaikyō shokuminchi gomuen jōto narabini torihiki seigen ni kansuru jōrei" [The Rubber Lands Transfer and Restriction Enactment in the Straits Settlements], in "Nan'yō ni okeru hompōjin kigyō kankei zakken" [Miscellaneous documents concerning companies managed by Japanese in the South Seas], vol. 2, Diplomatic History Archives, Ministry of Foreign Affairs.

[30] Ministry of Finance, Administration Bureau, "Nipponjin no kaigai katsudō," no. 32, "Malaya," p. 117.

Figure 9. Trends in the Japanese Agricultural Population of the Netherlands
East Indies and of Malaya and North Borneo, 1910–1936

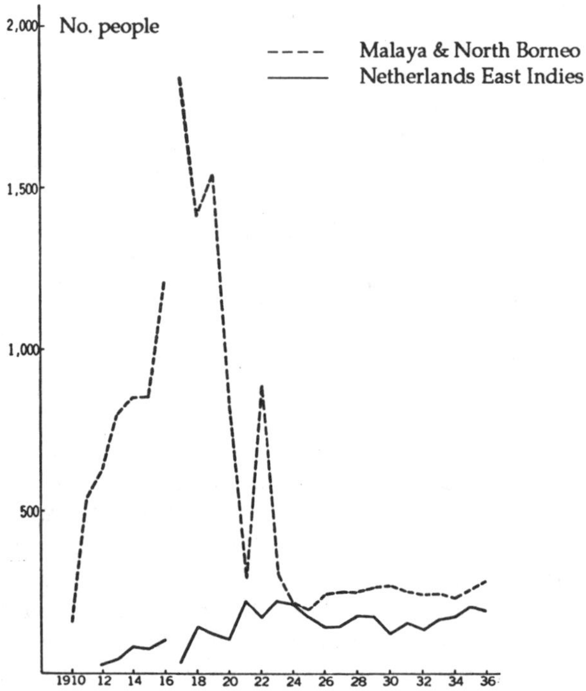

Source: Same as figure 1.

IV Conclusion

Except in the earliest period of the Japanese community in Singapore and Malaya,
Japanese penetration of the region between the two world wars was primarily economic, led by corporations attracted by the region's markets and natural resources—
a far cry from the popular stereotype of an "exodus of the dispossessed" from Japan.

The commercial penetration of Singapore, while of a dual structure that included small business, was for the most part led by employees of large Japanese corporations. These "migrant employees," primarily unmarried or unaccompanied by their
families, were highly responsive to changes in business conditions. The same can be
said of the workers employed by Japanese fishery companies, who contributed to
the rapid increase in the late 1920s in the number of Japanese in Singapore and
Malaya involved in the fishery industry. The fishery companies were attracted to
the region by its promise of new fishing grounds.

The bulk of the Japanese population in Malaya was involved in agriculture,
specifically rubber cultivation. While the pattern of involvement covered a wide
range—from large corporate plantations backed by big capital to small plantations
owned by individuals who had invested money earned in other occupations—only
the large corporate plantations, with their stable capital base, survived the drastic fluctuations in international rubber prices that marked the interwar period.
Most of the others were swept away by the economic tide. Another important Japanese concern in Malaya was the mining industry. Despite the large size and capi-

talization and the importance of mining concerns, however, I have not discussed the mining industry in this paper because it employed few Japanese.

I would like to emphasize once again that the pattern of Japanese economic penetration of Singapore and Malaya in the interwar period was characterized by the ebb and flow of Japanese company and bank employees who were either unmarried or unaccompanied by their families and whose numbers could be readily decreased or increased as business conditions warranted. This economic penetration was by no means led by lower-class Japanese who immigrated permanently in search of a new world in a foreign land where they could operate small-scale businesses or farms. The Japanese influx into Singapore and Malaya was, in fact, led by company and bank employees whose numbers could be controlled according to the economic conditions. It was an economic expansion motivated by modern capital in search of new markets and new resources.[31]

This paper was originally published under the title "Senzenki Shingapōru, Maraya ni okeru hojin keizai shinshutsu no keitai: Shokugyōbetsu jinkō chōsa o chūshin to shite" [The pattern of Japanese economic penetration of prewar Singapore and Malaya, with special reference to the Population Survey by Occupation], *Ajia keizai* [Developing economies] 26, no. 3 (March 1985): 13–32.

---

[31] Japanese economic penetration was made possible in large part by the relatively liberal policies of the British colonial government. Furthermore, for the most part Japanese agricultural and mining activities involved the development of previously unexploited resources and thus did not necessarily constitute an "economic invasion" (see Finance Ministry, Administration Bureau, "Nipponjin no kaigai katsudō," no. 32, "Malaya," pp. 174–75). Still, it cannot be denied that the high concentration of Japanese company and bank employees brought into Singapore and Malaya who were unmarried or unaccompanied by their families tends to give the impression that the Japanese saw the region purely in terms of the possibilities for exploiting its natural resources and markets. At a time when the global trade system was falling apart, the Japanese penetration of a region seen as one of the last bastions of the crumbling British empire could only have aggravated the British and aroused their suspicions.

4

THE PATTERN OF JAPANESE ECONOMIC PENETRATION OF THE PREWAR NETHERLANDS EAST INDIES

Yoshitada Murayama

I. The Netherlands East Indies and the Consular Population Survey

In this paper I will analyze the pattern of Japanese economic penetration of the Netherlands East Indies prior to World War II, using as my main source the "Consular Population Survey of Expatriate Japanese by Occupation," in the Diplomatic History Archives of the Ministry of Foreign Affairs.[1]

The Japanese population of the Netherlands East Indies (now Indonesia) began to be recorded in the consular population survey after a Japanese consulate was established in Batavia (now Jakarta) in 1909. There is only one earlier record of the Japanese population of the Netherlands East Indies: figures for 1897 were included in a report from the Japanese consulate in Singapore to the Foreign Ministry. According to that report, there were 125 Japanese, 25 males and 100 females, in "Jawa."[2] These figures were probably only an estimate, however, and it is unclear whether "Jawa" referred only to the island of Java or whether it included other parts of the Netherlands East Indies; nor do we know how these figures were collected. Furthermore, there are data only for 1897; Singapore consulate reports contain no figures for the Japanese population of the Netherlands East Indies in other years.

Although population reports were issued on a regular basis after the establishment of the consulate in Batavia, the reporting system was inadequate in the early years. The consular population survey for 1909 and 1910 recorded only the numbers of men and of women, classified under "miscellaneous occupations" for the sake of convenience, and the total population. In 1911 the population was not even classified by occupation; figures were given only for each sex and for the total popula-

---

[1] For a detailed discussion of this document and its character as a historical source, see Hajime Shimizu, "Gaimushō 'Kaigai zairyū homopōjin shokugyōbetsu jinkō chōsa ikken' no shiryōteki seikaku" [The character of the "Consular population survey of expatriate Japanese by occupation" of the Ministry of Foreign Affairs as a historical source], *Ajia keizai* [Developing economies] 26, no. 3 (March 1985).

[2] "Kaigai zairyū hompōjin shokugyōbetsu jinkō chōsa ikken" [Consular population survey of expatriate Japanese by occupation], Diplomatic History Archives, Ministry of Foreign Affairs, vol. 3, Batavia consulate message 13-12, January 31, 1898. This collection is referred to in subsequent citations as "Consular Population Survey."

tion. Figures for the population broken down by occupation did not appear until 1912.

These inadequacies in the consular population survey were due to the fact that at first reports from the Batavia consulate did not include occupationally based statistics. The Foreign Ministry then directed the consulate to provide figures by occupation, in keeping with the objective of the survey.[3] Accordingly, beginning with the June 1912 report such figures were provided, though for unknown reasons the 1912 report included figures based on occupation for the cities of Batavia, Semarang, and Surabaya but only the total population and its breakdown by sex for other parts of Java. The 1912 consular population survey listed most of these unclassified Japanese under the heading of "other occupations." Thus, the survey only began listing the Japanese population of the Netherlands East Indies by occupation in 1912, somewhat later than for other parts of Southeast Asia.

Initially, the survey was based on the figures in the population registers submitted to the Batavia consulate.[4] These figures were not accurate, however, since some Japanese failed to register, while some who had registered did not notify the consulate when they were leaving the area and thus remained on the rolls. The discrepancy between the number of Japanese actually in the Netherlands East Indies and the number registered was large in the early years. The Batavia consulate's 1909 report notes, after listing the registered population, that while 782 people were registered, more than 400 more were unregistered.[5]

This discrepancy gradually lessened as the years passed. For example, the Japanese population of Medan, on Sumatra, was recorded as 5 men and 1 woman in 1909. The next year it shot up to 278 people, 57 men and 221 women. This change probably reflected not a sudden increase in population but more accurate registration.

Because the Batavia consulate classified the Japanese population according to the occupations the registrants declared themselves, its 1913 report noted that prostitutes were classified under the categories of "miscellaneous occupations" and "unemployed."[6] That year 918 women were listed as "unemployed," and it is safe to assume that most were in fact prostitutes. The Netherlands East Indies had outlawed prostitution in 1912, earlier than other parts of Southeast Asia. Thus, that prostitutes continued to be counted after this date, albeit under different appellations, indicates that registration of Japanese residents of the Netherlands East Indies was now fairly thorough.

The Batavia consulate appears to have been well aware of the discrepancy between the registered and actual numbers of Japanese. To minimize the discrepancy, around 1918 the consulate began to rely most heavily for its figures on reports from Japanese organizations in each area.[7] Since no change affecting overall trends was evident after that year, we can assume that the number of registered Japanese and the actual population were quite close.

To recapitulate, the consular population survey figures issued by the Batavia consulate from 1909 to 1912 were unreliable, but after 1912 occupation-based figures

---

[3] Ibid., vol. 10, Ministry of Foreign Affairs message 20, March 20, 1912.

[4] Ibid., vol. 13, Batavia consulate message 61, April 10, 1913.

[5] Ibid., vol. 8, Batavia consulate message 139, December 31, 1909.

[6] Ibid., vol. 13, Batavia consulate message 229, October 29, 1913.

[7] Ibid., vol. 19, Batavia consulate message 117, October 22, 1919.

began to be kept and the survey became much more reliable. Since this paper deals mainly with the period between the two world wars, the inaccuracy of the records in the early years of the Batavia consulate can be ignored.

II. General Trends in the Japanese Population

Figure 1 charts trends in the Japanese population of the Netherlands East Indies from 1909 to 1936. The population grew rapidly from 1909 to 1916; from 1912 to 1916 it increased by an average of 500 people a year, a considerable rise compared with the corresponding figures of 350 and 120 for Singapore and the Philippines, respectively. Even allowing for an increased registration rate, by World War I the Netherlands East Indies was considered a good place for Japanese business activity and a rapid influx of Japanese was beginning.

Figure 1. Trends in the Japanese Population of the Netherlands East Indies, 1909–1936

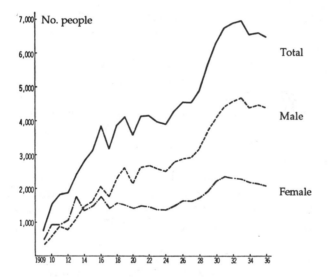

Source: "Kaigai zairyū hompōjin shokugyōbetsu jinkō chōsa ikken" [Consular population survey of expatriate Japanese by occupation], Diplomatic History Archives, Ministry of Foreign Affairs.

Between 1917 and 1927 the Japanese population fluctuated. It fell by nearly 500 people from 1916 to 1917 and from 1919 to 1920, a considerable drop for a one-year period. The decrease recorded in 1917 was most pronounced among people in the "agriculture," "manufacturing," "transportation," "civil service and self-employed," and "other occupations" categories. For example, 203 people listed manufacturing as their occupation in 1916; this figure plummeted to 1 person the following year. As this indicates, there is a marked discontinuity between the statistics for 1917 and those for the preceding year.[8] The decrease from 1919 to 1920,

---

[8] Two revised reports were issued for that year. The figures in the second revised report are close to those in "Kaigai kakuchi zairyū hompōjin shokugyōbetsu hyō" [Tables of expatriate Japanese in various regions by occupation], Diplomatic History Archives, Ministry of Foreign Affairs. Though some discrepancies in occupational classifications remain, I have used the figures from these tables in the interest of continuity with the figures for earlier and later years.

on the other hand, was evenly spread among all occupations. The figures for 1919 and 1921 are similar, however; it is those for 1920 that seem divergent.

This disarray in the statistics indicates problems with the survey itself. In 1919 a new consulate was opened in Surabaya, and the Batavia consulate was elevated to the status of consulate general. The occupation-based consular population survey of Japanese in the Netherlands East Indies was subsequently divided between the two. The first year of the survey under this new arrangement was 1920. This is probably the main reason for the lack of uniformity in the statistics.

The next drop in the Japanese population took place from 1922 to 1924, the first time that the number of Japanese in the Netherlands East Indies decreased for two consecutive years. As I will discuss later, this reflected the drop in the commercial population resulting from the recession following World War I.

Thus, the Japanese population decreased on three occasions between 1917 and 1927, but flawed statistics may be a factor in the first two. What is important here is that even though troughs were registered in 1917 and 1920, the population in 1920 was larger than it had been in 1917, and in the case of the 1924 trough, caused by the postwar recession, the population was larger than it had been in 1920. Thus, even though the Japanese population in the Netherlands East Indies fluctuated from 1917 to 1927, the general trend was one of slow growth.

In 1927 the Japanese population started to climb rapidly once more. In the four-year period between 1927 and 1931, when the upward trend began to flatten again, the population increased by more than 500 people a year. After peaking in 1933, the population began to fall because the commercial population, the driving force behind the increase, stopped growing and the number of people in other occupations began to drop. The commercial population peaked in 1933 because of policies introduced that year by the Netherlands East Indies government, such as the Emergency Import Restriction Ordinance and the Emergency Ordinance Restricting Foreign Entry. The aim of these policies was to combat low-priced Japanese goods, which had been rapidly expanding their share of the Netherlands East Indies market since 1929.

Let us now consider overall trends in the Japanese population of the Netherlands East Indies. The Japanese population also increased, though at different rates, in British colonies around the begimaing of World War I, and the number of Japanese in the Philippines grew from the late 1920s through the early 1930s. The difference in population trends between those areas and the Netherlands East Indies was that in the latter the number of Japanese increased so gradually between 1917 and 1927.

What was the reason for this gradual increase? To arrive at the answer, let us examine changes in the population more closely. Looking at trends in the female population first, from 1913 onward the number of women fluctuated, while showing an overall downward curve, until 1924, after which it rose until 1931, then began to fall again. The decrease between 1913 and 1924 probably had to do largely with various measures taken to eradicate prostitution. In figure 2, which charts changes in the female population, divided into working women and dependent women, from 1917 to 1936, we note a sharp drop in the number of working women from 1918 to 1927. As the 1913 consular population survey noted, most women classified under "miscellaneous occupations" or "unemployed" were in fact prostitutes. Although

Figure 2. Trends in the Japanese Female Working and Dependent
Population of the Netherlands East Indies, 1917–1936

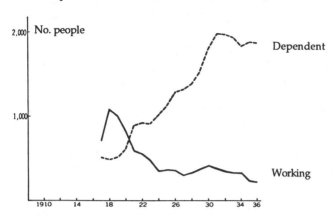

Source: Same as figure 1.

they were also described at various times as "serving women" or "foreign-employed," most working women were prostitutes.[9]

Prostitution was prohibited somewhat earlier in the Netherlands East Indies than in other parts of Southeast Asia. A. W. F. Idenburg, the Netherlands East Indies governor general who took office in 1909, ordered prostitution eliminated by 1912. To enforce the ban, entry to Java through Madura was restricted in 1912, and the penal code was amended the following year to clamp down on pimps and others living off prostitutes.[10] This put teeth in the drive to eradicate prostitution on Java, the seat of the Netherlands East Indies government, and the number of Japanese prostitutes dropped sharply. Some women, however, left Java for the outer islands to escape the prohibition, joining those already there. This population shift was especially noticeable on Sumatra, particularly in the city of Medan. In 1917, of the 584 Japanese women listed as "domestic employees," "entertainers, prostitutes, serving women, etc.," and "unemployed," 355 were living on Sumatra, while only 49 were living on Java.

Though the number of working women decreased, the number of dependent women grew until 1931. The number of dependent women overtook the number of working women in 1921 and continued to grow steadily thereafter, the gap between

_____

[9] The Batavia consulate's 1909 report for the consular population survey contained the following note: "Occupations are divided into six classifications: direct imports, sales of medicines and general merchandise, traveling sales, fishing, operation of eating and drinking establishments, *and prostitution. The majority of women are engaged in prostitution,* and the largest number of men are fishermen, followed by shop employees and traveling salesmen" (emphasis in original). "Consular Population Survey," vol. 8, Batavia consulate message 139, December 31, 1909. The words underlined by the original writer have been crossed out with blue and replaced with "etc.," also in blue. This change, probably made at the Foreign Ministry, is an interesting example of the authorities' reluctance to acknowledge the existence of prostitution, even though such reports were not actually printed and circulated.

[10] Toraji Irie, *Hōjin kaigai hattenshi* [A history of Japanese development overseas] (Tokyo: Hara Shobōo, 1981), p. 230; Toraji Irie, "Hōjin nan'yō hatten jijō" [Japanese development in the South Seas], in *Shōwa 17 nen dai nan'yo nenkan* [1942 Greater South Seas Annual], ed. Nan'yō Dantai Rengōkai [Federation of South Seas Organizations] (Tokyo: Nan'yō Dantai Rengōkai, 1942), p.346.

the two categories increasing yearly. This factor was responsible for the upswing, after some years of decline, in the Japanese female population from 1924 on.

Trends in the Japanese male population, on the other hand, corresponded closely to the curve for the total Japanese population of the Netherlands East Indies shown in figure 1. Until about 1913, women outnumbered men, but in 1914 men overtook women in numerical terms. Thereafter the number of men was consistently greater. Figure 3 shows changes in the numbers of working men and dependent men from 1917 to 1936. There was a great difference in the numbers of working men and male dependents; the overall trends have to do largely with working men.

Figure 3. Trends in the Japanese Male Working and Dependent Population of the Netherlands East Indies, 1917–1936

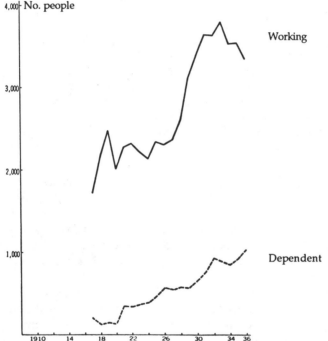

Source: Same as figure 1.

Thus, when the Japanese population is classified in terms of working and dependent men and women, it is clear that working men were the determining factor in overall population trends. Although working women, including those sent to the Netherlands East Indies to work as prostitutes, were a major factor until about 1913, their effect on overall population trends waned after 1914, when men began to outnumber women. The gradual rise in total population from 1917 to 1927 reflected the trend for working men during that period, meaning that the number of working men maintained a certain level. The number of male and female dependents also grew, compensating for the drop in the number of working women. The number of working men began to grow rapidly in 1927, as a result of which the total Japanese population of the Netherlands East Indies shot up.

III. POPULATION TRENDS BY OCCUPATION

1. AGRICULTURE AND FISHERIES

As already mentioned, the Japanese population of the Netherlands East Indies began to be listed by occupation in the consular population survey in 1912. Although we have no information on the occupational breakdown of the population prior to that, in 1909 the Batavia consulate reported that Japanese women most commonly worked as prostitutes and men as fishermen, though precise figures were not given. Most of the men classified as fishermen were pearl-oyster divers. Many of these men lived on the island of Alor, whose Japanese population in 1909 totaled 155, 94 men and 61 women, 19.8 percent of the Japanese population of the Netherlands East Indies that year.

The occupational breakdown of the Japanese population changed radically after 1912. As mentioned above, the prohibition of prostitution led to a decrease in the female population, and by 1914 men exceeded women in number. Fishermen were overtaken in number by the rapidly growing commercial population, a trend touched off by the traveling medicine salesmen who had become a noticeable presence around the time of the Russo-Japanese War (1904–1905). In 1912, the first year that occupational statistics for the Japanese population of the Netherlands East Indies appeared in the consular population survey, the male commercial population accounted for 46.9 percent, or nearly half, of the Japanese male population. This concluded the first period of the Japanese community in the Netherlands East Indies.

Table 1 shows changes in the occupational structure of the Japanese population from 1912 to 1935, in five-year periods from 1915 onward. The first characteristic the figures reveal is that the agricultural population was quite small. In view of the relatively large Japanese agricultural populations in the Philippines and Malaya, it seems strange that there were so few Japanese engaged in agriculture in the Netherlands East Indies, a treasure-trove of tropical crops. As figure 4 indicates, the Japanese agricultural population in the Netherlands East Indies was smaller both proportionately and in actual numbers, and showed less fluctuation, than the Japanese agricultural population of Malaya and North Borneo. Was this because Japanese agriculture failed to develop in the Netherlands East Indies?

According to figures for 1936–1937 (a much later period, to be sure) in a survey conducted by the Taiwan government general, Japanese plantations in the Netherlands East Indies covered a total of 180,700 hectares, accounting for 66.8 percent of the total area of Japanese plantations in Southeast Asia.[11] Investment amounted to ¥48.18 million, or 61.8 percent of all Japanese investment in the region. These figures far surpass those for Malaya, ranked second at the time, where Japanese plantations occupied 36,000 hectares and investment was ¥26.48 million. Nevertheless,

---

[11] Secretariat of the Governor General of Taiwan, External Affairs Division, *Nan'yō kakuchi hōjin kigyō yōran* [Survey of Japanese companies in the South Seas], Minami Shina oyobi nan'yō chōsa dai 238 shū [South China and South Seas survey 238] (Taipei: Secretariat of the Governor General of Taiwan, 1937), p. 2.

Table 1. The Japanese Population of the Netherlands East Indies, by Occupation, 1912–1935

Unit: %

Occupation (by sex & total)	1912	1915	1920	1925	1930	1935
Agriculture						
Male	2.2	4.2	4.9 (5.2)	6.0 (7.2)	2.9 (3.4)	4.6 (5.8)
Female	0.5	0.2	0.0 (0.1)	0.2 (0.8)	0.1 (0.9)	0.0 (0.8)
Total	1.2	2.3	2.9 (3.7)	4.0 (6.4)	1.9 (3.1)	3.1 (5.5)
Fisheries						
Male	9.5	0.2	1.4 (1.4)	5.7 (6.9)	10.8 (12.7)	11.5 (14.6)
Female	0.0	0.0	0.0 (0.0)	0.0 (0.0)	0.0 (0.0)	0.0 (0.4)
Total	4.1	0.1	0.8 (1.0)	3.7 (6.0)	6.9 (11.3)	7.8 (13.7)
Mining						
Male	0.0	0.0	0.0 (0.0)	0.0 (0.0)	1.1 (1.2)	0.4 (0.5)
Female	0.0	0.0	0.0 (0.0)	0.0 (0.2)	0.0 (0.0)	0.0 (0.0)
Total	0.0	0.0	0.0 (0.0)	0.0 (0.0)	0.7 (1.1)	0.3 (0.5)
Manufacturing						
Male	9.3	6.8	7.3 (7.8)	6.7 (8.1)	7.8 (9.2)	4.8 (6.1)
Female	1.5	0.5	0.2 (0.3)	0.4 (1.9)	0.4 (2.2)	0.7 (7.0)
Total	4.9	3.9	4.5 (5.6)	4.5 (7.3)	5.3 (8.5)	3.5 (6.2)
Commercial						
Male	46.9	48.3	68.3 (72.6)	55.0 (65.9)	51.4 (60.5)	50.7 (64.0)
Female	11.7	7.3	39.5 (69.0)	16.4 (67.2)	5.1 (27.9)	4.8 (46.2)
Total	26.8	29.3	56.8 (71.6)	41.6 (66.1)	34.9 (57.1)	35.8 (62.9)
Transportation						
Male	0.0	7.4	1.4 (1.4)	1.7 (2.1)	1.4 (1.7)	0.6 (0.8)
Female	0.0	0.0	0.0 (0.0)	0.0 (0.0)	0.0 (0.2)	0.0 (0.0)
Total	0.0	3.9	0.8 (1.0)	1.1 (1.8)	0.9 (1.5)	0.4 (0.8)
Civil service & self-employed						
Male	4.6	3.8	5.0 (5.4)	5.5 (6.6)	5.2 (6.2)	4.6 (5.8)
Female	0.7	0	0.2 (0.4)	0.7 (3.0)	0.4 (2.4)	0.5 (5.2)
Total	2.4	2.0	3.1 (3.9)	3.8 (6.1)	3.5 (5.8)	3.2 (5.7)
Other occupations						
Male	26.6	7.4	3.2 (3.4)	1.0 (1.2)	1.4 (1.6)	1.1 (1.3)
Female	80.2	13.8	0.0 (0.0)	0.3 (1.3)	0.0 (0.4)	0.0 (0.0)
Total	57.2	10.3	1.9 (2.4)	0.7 (1.2)	0.9 (1.5)	0.7 (1.3)
Domestic employee						
Male	0.1	0	0.4 (0.4)	1.0 (1.2)	0.4 (0.5)	0.2 (0.3)
Female	5.1	8.8	7.9 (13.9)	4.2 (17.3)	10.7 (58.6)	3.9 (37.4)
Total	2.9	4.7	3.4 (4.3)	2.1 (3.4)	4.1 (6.6)	1.4 (2.5)
Unemployed						
Male	0.4	21.5	7.8 (2.0)	16.9 (0.4)	17.1 (0.7)	20.9 (0.3)
Female	0.0	69.2	51.9 (16.0)	77.5 (7.9)	82.9 (6.9)	89.7 (24.6)
Total	0.2	43.5	25.4 (6.0)	37.9 (1.4)	40.5 (1.4)	43.3 (1.8)

Figures in parentheses indicate working population (total population minus dependent family members).

Source: Same as figure 1.

Figure 4. Trends in the Japanese Agricultural Population of the Netherlands
East Indies and of Malaya and North Borneo, 1910–1936

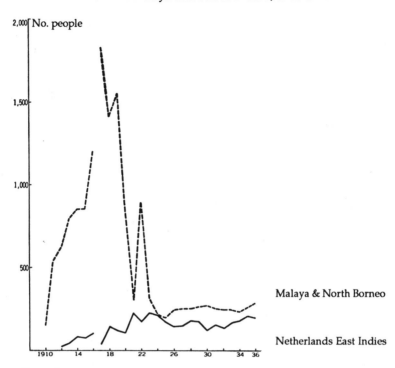

Source: Same as figure 1.

there were only about 200 Japanese engaged in agriculture in the Netherlands East
Indies, an exceedingly small number. Why was this?

Stimulated, among other things, by the rubber-plantation boom in Malaya,
there was a proliferation of Japanese plantations in Southeast Asia around the
beginning of World War I. This is clear from the changes in the Japanese agricultural population Malaya and North Borneo shown in figure 4. The influx of Japanese in the plantation sector of the Netherlands East Indies, however, did not peak
until the 1920s. The 1917 Rubber Lands Restriction Enactment, severely limiting the
sale of land in Malaya and the Straits Settlements, caused Japanese plantation
investment, which had centered on Malaya, to shift to the Netherlands East
Indies.[12]

Most of the new plantations established in the Netherlands East Indies were
large-scale operations run by companies having relatively large amounts of capital. These company plantations, the main form of Japanese agricultural enterprise
in the Netherlands East Indies, differed from the numerous small farms run by
individuals in Malaya. The reason the Japanese agricultural population of the
Netherlands East Indies was so small is that most Japanese-run plantations there

---

[12] See Hajime Shimizu, "Senzenki Shingapōru, Maraya ni okeru hōjin keizai shinshutsu no
keitai: Shokugyōbetsu jinkō chōsa o chūshin to shite" [The pattern of Japanese economic
penetration of prewar Singapore and Malaya, with special reference to the Population Survey
by Occupation], *Ajia keizai* [Developing economies] 26, no. 3 (March 1985). [A translation
appears in this volume.—Ed.]

employed only a handful of Japanese; the rest of the work force was Chinese and Indonesian.

For example, in 1918 and 1919 Nangoku Sangyō bought three plantations on Java: Wonosari, Tempor Sewu, and Cimulang. These three plantations, with a combined area of 2,435 hectares, occupied 17.9 percent of the total area occupied by Japanese plantations on Java. Like other plantations on Java, they cultivated a variety of agricultural products, including rubber, tea, cinchona, coffee, and coca. The Tempor Sewu and Cimulang plantations had Japanese managers, while the manager of the Wonosari plantation was European. The staff of the three plantations included six Europeans and six Indonesians but no Japanese; all the other workers were Chinese and Indonesian.[13] As the example of the Nangoku Sangyō plantations shows, the large Japanese plantations in the Netherlands East Indies employed very few Japanese. This is why the number of Japanese engaged in farming did not grow even though agriculture developed.

The largest occupational category for Japanese men listed in the Batavia consulate's 1909 report was fishing. The number of Japanese fishermen began to rise rapidly in the mid-1920s. As illustrated by figure 5, not only did the ratio of this occupational group to the total population grow, but the absolute numbers shot up, as well.

Figure 5. Trends in the Japanese Fishery Population of the Netherlands East Indies, 1912–1936

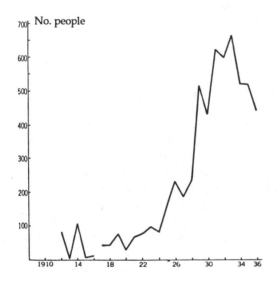

Source: Same as figure 1.

Around 1912, as already mentioned, most Japanese fishermen were engaged in gathering pearl oysters, but a changeover to fishing in the true sense of the word took place in the next few years. The first genuine Japanese fishermen to arrive in the Netherlands East Indies were Okinawans who moved there from Singapore. Their fishing techniques were very different from those previously used in the

---

[13] Secretariat of the Governor General of Taiwan, Nan'yō kakuchi hōjin kigyō, p. 49.

Netherlands East Indies: they used motorized vessels and hauled in large catches by driving schools of fish into nets.

The main factor limiting the expansion of fisheries was the small market,[14] but as transportation routes from harbors to inland regions were established and refrigeration methods improved, the market slowly grew, and with it the population of Japanese engaged in fisheries.

Far fewer companies were involved in the fishery industry than in agriculture, however. In 1937 only two Japanese fishery companies were operating in the Netherlands East Indies: Nichiran Gyogyō, based on Menado in the Celebes (Sulawesi), and Daishō Kōshi, a Singapore-based concern with a branch office in Batavia.[15] The increase in the number of fishermen in the Japanese population was due mainly to the expansion of the latter company. In 1937 it operated 100 fishing vessels (50 of them motorized) and employed 790 Japanese. When this number is compared with the figure for Japanese engaged in fisheries in the consular population survey, it is evident that the majority worked for Daishō Kōshi.

2. COMMERCE

Whereas the agricultural and fishery populations recorded in the consular population survey showed pronounced changes, their combined number was not large enough to influence overall trends in the Japanese population of the Netherlands East Indies. As table 1 shows, the deciding factor was the commercial population, which accounted for the largest segment of the working population.

From 1917 to 1927 the number of Japanese in the Netherlands East Indies increased gradually, showing little change when compared with the years of rapid growth before and after this period. In 1920 the largest number of working Japanese belonged to the commercial sector: 72.6 percent of men and 69.0 percent of women, or 71.6 percent of all working Japanese. That this sector continued to grow while the Japanese population as a whole remained fairly constant indicates the sector's influence on the overall population. Clearly, then, to elucidate the population changes in the 1917–1927 period, whose salient feature was gradual growth, it is important to analyze the trends in the commercial population.

Because of the relatively small number of women in this sector, they had little effect on the commercial population as a whole. However, since the changes in the female commercial population exhibit a few discontinuities, let us examine this group first. Table 1 indicates that the female commercial population accounted for a very high proportion of all women in the 1920s: 69.0 percent in 1920 and 67.2 percent in 1925. This is suspiciously high, when compared with the trends in the previous decade and in the 1930s. In large part, these apparent population fluctuations had to do with the categories in which prostitutes and women in related occupations were placed at different times. As I have already stated, in the early years of the consular population survey Japanese were registered under self-reported occupations and the population was classified by occupation on the basis of those registers. Even after occupations began to be classified on the basis of surveys carried out by local Japanese organizations, prostitution was not necessarily classified as such.

---

[14] Jagatara Tomo no Kai [Friends of Jakarta], ed., *Jagatara kanwa* [Jakarta chitchat] (Tokyo: Jagatara Tomo no Kai, 1978), p.110.

[15] Secretariat of the Governor General of Taiwan, *Nan'yō kakuchi hōjin kigyō*, pp. 73–74.

Table 2 shows figures for the various categories in which prostitutes are likely to have been placed from 1912 to 1935, again in five-year periods from 1915 onward. It is immediately evident that there were large fluctuations in each category. Whereas 905 women were listed under "miscellaneous occupations" in 1912, that number fell to 206, less than one-quarter the 1912 figure, in 1915. Meanwhile, the number of "unemployed" women jumped from zero to 1,027 over the same three years. These figures do not reflect the actual situation; they merely demonstrate that prostitutes were classified under different labels according to the exigencies of the time. The figures in all the categories combined probably better reflect the actual trend in the number of prostitutes. The total for these categories declined over the long term, both in absolute numbers and as a percentage of working women, as a result of the ban on prostitution. Thus, the apparent growth in the female commercial population in 1920 and 1925 was due simply to the fact that prostitutes happened to be classified in the commercial category in those years; it does not indicate a significant rise in the female commercial population.

Table 2. Trends in the Japanese Female Population of the Netherlands East Indies Engaged in Prostitution and Related Occupations, 1912–1935

Unit. No. people

Classification	1912	1915	1920	1925	1930	1935
Serving women	0	0	463	136	2	13
Miscellaneous occupations	905	206	0	5	2	0
Domestic employees	58	131	113	63	237	85
Unemployed	0	1,027	130	29	28	56
Subtotal (A)	963	1,364	706	233	269	154
Total female working population (B)	1,052	1,484	812	363	404	227
A/B x 100 (%)	91.5	91.9	86.9	64.1	66.5	67.8

Source: Same as figure 1.

Whereas the apparent shifts in the female commercial population in the 1920s do not reflect the situation accurately, changes in the male commercial population did have a profound impact on Japanese population trends in the Netherlands East Indies. Figure 6 shows that the male commercial population in the Netherlands East Indies reached a peak in 1919, bottomed out in 1923, and only resumed rapid growth in 1928. The decrease in the male commercial population, the largest sector of working people, contributed to the sluggish growth of the total Japanese population in this period despite the increase in the number of Japanese families. However, it should be remembered that the increase in the number of Japanese families more than offset the decrease in the commercial population. In short, the gradual increase in the Japanese population between 1917 and 1927 was the product of a small decrease in the male commercial population and a proportionately larger increase in the number of families. This becomes even clearer when changes in the male commercial population of the Netherlands East Indies are compared with those of other parts of Southeast Asia (fig. 6). Whereas the Japanese male commercial population of Malaya, North Borneo, and Singapore plummeted during the recession following World war I, the decrease in the Netherlands East Indies even in the worst year, 1923, was only 240 people, a 14.6 percent drop from 1919, when the population of this sector had reached a peak.

Figure 6. Trends in the Japanese Male Commercial Population of the Netherlands East Indies, of Singapore, and of Malaya and North Borneo, 1912–1936

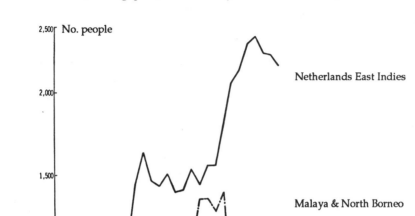

Source: Same as figure 1.

Why did the Japanese commercial population of the Netherlands East Indies decrease so little during the postwar recession? Let us address this question by analyzing the changes on Java, where the Japanese commercial population was concentrated. The commercial population on Java had increased markedly until that time: around 1912 the commercial populations of Sumatra and Java were roughly equivalent, but in 1919 the commercial population of Java was double that of Sumatra.

The first wave of Japanese merchants in the Netherlands East Indies was made up of traveling salesmen; the second comprised shopkeepers. By 1912 or so, shopkeeping had become the main type of commercial activity. In 1914 there were 74 shopkeepers and 144 shop employees on Java. That year there were 56 traveling salesmen, of whom 38 sold medicines, the remnant of the first wave of merchants.[16]

The changeover from traveling salesmen to shopkeepers involved a shift not only in the type of commercial operation but also in the kinds of goods sold. Only 22, or 29.7 percent, of the 74 shopkeepers on Java in 1914 sold medicines, whereas 34,

---

[16] "Consular Population Survey," vol. 15, Batavia consulate message 157, July 1, 1914.

or 45.9 percent, handled general merchandise, an indication that the mainstream of commerce had shifted from medicines to general merchandise. The influx of Japanese goods into the Netherlands East Indies during World War I accelerated this shift, boosted the commercial population, and led some retailers, such as Kazue Tsutsumibayashi, to switch to importing.[17]

The growth of Japanese commercial operations during this period was centered on the three port cities of Batavia, Semarang, and Surabaya. In 1914, as table 3 indicates, 60.8 percent of the above-mentioned 74 shopkeepers were concentrated in these three cities. If shop employees are included, the figure rises to 64.2 percent. Most shopkeepers were located in these cities because they were the ports of entry for imported goods. Even earlier, when most merchants had been traveling salesmen, many had probably based themselves in one or another of these cities.

Table 3. Trends in the Japanese Population of Merchants and Shop Employees of the Netherlands East Indies, by Locale, 1913–1919

Unit: No. people

Locale	1913	1914	1915	1916	1917	1918	1919
Batavia	(35)	(26)	(35)	(31)	(58)	(54)	(55)
	15	8	10	10	12	12	17
Semarang	(68)	(65)	(82)	(88)	(58)	(87)	(88)
	25	15	17	18	8	23	10
Surabaya	(48)	(49)	(54)	(74)	(111)	(109)	(187)
	21	22	10	13	19	27	41
Subtotalf (A)	(151)	(140)	(171)	(193)	(227)	(250)	(330)
	61	45	37	41	39	71	68
Rest of Java		(78)	(79)	(109)	(107)	(274)	(234)
		29	33	50	37	126	116
Total for Java (B)		(218)	(250)	(302)	(334)	(524)	(564)
		74	70	91	76	197	184
A/B x 100 (%)		(64.2)	(68.4)	(63.9)	(67.9)	(47.7)	(58.5)
		60.8	52.8	45.0	51.3	36.0	36.9

Figures in parentheses include shop employees.

Source: Same as figure 1.

As Japanese commercial activity grew, however, the commercial population of these cities slowly dwindled as merchants spread out to other areas (table 3), though if shop employees are counted, the shift was less marked. This probably means that, while some shops in the three cities were relatively large and could afford to hire employees, many of those in outlying areas were small businesses operated by individuals.

---

[17] Tōru Yano, *"Nanshin" no keifu* [The lineage of southern expansion] (Tokyo: Chuo Koronsha, 1975), pp. 85–97. People like Kazue Tsutsumibayashi, who started out as traveling salesman and then became a retailer and finally an importer, were rare exceptions. Wholesalers stood between retailers and importers. Quite a few retailers became wholesalers early in the second decade of this century, but it was much more difficult to make a successful transition from wholesaler to importer. It was more common for importers operating elsewhere to enter the Netherlands East Indies when they saw the possibilities this market offered.

Semarang had the most shops and shop employees in 1913, but Surabaya took the lead in 1917. This indicates that some shops progressed from retailing or wholesaling small lots of imported goods to importing relatively large amounts of goods in order to sell them wholesale. Surabaya, the Netherlands East Indies' largest commercial port city, was the center for imports and exports, so that it was advantageous for import-export businesses to locate there. This is supported by the fact that of the 29 people on Java classified as "traders" in 1918, 19 were in Surabaya.[18]

The interruption in the supply of goods from Europe caused by World War I provided a good opportunity for Japanese merchandise to enter the Netherlands East Indies' market, and Japanese commerce expanded. With the end of the war, European goods again became available, which meant that Japanese businesses could no longer grow as quickly. Japanese businesses were also hard hit by the recession of 1921. A 1922 report from Kawai Shoten, an establishment with its main store in Mojokerto and two branches, stated: "This year sales are up 20 percent over last year but net profit has dropped 40 percent. This is probably because we concentrated on high-volume, low-profit sales to ride out the recession and because general purchasing power is decreasing. The recession will probably continue into the first half of 1923.[19]

The recession severely affected merchants based in the three port cities, particularly Surabaya. As table 4 indicates, the number of merchants in the three cities grew until 1922 but dropped sharply in 1923. The decrease was especially marked in Surabaya, which had 142 merchants in 1922 but only 17 in 1923. This drop is so precipitous that one wonders whether there was a change in the survey method, but figures for the same period from the Batavia consulate, which had a different area under its jurisdiction, showed a nearly 30 percent drop, from 31 to 24, in the number of merchants. Whatever the actual figures, it is clear that a large number of merchants left the three northern port cities.

Why was the recession-related drop in commercial population so much greater in Malaya, North Borneo, and Singapore than in the Netherlands East Indies (fig. 6)? One reason was that shopkeepers in the Netherlands East Indies outside the

Table 4. Trends in the Japanese Merchant Population of the Netherlands East Indies, by Locale, 1920–1927

Unit: No. people

Locale	1920	1921	1922	1923	1924	1925	1927
Batavia	22	20	33	24	13	4	
Semarang	7	15	20	14	(14)	(14)	
Surabaya		70	142	17	26	18	31
Subtotal		105	195	55	(53)	(36)	
Rest of Java		190	374	313	(298)	(350)	
Total for Java	179	295	569	368	351	386	327

Figures in parenthese assume a figure of 14 for Surabaya.

Source: Same as figure 1.

[18] "Consular Population Survey," vol. 19, Batavia consulate message 117, October 22, 1919.

[19] "Zai nan'yō hompojin keiei kigyō chōsa ikken" [Survey of companies managed by Japanese in the South Seas], Diplomatic History Archives, Ministry of Foreign Affairs, Batavia consulate secret message 2, January 23, 1924.

three big port cities were affected relatively little. Their number fell from 374 to 313, a 16.3 percent decrease, from 1922 to 1923, but changed relatively little thereafter. For example, table 4 shows that the number of merchants on Java, 298 in 1924, increased to 350 in 1925 (assuming that the number of merchants in Semarang, for which figures are not available from documents, remained unchanged at 14). That Japanese merchants in outlying areas were not as severely affected by the economic downturn as their counterparts in the three port cities is attested to by this report from Harima Shōten in Kediri, an inland city in East Java: "We are engaged mainly in selling daily necessities to the natives, so we are not affected by the depression like merchants in the cities. With diligence, it is not hard to do fairly well."[20]

Thus, despite the recession the drop in demand was not too great for merchants selling daily necessities to Indonesians. Furthermore, many local merchants were, as mentioned earlier, running one-man businesses, so they were able to continue operating on a small scale. Thus, when the number of merchants in the northern port cities plummeted, the traders in outlying areas kept Japanese commerce going.

Learning from the recession, small local merchants began to build up businesses directed at Indonesian customers. One leading business of this type was Fuji Yoko, owned by Masao Sawabe and based in Yogyakarta, which spread the method of high-volume, low-profit sales to Indonesians throughout Java. After the Great Depression that followed the Wall Street crash of 1929, this business sold low-priced Japanese goods even more cheaply and laid the groundwork for establishing far-reaching distribution routes to flood the depression-hit Netherlands East Indies with Japanese merchandise.

Another reason the number of merchants in outlying areas remained steady was the presence of Japanese merchants known as "commodity traders" (*bussanshō*), though their numbers are not recorded in the consular population survey. These commodity traders were primary freight collectors who bought produce from Indonesian farmers and sold it to brokers. They also owned small shops and sold miscellaneous daily necessities, recovering the money they had spent to buy agricultural products by selling general merchandise and using agricultural products as collateral for selling on credit. These commodity traders appear to have established themselves in the 1920s in Lumajang and a few other areas of eastern Java.[21] According to the December 1924 "Survey of Expatriate Japanese Businessmen," compiled annually by the Foreign Ministry's Bureau of Commercial Affairs from consular reports on the leading Japanese commercial and financial enterprises in the areas under the consulates' jurisdiction, there were eight shops dealing in daily necessities and general merchandise in Lumajang. Four had no shop name but were registered under individuals' names. They were probably businesses so small that they did not warrant a shop name. All eight establishments were operated by commodity traders.[22]

Yet another reason the Japanese commercial population in the Netherlands East Indies did not decrease substantially had to do with the port cities. Figure 7

---

[20] Ibid.

[21] Sadaaki Kondō, *Rumajan hōjin no kiroku* [A record of Japanese in Lumajang] (privately published, 1978), pp. 8–22.

[22] See Shimizu, "Senzenki Shingapōru, Maraya," for more detailed information on this survey.

shows the changes in the total and merchant Japanese populations of Surabaya from 1913 to 1927. As mentioned above, until 1922 the total Japanese population of Surabaya followed the same curve as the city's Japanese merchant population. In 1923, however, the curves diverged; despite a drop in the number of merchants, the total population increased. Why?

Figure 8 shows the changes in the number of Japanese shop and company employees in Surabaya from 1913 to 1927. In 1923 and 1924 the curve diverged from that of the total population, although the number of people in the "shop and company employee" category was growing, following roughly the same trend as that of the total Japanese population. If the number of merchants decreased, as noted above, it is hard to believe that the number of shop employees grew. This probably means that the population rose because of an increase in company employees.

Table 5 shows the number of employees in the leading Japanese trading companies and banks in Surabaya, according to the "Survey of Expatriate Japanese Businessmen." Perhaps due to differences in the survey period or method, the figures from the consular population survey and the "Survey of Expatriate Japanese Businessmen," both based on data provided by the Surabaya consulate, differ somewhat, although both reveal similar trends.

It is also worth noting that a number of leading Japanese trading companies established branches in the Netherlands East Indies during the postwar recession. In addition to Mitsui & Co., the pioneer among large trading companies in the Netherlands East Indies, by 1921 Suzuki Shōten, Mitsubishi Trading Co., Nippon Menka, Gōshō, and Tōyō Menka all had offices there. These trading companies moved into the Netherlands East Indies to buy sugar and other agricultural products and sell cotton cloth, one of Japan's major exports at the time. Along with the large trading companies, numerous import-export businesses established themselves. In general, these new arrivals had plentiful capital and numerous employees.

Thus, around the time of the postwar recession the configuration of Japanese commerce in Surabaya underwent a transition from shopkeepers who had built up their businesses locally to newly arrived import-export trading houses. The number of merchants dropped markedly, while the number of trading companies grew. The latter brought in employees, which increased Surabaya's Japanese population. Although Surabaya was a special case, being the Netherlands East Indies' primary commercial city, this development had a major effect on subsequent changes in the Japanese population of the Netherlands East Indies as a whole.

While the postwar recession also affected the trading companies, they did not drastically cut back their operations or leave the colony, although some did reduce their staffs (table 5). The reason is that the recession did not have a decisive impact on trade between Japan and the Netherlands East Indies. Figure 9 charts the changes in the total value of trade between Japan and the Netherlands East Indies from 1909 to 1932. The value of trade dropped in the recession period from 1921 to 1923, but recovered quickly thereafter. And although there was a drop in those three years, the level was still quite high compared with the levels up to 1919.

The main export product handled by the trading companies was sugar, and the main import from Japan was cotton goods. The value of sugar exports to Japan dropped from 108.24 million guilders in 1920 to 66.55 million guilders in 1921.

Figure 7. Trends in the Japanese Total Population and
Merchant Population of Surabaya, 1913–1927

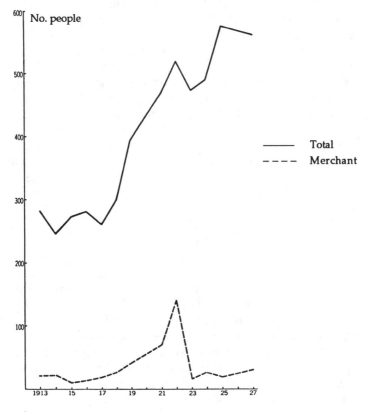

Source: Same as figure 1.

Figure 8. Trends in the Japanese Population of Shop and Company
Employees of Surabaya, 1913–1927

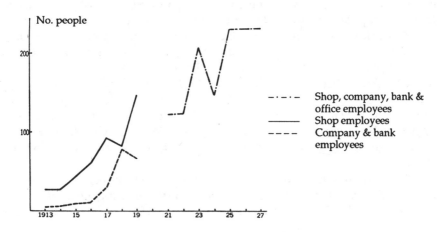

Source: Same as figure 1.

Table 5. The Number of Employees of Japanese Trading Companies and Banks in Surabaya

Unit: No. people

1919		1921		1924	
Mitsui & Co.	4	Mitsui & Co.	26	Mitsui & Co.	23
Daitō Bussan	10	Yokohama Specie Bank	11	Mitsubishi Trading Co.	6
Arima Yōkō	10	Bank of Taiwan		Yokohama Specie Bank	8
Chōya Shōkai		Arima Yōkō	12	Bank of Taiwan	13
Tō Indo Bōeki	12	Suzuki Shōten	13	Suzuki Shōten	13
Ajia Bōeki	4	Ōtake Yōkō	2	Arima Yōkō	16
Fukushima Yōkō	4	Senda Shōkai	3	Nippon Menka	3
Tōyō Bōeki Takushoku		Mitsubishi Trading Co.	6	Tōyō Menka	6
Takamura Shōten	6	Tō Indo Bōeki	5	Nan'yō Shōkai	
Yoko Shōten	7	Horikoshi Shōkai	3	Nakamura Shōten	5
Furukawa	6	Nakamura Shōkai	7	Daikyūsha	1
Yokohama Specie Bank	4	Tōyō Shōkai	5	Jawa Bōeki	2
Bank of Taiwan	14	Daishin Yōkō	12	Gōshō	4
Nakamura Shōten	4	Shimosato Shōten	1	Senda Shōkai	4
		Ōtsu Shōten	4	Nichiran Bōeki	7
		Kawahara Shōten	4	Daidō Bōeki	8
		Nichiran Bōeki	3	Nippon Satō Bōeki	1
		Kumazawa Shōten	10	Daishin Yōkō	15
		Yamato Shōkai	5	Yuasa Bōeki	2
		Takamura Shōten	2	Shimosato Shōkai	2
		Nippon Baiyaku	2	Wataya Shōten	5
		Wataya Shōten	2	Yamato Shōkai	4
		Yahirowa Shōten	3	Yafujiwa Shōten	2
		Yuasa Bōeki	2	Tōmei Shōkai	
		Yoko	7	Nakagawa Shōten	1
		Nan'yō Shōkai	13	Ōtomi Shōkai	3
		Nippon Menka	4	Yoko	4
		Gōshō	6	Matsunaga Yōkō	3
		Tōyō Menka	6	Endō Yōkō	5
		Akatsu Shōten	2	Katō Suishōdō	8
		Kaneko Shōten	2	Nan'in Shōkai	5
		Matsunaga Shōten	3	Ajia Bōeki	4
				Shikishima Shōkai	3
				Takamura Shōten	1
				Taiyō Shōkō	2
				Tōyō Shōkai	5
Total	85	Total	186	Total	194

Source: Ministry of Foreign Affairs, Bureau of Commercial Affairs, "Zaigai hompō jitsugyōsha shirabe" [Survey of expatriate Japanese businessmen].

Volume, on the other hand, increased from 155,471 tons to 265,460 tons.[23] And if third-country trade is taken into account, the volume of sugar from the Netherlands East Indies handled by the big Japanese trading companies was still greater.

After the war European cotton goods became available again, but Japan's share of the Netherlands East Indies' market for cotton cloth grew even larger, though

[23] Ministry of Foreign Affairs, Bureau of Commercial Affairs, *Ranryō Higashi Indo jijō* [Netherlands East Indies Affairs] (Tokyo: Ministry of Foreign Affairs, 1924), p. 872.

there were some fluctuations in the value of this trade (table 6). In terms of the total value of exports of cotton goods, Japan's share of the Netherlands East Indies' market rose from an average of 3 percent in 1910 to an average of 12 percent in 1920. This market, replacing the faltering Chinese market, became almost as important to Japan as the Indian market. Furthermore, Japan's share of the Netherlands East Indies' market for bleached and processed cotton cloth began to expand in the 1920s.[24] Thus in the first half of the 1920s the Netherlands East Indies' market was becoming more rather than less valuable to Japanese trading companies.

Figure 9. Trends in the Total Value of Trade between Japan and the
Netherlands East Indies, 1909–1932

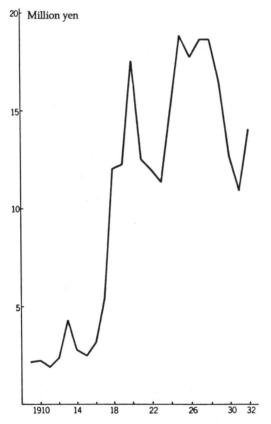

Source: Tōyō Keizai Shimpōsha, ed., *Nihon bōeki seiran* [Data on Japanese trade], reprint with supplementary material (Tokyo: Tōyō Keizai Shimpōsha, 1975).

---

[24] Yoshitada Murayama, "Ryōtaisenkanki Nihon men orimono no Tōnan Ajia shinshutsu: Ranryō Higashi Indo o chushin ni" [The penetration of Southeast Asia by Japanese cotton goods in the interwar period, with special reference to the Netherlands East Indies], *Tōnan Ajia: Rekishi to bunka* [Southeast Asia: History and culture] 11 (1982): 43–44.

Table 6.1. The Value of Cotton Cloth Imported to Java and Madura from Various Countries

Unit: Thousand guilders

Year	Japan	Netherlands	Britain	China	Total
1916	96	2,633	4,305		7,807
1920	22,740	4,897	12,297		41,135
1921	15,795	2,901	3,319		22,877
1922	10,402	2,662	3,341		16,616
1923	7,624	2,144	2,517		12,606
1924	11,450	933	2,174		15,576
1925	12,532	1,122	2,121		16,650
1926	9,709	1,005	581	859	12,177
1927	8,778	471	811	1,250	11,322
1929	8,485	456	606	1,318	10,880
1930	7,217	211	253	795	8,483
1931	6,175	237	76	599	7,095
1932	5,975	39	66	264	6,366
1933	4,767	11	26	278	5,114
1934	6,081	19	11	241	6,394
1935	5,438	10	19	24	5,534
1936	6,818	5	14	46	7,140

Table 6.2. Proportionate Shares of the Value of Cotton Cloth Imported to Java and Madura from Various Countries

Unit: %

Year	Japan	Netherlands	Britain	China	Total
1916	1.2	33.7	55.1		100.0
1920	55.3	11.9	29.9		100.0
1921	69.0	12.7	14.5		100.0
1922	62.6	16.0	20.1		100.0
1923	60.5	17.0	20.0		100.0
1924	73.5	6.0	14.0		100.0
1925	75.3	6.7	12.7		100.0
1926	79.7	8.3	4.0	7.1	100.0
1927	77.6	4.3	7.2	11.0	100.0
1928	73.4	5.1	5.7	15.4	100.0
1929	78.0	4.2	5.6	12.1	100.0
1930	85.1	2.5	3.0	9.4	100.0
1931	87.0	3.3	1.1	8.4	100.0
1932	93.9	0.6	1.0	4.1	100.0
1933	93.2	0.2	0.5	5.4	100.0
1934	95.1	0.3	0.2	3.8	100.0
1935	98.3	0.2	0.3	0.4	100.0
1936	95.5	0.1	0.2	0.6	100.0

Source: Yoshitada Murayama, "Ryōtaisenkanki Nihon men orimono no Tōnan Ajia shinshutsu: Ranryō Higashi Indo o Chūshin ni" [The penetration of Southeast Asia by Japanese cotton goods in the interwar period, with special reference to the Netherlands East Indies], *Tōnan Ajia: Rakishi to bunka* [Southeast Asia: History and culture] 11 (1982). Figures for 1916 are from Tokyo Shin'yō Kōkanjo [Tokyo Credit Exchange], *Nan'yō orimono jijō* [South Seas textile conditions] (Tokyo: Tokyo Shin'yō Kōkanjo, 1919); those for 1920–1924 are from *Kaigai shijō ni okeru hompō mempu* [Japanese cotton cloth in overseas markets]; those for 1925 are from Nippon Yushutsu Men Orimono Dōgyō Kumiai Tengōkai [Japan Federation of Cotton Texport Builds], *Jawa ni yunyū saruru mempu ni tsuite* [On cotton cloth imported to Java] (Nippon Yushutsu Men Orimono Dōgyō Kumiai Rengōkai, 1926); those for 1926 and 1927 are from *Hompō yushutsu men orimono no gensei* [The state of Japanese exports of cotton goods]; those for 1928 and 1929 are from Kiichirō Kamo, *Nan'yō mempu shijō shisatsuki* [Observations on the South Seas cotton cloth market] (privately published, 1930); those for 1930–1936 are from Nichi-Ran Kaishō Iinkai [Japan-Netherlands Conference Committee], *Nichi-Ran bōeki sankō shiryō* [References on Japan-Netherlands trade] (Nichi-Ran Kaishō Iinkai, 1937).

Let us now examine the period from 1919 to 1928, when the commercial population dropped. The operative factor was the decrease in the number of merchants in the cities. There was little diminution in the number of merchants in outlying areas, and commodity traders, a new type of merchant, emerged in some localities. In addition, large and medium-sized trading companies were established in Surabaya, which meant that the number of company employees increased. As a result, the overall drop in the Japanese commercial population was quite small. This change in the composition of the commercial population in the 1920s not only served to keep the decrease in the commercial population small but also laid the foundation for the expansion of commercial operations that would occur in the 1930s.

In the 1920s the relationship between importers and retailers, the two poles of the distribution chain, was epitomized by the geographical relationship between Surabaya and other locales. This period also saw the formation of distribution networks (*keiretsu*). For example, Nippon Menka began its operations in the Netherlands East Indies with the establishment of a South Seas agency in Surabaya in 1919. In 1920 it added a subagency in Semarang, and the following year it upgraded the Surabaya agency to a branch. In 1924 it set up subagencies in Batavia and Cirebon, completing its network on Java.

Concurrently, Nippon Menka organized sales routes to outlying areas, signing up as partners wholesalers who had ridden out the recession to gain access to their retail routes. In its first such arrangement, Nippon Menka concluded an exclusive contract with Nakamura Shōten, based in Surabaya, in 1923. It also had a tie-up with Nan'yō Shōkai, which had a network of branches on Java and Borneo. On Sumatra, Meiji Shōkai, based in Padang and with close ties to Nichiran Bōeki in Batavia, became the company's agent. In this way Nippon Menka established a sales network and expanded its operations in the Netherlands East Indies.[25]

With the Great Depression, Japanese products flooded the Netherlands East Indies' market and the commercial population increased. Japanese goods were imported because their low prices ensured them a ready market among the indigenous population, but the role of the aforementioned distribution routes in bringing these goods to the public should not be overlooked. These routes had been set up when economic restructuring was taking place in the aftermath of the recession following World War I. Because of this, as mentioned in part two, in 1933 the colonial authorities, disturbed by the influx of Japanese goods, enacted not only an Emergency Import Restriction Ordinance but also an Emergency Ordinance Restricting Foreign Entry, which put pressure on shops operated by Japanese. As a result, the Japanese commercial population decreased after 1933, and the total Japanese population in the Netherlands East Indies inevitably began to drop, as well.

CONCLUSION

The main purpose of this paper is to elucidate the reasons for the gradual increase in the Japanese population of the Netherlands East Indies between 1917 and 1927, the distinctive feature of Japanese population trends in that part of Southeast Asia. As we have seen, the modest drop in the male commercial population during

---

[25] Nippon Menka Kabushiki Kaisha, *Nippon Menka Kabushiki kaisha gojū nen shi* [Nippon Menka Kabushiki Kaisha's fifty years of history] (Tokyo: Nippon Menka Kabushiki Kaisha, 1943), pp. 139–41.

this period, coupled with the increase in the population of male and female dependents, contributed to an overall increase in the Japanese population.

The reason the male commercial population did not drop significantly is that merchants who had dispersed to outlying areas were able to survive and that large and medium-size trading companies established themselves in the northern port cities, offsetting the marked drop in the number of merchants there. As a result, a structure similar to that of the *"gudang* [godown] people" and "lower-town people" of Singapore described by Tōru Yano[26] developed between Surabaya and the other regions of Java. With the reemergence of merchants in Surabaya at the end of the 1920s, a similar pattern was established within Surabaya itself. In 1934, at the time of the first Japan-Netherlands Conference, relations between the trading companies and independent merchants were poor. Shun'ichi Nagaoka, Japan's ambassador plenipotentiary to the conference, commented: "Upon our arrival in the Netherlands East Indies, relations within the Japanese community, the fusion of big trading companies and small and medium-sized merchants, seemed to us rather strained, even mutually antagonistic."[27]

Like the relationship between Surabaya and the other regions of Java, the relationship between the Japanese community on Java and that on Sumatra is of interest. Until about 1912 both Java and Sumatra saw an influx of Japanese. At one point Sumatra even had a larger Japanese population than Java. Whereas the Japanese population on Java continued to grow, however, that on Sumatra remained flat. Some attribute the stagnancy of Japanese activities on Sumatra to psychological factor—a lack of the will to abandon the old ways and pursue vigorous development.[28]

The old ways certainly held on longer on Sumatra than on Java. There continued to be more women than men on Sumatra for many years; even after prostitution was outlawed on Java, many prostitutes were to be found in Medan. Merchants on Java switched to handling general merchandise earlier than their counterparts on Sumatra, where the proportion of medicine sellers and traveling salesmen remained high. In other words, the factors that led to the development of the Japanese community on Java were absent on Sumatra. Analysis of the Japanese community on Sumatra would further clarify the factors that stimulated the development of the Japanese community on Java.

This paper was originally published under the title "Senzenki Orandaryō Higashi Indo ni okeru hōjin keizai shinshutsu keitai: Shokugyōbetsu chōsa o chushin to shite" [The pattern of Japanese economic penetration of the prewar Netherlands East Indies, with special reference to the Population Survey by Occupation], *Ajia keizai* [Developing economies] 26, no. 3 (March 1985): 52–69.

---

[26] Yano, *"Nanshin" no keifu*, pp. 124–27.

[27] Shun'ichi Nagaoka, "Nichi-Ran kaishō yori kaerite" [On returning from the Japan-Netherlands Conference], *Nan'yō Kyōkai zasshi* [Journal of the South Seas Association] 3 (1935): 5.

[28] Tamizo Tsujimori, *Hōko Sumatora no zembō* [An overview of the treasure-trove of Sumatra] (Tokyo: Ritsumeikan Shuppanbu, 1934), p. 229.

5

THE PATTERN OF JAPANESE ECONOMIC PENETRATION OF THE PREWAR PHILIPPINES

Hiroshi Hashiya

In this paper I will analyze the pattern of Japanese economic penetration of the prewar Philippines, using statistics primarily from the "Consular Population Survey of Expatriate Japanese by Occupation," in the Diplomatic History Archives of the Ministry of Foreign Affairs. A detailed description of the survey's content and a discussion of its nature as a historical source are found elsewhere.[1]

I. TRENDS AND TRAITS OF THE JAPANESE POPULATION OF THE PHILIPPINES

The number of Japanese living in the Philippines represented about 30 percent of the Japanese in Southeast Asia from 1907 to 1917. This proportion rose to 45 percent in 1918 and hovered around 40 percent for several years thereafter. In 1929 the proportion rose to 50.3 percent and eventually passed 60 percent. The lowest proportion was 30.5 percent, in 1911; the highest was 63.7 percent, in 1940. The number of Japanese in the Philippines was thus quite high, especially in the 1930s, when more than half the Japanese in Southeast Asia were living in the Philippines.

The ratio of Japanese men to women was also much higher in the Philippines than in other parts of Southeast Asia. In the region as a whole, 62 percent of the Japanese population was male in 1915, 66 percent in 1925, and 67 percent in 1935. In the Philippines, however, males represented 83 percent, 81 percent, and 69 percent, respectively, of the Japanese population in the same years. Although the proportion of Japanese women in the Philippines rose somewhat during the 1930s, accompanying an increase in the total Japanese population, prior to that period the male population far outnumbered the female. Around 1911, when a high percentage of Japanese in Southeast Asia were female, the Japanese male population of the Philippines was already much greater than the female. As will be seen in the discussion of occupational patterns of Japanese in the Philippines, this fact was related to the high proportion of male-dominated occupations, such as engineering, construction, and agriculture.

Figure 1 charts the fluctuations in the Japanese population of the Philippines. The population increased from around 1912 to the middle of World War I but

---

[1] Hajime Shimizu, "Gaimushō 'Kaigai zairyū hompōjin shokugyōbetsu jinkō chōsa ikken' no shiryōteki seikaku" [The character of the "Consular population survey of expatriate Japanese by occupation" of the Ministry of Foreign Affairs as a historical source], *Ajia keizai* [Developing economies] 26, no. 3 (March 1985).

Figure 1. The Japanese Population of the Philippines, 1907–1940

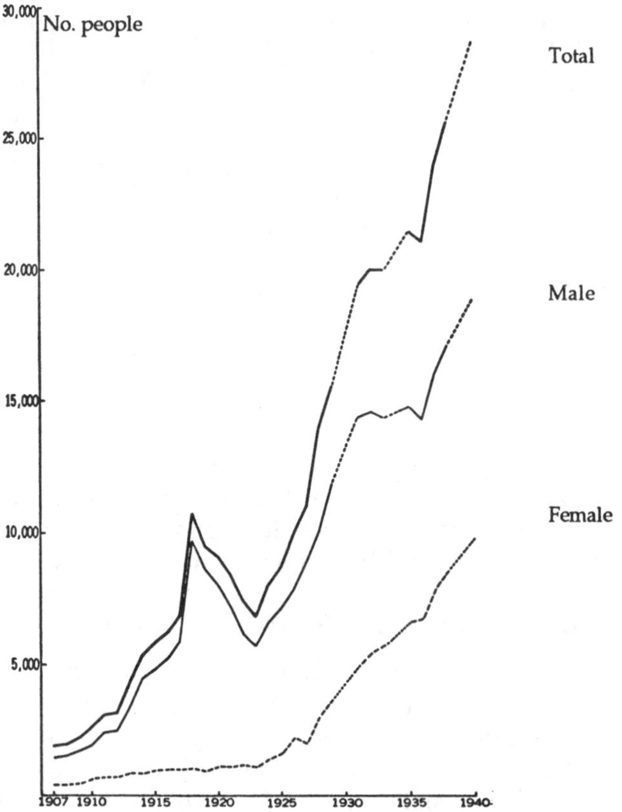

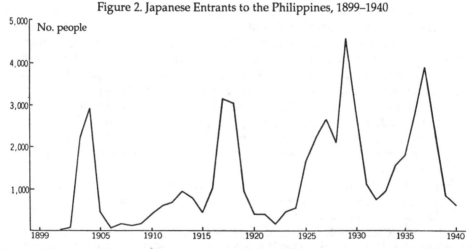

Source: "Kaigai zairyū hompōjin shokugyōbetsu jinkō chōsa ikken" [Consular population survey of expatriate Japanese by occupation], Diplomatic History Archives, Ministry of Foreign Affairs.

Figure 2. Japanese Entrants to the Philippines, 1899–1940

Source: Ministry of Foreign Affairs, Consular and Emigration Affairs Department, *Waga kokumin no kaigai hatten: Ijū hyaku nen no ayumi* [Japanese nationals overseas: One hundred years of migration] (Tokyo: Ministry of Foreign Affairs, 1971), "References," p. 143.

decreased at the end of the war. If the population in 1918 is designated as 100, by 1923 it had decreased to 63, representing a much greater drop than the 72 registered for the Japanese population of Southeast Asia as a whole. After that the population began to increase once again, growing at an especially rapid rate in the late 1920s. Although it grew only moderately in the early 1930s, another marked rise occurred in the late 1930s. This trend is corroborated by the statistics on the number of Japanese entrants (fig. 2).

Thus, the Japanese population of the Philippines increased in four distinct periods: the early 1900s, the latter half of the second decade, the late 1920s, and the late 1930s. As will be discussed below, this pattern of population fluctuations was closely related to the market price of abaca (Manila hemp), in whose production the majority of Japanese in the Philippines were engaged.

With regard to the difference in male and female population trends, it is clear that the male population exhibited the same trend as the Japanese population as a whole and, in effect, determined the pattern of the latter. Fluctuations in the female population followed quite a different pattern. The female population remained relatively stable throughout World War I and the early 1920s, growing rapidly thereafter. Moreover, in contrast to the slow growth of the overall population in the early 1930s, the female population continued to increase steadily.

This trend was the result of the predominance of dependent women as opposed to working women in the female population, as shown in table 1. In 1920, for example, the percentage of working women was greater than the number of dependent women in Southeast Asia as a whole. Only in the Philippines were more than 80 percent of Japanese women classified as dependents. Since the majority of women classified as working women were prostitutes, this figure indicates that there were few prostitutes in the Japanese community in the Philippines during the early period and that the number of women other than prostitutes began to increase at a relatively early date. Economic changes around the time of World War I and the antiprostitution movement of the early 1920s thus had little effect on the female population, which remained fairly stable until the mid-1920s. In the mid-1920s the male population began to increase, and as the men's livelihood stabilized the number of women arriving as wives also increased, resulting in a rapid rise in the female population.

Table 1. The Percentage of Dependents in the Japanese Female Population of Southeast Asia, 1920–1935

Unit: %

	Philippines	Singapore	Malaya & North Borneo	Netherlands East Indies
1920	81.9	49.4	36.9	42.7
1925	86.8	53.8	46.3	75.6
1930		73.3	62.0	81.7
1935	98.3			89.2

Source: Same as figure 1.

From the above it is clear that the Philippines had the largest Japanese population in Southeast Asia, that fluctuations in the Japanese population were dictated by changes in the male population, and that changes in that population were caused by changes in the market price of abaca. Moreover, in contrast to other parts of Southeast Asia, the majority of the Japanese female population of the Philippines was made up of dependents from an early date, and this female population exhibited a different pattern from both the Japanese population as a whole and the Japanese male population.

II. The Early Japanese Community

Below I will examine some of the economic activities of Japanese living in the Philippines through analysis of the population by occupation. Since few Japanese were engaged in abaca cultivation before 1910, their economic activities in the early period differed significantly from those of later periods. Accordingly, the Japanese community in the pre-1910 period deserves to be considered independently.[2]

A Japanese consulate was established in the Philippines in December 1888, and in December 1889 a total of 35 Japanese residents were registered, as shown in table 2. However, since 27 were short-term residents, such as sailors and acrobats, the number of Japanese residents dropped to only 5 in 1891. The consulate was closed from mid-September 1893 until late October 1896.

The next opportunity for large-scale Japanese immigration to the Philippines was construction of the Benguet highway, linking Manila and Baguio. Because of difficulties during the project's early stages, the construction supervisor, an American, Major W. V. Kennon, decided to employ Japanese rather than Filipino and Chinese laborers and commissioned Kōbe Tokō Kaisha to recruit immigrants to the Philippines. The first group of 125 immigrants, assembled by Kōbe Tokō and other immigration companies, reached Manila in 1903, followed by 3,096 immigrants the next year. If those who went to the Philippines independently are included, some 5,000 Japanese are reported to have entered the Philippines during those two years.[3]

Figure 2, which is based on existing statistics on the flow of Japanese overseas, supports this estimate, showing a total of over 5,000 entrants in 1903 and 1904. According to the consular population survey statistics presented in table 2, however, the total Japanese population in the Philippines in December 1904 was 2,652, representing an increase of only 1,688 over the population of December 1902. This survey attempted to determine the actual Japanese population, not only the number of legal entrants, and it is inconceivable that its figures would be significantly lower than the actual numbers. Therefore, regardless of minor discrepancies in the annual surveys, the fact remains that the statistics on population flow and those on the stock of resident Japanese differed by as much as 3,000 people. This indicates that the majority of Japanese lured by the Benguet highway construction project were unable to disembark in the Philippines and returned to Japan forthwith.[4]

---

[2] For case studies of Japanese commercial activities in the Philippines during the early period, see Yōko Yoshikawa, "Beiryōka Manira no shoki Nihonjin shōgyō, 1899–1920: Tagawa Moritarō no nampō kan'yo" [Early Japanese commerce in Manila under American rule, 1899–1920: Moritarō Tagawa's involvement in the southern region], *Tōnan Ajia kenkyū* [Southeast Asian studies] 18, no. 3 (December 1980).

[3] Toraji Irie, *Hōjin kaigai hattenshi* [History of Japanese development overseas] (Tokyo: Ida Shoten, 1942; reprint, Tokyo: Hara Shobō, 1981), vol. 1, pp. 428, 432 (page references are to the reprint edition).

[4] Although many construction workers were reportedly killed in accidents, the number was insufficient to account for so large a discrepancy.

Table 2. The Population of the Early Japanese Community in the Philippines, by Occupation, 1889–1906

Unit: No. people

	1889			1891			1896			1897			1898		
	M	F	T	M	F	T	M	F	T	M	F	T	M	F	T
Civil service	3	0	3	2	0	2	2	0	2	2	0	2	2	0	2
Commerce	3	0	3	2	0	2	5	0	5	7	0	7	13	5	18
Study	0	0	0	0	0	0	0	0	0	0	0	0	0	0	0
Other	29	0	29	1	0	1	0	0	0	4	3	7	1	3	4
Total	35	0	35	5	0	5	7	0	7	13	3	16	16	8	24

	1899			1900			1901			1902			1903		
	M	F	T	M	F	T	M	F	T	M	F	T	M	F	T
Civil service	3	0	3	4	0	4	4	0	4	3	0	3	2	0	2
Commerce	28	3	31	25	0	25	75	0	75	120	0	120	80	12	92
Study	1	0	1	0	0	0	1	0	1	1	0	1	1	0	1
Other	50	7	57	74	64	138	146	170	316	480	360	840	1,400	500	1,900
Total	82	10	92	103	64	167	226	170	396	604	360	964	1,483	512	1,995

	1904			1905			1906		
	M	F	T	M	F	T	M	F	T
Civil service	2	0	2	2	0	2	3	0	3
Commerce	120	30	150	126	33	159	121	40	161
Study	0	0	0	0	0	0	0	0	0
Other	1,900	600	2,500	1,674	600	2,274	1,401	620	2,021
Total	2,022	630	2,652	1,802	633	2,435	1,525	660	2,185

The number of people in each occupational category is broken down into M (males), F (females), and T (total). The figures are for December of each year.

Source: Same as figure 1.

With the completion of the Benguet highway in the autumn of 1904 and its opening in January 1905, Japanese laborers were laid off and the Japanese population decreased by 760 people, dropping from 2,652 in 1904 to 1,892 in 1907. This figure, and the fact that many Japanese returned home during the course of the highway construction project, indicates a highly mobile Japanese population in the Philippines during the early period, a supposition corroborated by the statistics on the number of passports issued and returned (table 3). (The numbers in table 3 do not always correspond to the actual number of entrants, since many people did not carry passports.)

Table 3. The Number of Passports Issued to and Returned by Japanese Entrants to the Philippines, 1892–1910

Year	No. issued	No. returned	Year	No. issued	No. returned
1892	5		1902	379	6
1893	26		1903	391	15
1894	5		1904	646	24
1895	?		1905	542	609
1896	12		1906	226	387
1897	20		1907	271	199
1898	10		1908	197	202
1899	90		1909	227	173
1900	61		1910	396	133
1901	192	7			

Source: Bureau of Statistics, *Nippon teikoku tōkei nenkan* [Statistical yearbook of the Empire of Japan].

Let us look next at the occupational structure of the early Japanese community in the Philippines. During this period the consular population survey included detailed occupational statistics only for 1903 and 1907 (table 4). Carpentry was the major occupation for males, accounting for 33 percent of the male population in 1903 and 46 percent in 1907. Many Japanese men, attracted by high wages, were hired for construction of wooden bridges and other structures from the beginning of the Benguet highway project onward, resulting in a group of hastily trained amateur carpenters known as "Manila carpenters." Upon completion of the Benguet highway, approximately 300 such carpenters were hired to build barracks for the United States Army in Malabato, Rizal Province, and were subsequently employed in barracks construction and engineering projects in Manila, Baguio, and Olongapo on Luzon, Iloilo on Panay, Malawe on Mindanao, and other parts of the Philippines.[5]

Agriculture was the second most common male occupation, growing from only 1 person in 1903 to 306 people in 1907. As discussed below, this increase was caused by a resettlement policy designed to aid Japanese immigrants by settling them on abaca plantations in Davao from 1904 onward. Agriculture, however, accounted for only 21 percent of the male population. Other significant occupations were fishery and, in 1907, "resident foreign employee," but the percentage of men engaged in both occupations was quite low.

The above statistics indicate that the majority of Japanese men entering the Philippines to work on the Benguet highway project returned to Japan in two or

---

[5] Irie, *Hōjin kaigai hattenshi*, vol. 1, p. 439.

Table 4. The Occupational Structure of the Early Japanese Community in the Philippines, 1903 and 1907

Unit: No. people

1903				1907			
	M	F	T		M	F	T
Carpenters & dependents	253	15	268	Carpentry	674	10	684
Fishermen	50	0	50	Fisheries	120	5	125
Construction workers	45	0	45	Agriculture	306	1	307
Serving women	0	280	280	Miscellaneous occupations	18	290	308
Sake retailers	0	33	33	Resident foreign employees	96	93	189
Other	425	114	539	Other	247	32	279
Total	773	442	1,215	Total	1,461	431	1,892

The number of people in each occupational category is broken down into males (M), females (F), and total (T). The 1903 figures are for June; the 1907 figures are for December.

Source: Same as figure 1.

three years at most, and that most of those who managed to stay on were carpenters. Although some resettled on abaca plantations in Davao, they would have to wait more than ten years before abaca production really flourished.

As for the female population, the overwhelming majority of females classified as working women were prostitutes. In 1903 there were 280 prostitutes, 63 percent of the female population. In 1907, since the statistics for that year do not include a category for "entertainers, prostitutes, serving women, etc.," prostitutes are thought to have been classified under "miscellaneous occupations," which included 290 women, or 67 percent of the female population. There were probably prostitutes who were not registered, as well.

The high proportion of prostitutes in the female population corresponds to the pattern indicated by the statistics on Japanese in other parts of Southeast Asia. Certain factors, however, were unique to the Japanese female population of the Philippines. First, the female population there began to increase later than elsewhere in Southeast Asia. It began to grow in 1900, when it reached 64. In Singapore, however, it was 518 and in Malaya it was 200 that year, according to the consular population survey. Although the 1900 figure for the Netherlands East Indies is unavailable, there were already 100 Japanese women there in 1897.

Second, the Japanese populations of other parts of Southeast Asia were characterized by an increase in the number of prostitutes followed by a slight increase in the male population, whereas in the Philippines the male population increased first and consistently outnumbered the female population. This was because Japanese men in other parts of Southeast Asia were engaged mainly in prostitution-dependent occupations, whereas the majority of Japanese men in the Philippines were engaged in engineering, construction, carpentry, and other occupations unrelated to prostitution. This characteristic ties in with the fact that by about 1920 most Japanese women in the Philippines were dependents.

The early Japanese community in the Philippines was thus made up mainly of male laborers engaged in construction and engineering projects, a large percentage of whom were unable to stay. Moreover, in contrast to other parts of Southeast Asia, where prostitutes were the forerunners of the Japanese presence, prostitution was of only secondary importance in the Philippines.

III. Changes in Occupational Patterns

Let us now examine occupational patterns of Japanese in the Philippines in comparison with those of Japanese in other parts of Southeast Asia. The majority of Japanese in other parts of the region were engaged in commerce. A large percentage of the Japanese population of the Philippines, however, was engaged in agriculture. Moreover, almost all Japanese in the agricultural sector were engaged in abaca cultivation, accounting for about half the working population once the economic base of the abaca plantations was stabilized.

As I have discussed elsewhere,[6] the predominance of agricultural immigrants resembles both "strategic immigration" to the South Pacific islands, Central and South America, and Manchuria and immigration to North America. However, in view of the facts that the Japanese government did not have a strategic-immigration policy for the Philippines and that the Philippines lacked a large-scale anti-Japanese policy, we must acknowledge that immigration to the Philippines differed fundamentally from immigration to the above-mentioned regions. Moreover, fluctuations in the Japanese population of the Philippines, as of other parts of Southeast Asia, were closely linked to economic factors, a clear indication that immigration to the Philippines followed the general pattern for Southeast Asia.

Abaca, in whose production a large proportion of the Japanese population was engaged, was an international commodity whose price fluctuated according to world economic conditions. Fluctuations in the market price of abaca (fig. 3) and in the Japanese population (fig. 1) followed the same pattern, with a slight time lag. Although the two curves diverged in the latter half of the 1920s, the low price of abaca was apparently compensated for by improved production, resulting in a more stable livelihood and an increase in the number of dependents. Clearly, fluctuations in the Japanese population of the Philippines were generally dependent upon changes in the market price of abaca and in the profits obtained from abaca plantations.

Next let us consider population trends by occupation (fig. 4). As already stated, the majority of Japanese in the Philippines were engaged in agriculture. The percentage rose rapidly from 1916 to 1918, dropped rapidly from 1919 to 1923, rose rapidly from 1924 to 1931, fell from 1932 to 1936, and rose from 1937 onward. As mentioned, these large fluctuations in the agricultural population reflected changing profits from abaca and also determined the pattern of the Japanese population of the Philippines as a whole.

The proportion of the population engaged in commerce and fishery was much smaller than that engaged in agriculture. Nevertheless, in absolute numbers more Japanese in the Philippines were engaged in commerce and in fishery in the 1920s and 1930s than anywhere else in Southeast Asia, with the exception of the Netherlands East Indies (commerce) and Singapore (fisheries). Fluctuations in the commercial population were less drastic than those in the agricultural population, with increases occurring during the early part of the second decade of the century

---

[6] Hiroshi Hashiya, "Senzenki Tōnan Ajia zairyū hōjin jinkō no dōkō: Tachiiki to no hikaku" [Trends in the prewar Japanese population of Southeast Asia: A comparison with other regions], *Ajia keizai* [Developing economies] 26, no. 3 (March 1985).

Figure 3. The Average Market Price of Abaca, 1915–1937

Prices are per picul of low-grade abaca.

Source: Hiroji Kamohara, *Dabao hōjin kaitakushi* [History of Japanese development of Davao] (Davao: Nippi Shimbunsha, 1938).

Figure 4. The Japanese Population of the Philippines, by Occupation, 1907–1940

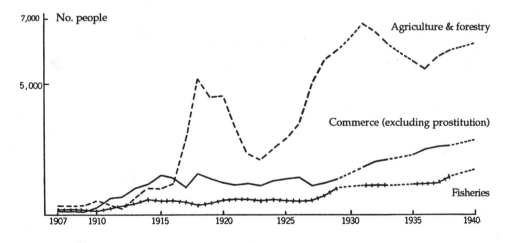

Source: Same as figure 1.

and in the 1930s. As suggested by figure 5, these increases were related to growth in the value of trade between Japan and the Philippines during those two periods—an indication that changes in the commercial population, as in the agricultural population, were closely tied to economic factors, though the causes and patterns of change differed.

One discrepancy can be seen, however, between the trends in the commercial population and in the value of trade. Despite a large reduction in the value of imports from Japan from 1921 to 1923, the commercial population remained fairly stable. As discussed in detail below, the drop in the value of trade during those years was mainly the result of a reduction in the unit price of Japanese goods; the volume of goods handled did not diminish much. Moreover, the share of Japanese goods in the Philippine market actually increased, so that the drop in the value of trade did not affect individual Japanese businessmen enough to cause them to pull out. Thus, despite this one apparent discrepancy, fluctuations in the commercial population were still closely tied to economic factors.

Fluctuations in the population engaged in fisheries were even less pronounced, although a slight and gradual increase occurred in the 1930s. The proportion of Japanese involved in the Philippine fishery industry was extremely high in the 1930s. Japanese contributed $1 million of the $5.5 million invested in fisheries in 1932, and 41 of the 150 large fishing vessels in 1935 were under Japanese ownership.[7] Despite the added restrictions placed on Japanese fisheries by the 1932 revision of the Fishery Act, the Japanese continued to expand their operations by various means, including registration under Filipino names. A considerable number of Japanese were engaged in industry as well, but because this category in the consular population survey included the construction industry, the statistics reflect the presence of a large number of carpenters.

In summary, most Japanese in the Philippines were engaged in agriculture and commerce. Fluctuations in the population reflected fluctuations in the economic factors governing these sectors, and in this sense Japanese population patterns in the Philippines were typical of those in Southeast Asia as a whole. Detailed analyses of the Japanese agricultural and commercial populations of the Philippines follow.

IV. Analysis of the Agricultural Population

The major agricultural activity of Japanese living in the Philippines was abaca cultivation in Davao,[8] which began with completion of the Benguet highway and the resultant rise in unemployed Japanese. Kyōsaburō Ōta, who ran a general-merchandise business in Manila, sent 180 unemployed immigrants to Davao abaca plantations in 1904. He sent another 100 in January 1905 and 70 more in August, after which he moved to Davao himself and began operating his own plantation in 1906.

---

[7] Ministry of Finance, Administration Bureau, "Nipponjin no kaigai katsudō ni kansuru reki-shiteki chōsa" [A historical survey of Japanese overseas activities], "Nampōhen" [Southern region], vol. 5, pp. 65–66.

[8] Major studies of the Japanese community in Davao include G. P. Provido, "Japanese Interests in the Philippines" (Ph.D. diss., Stanford University, 1936); C. E. Cody, "The Consolidation of the Japanese in Davao," *Comment*, no. 3, 1958; G. K. Goodman, *Davao: A Case Study in Japanese-Philippine Relations* (Lawrence, Kansas: Center for East Asian Studies, University of Kansas, 1967).

In 1907 he established a company named Ōta Kōgyō and began expanding his sphere of business.[9] According to the 1907 consular population survey, 307 of the 1,892 Japanese in the Philippines were engaged in agriculture, which corresponds fairly closely to the above total of 350 immigrants in Davao.

Abaca plantations did not develop as a direct result of resettlement of unemployed Japanese from the Benguet highway project, however. The agricultural population did not increase significantly until much later, around 1916, when World War I led to a rise in demand for rope for naval use. With the corresponding rise in the price of hemp, Japanese-run abaca plantations employing immigrant Japanese proliferated, and the number of new Japanese entrants also increased rapidly. In 1915 Furukawa Takushoku was established, a company destined to control half the hemp business; Ōta Kōgyō controlled the rest.

In 1918 the agricultural population peaked at 5,216 people, 54 percent of the Japanese working population. When this figure is compared with the 16 percent of 1907, it is apparent that the Japanese population of the Philippines had become predominantly agricultural. Subclassification of the Japanese engaged in agriculture in Davao (table 5) reveals that most were plantation workers—94 percent of the agricultural population in 1919. Moreover, only 127 of the Japanese living in the Davao area that year were classified as dependents of plantation workers, a clear indication that the majority were migrant workers unaccompanied by their families.

These figures should also be examined in relation to the phenomenon of "independent cultivators," a system peculiar to the Japanese plantations in Davao. This was in fact a tenant-farming system under which immigrant Japanese cultivated land owned by agricultural companies. Since tenants were required to hand over only 5 to 15 percent of the harvest to the company as a "sale handling fee," the system was considered to be quite advantageous to tenants. Meanwhile, immigrants with no capital were employed as plantation workers under direct company management.

There is some disagreement as to when a stable independent-cultivator system was established. Gizō Furukawa maintains that it was the main system of cultivation as early as 1918, and estimates that there were 3,000 independent cultivators and 1,700 hired workers.[10] This estimate, however, is in sharp contrast to the picture presented by the consular population survey statistics, which clearly indicate the continued predominance of plantation-style management at that time. In 1920, though, the ratio of independent cultivators to plantation workers was abruptly reversed, with the former predominating. Such a drastic change may have been due in part to changes in survey methods or other factors, but it is inconceivable that the figures were totally divorced from reality. They are in fact confirmed by various recorded statements from about that time, such as the following: "Due to the shortage of labor, wages for plantation workers were extremely high, and one could save quite a lot of money in a year or two." Moreover, "since the company helped

---

[9] Hiroji Kamohara, Dabao hōjin kaitakushi [History of Japanese development of Davao] (Davao: Nippi Shimbunsha, 1938), p. 59; Gizō Furukawa, *Dabao kaitakuki* [A record of the development of Davao] (Tokyo: Furukawa Takushoku, 1956), pp. 120–22. According to these two works, 30 Japanese immigrants were recruited by a Syrian but returned to Manila a year later, after the venture failed.

[10] Furukawa, *Dabao kaitakuki*, pp. 425–26. It should be noted that these figures are speculative.

Table 5. The Japanese Agricultural Population of Davao, 1917–1940

Units: No. people, %

Year	Plantation workers No. people M	F	T	% of total	Independent cultivators No. people M	F	T	% of total	Total agricultural population	Dependents M	F	T
1917	1,549	0	1,549	63	881	39	920	37	2,469	18	46	64
1918	4,611	1	4,612	94	295	0	295	6	4,907	42	85	127
1919	4,011	5	4,016	94	244	0	244	6	4,260	44	85	129
1920	1,623	0	1,623	37	2,680	33	2,713	63	4,336	49	82	131
1921	1,109	4	1,113	36	1,941	3	1,944	64	3,057	79	262	341
1922	892	0	892	43	1,204	0	1,204	57	2,096	113	225	338
1923	1,045	0	1,045	56	815	0	815	44	1,860	69	151	220
1924	1,106	0	1,106	50	1,101	0	1,101	50	2,207	112	288	400
1925	1,603	0	1,603	58	1,138	1	1,139	42	2,742	192	388	580
1926	1,852	0	1,852	56	1,446	0	1,446	44	3,298	242	564	806
1927	2,606	0	2,606	57	2,005	0	2,005	43	4,611	384	889	1,273
1928	3,047	0	3,047	56	2,407	0	2,407	44	5,454	513	1,368	1,881
1929	3,187	0	3,187	54	2,708	0	2,708	46	5,895	608	1,685	2,293
1930			4,108	59			2,865	41	6,973	831	2,219	3,050
1931	4,039	0	4,039	59	2,816	1	2,817	41	6,856	1,060	2,527	3,587
1932	2,953	0	2,953	45	3,644	3	3,647	55	6,600	1,367	2,778	4,145
1933	2,563	0	2,563	42	3,553	4	3,557	58	6,120	1,576	2,965	4,541
1934	2,936	0	2,936	45	3,630	3	3,633	55	6,569			
1935	2,049	0	2,049	38	3,285	0	3,285	62	5,334	1,758	3,337	5,095
1936	1,757	0	1,757	34	3,375	0	3,375	66	5,132	1,962	3,750	5,712
1937	2,178	0	2,178	39	3,406	0	3,406	61	5,584	2,113	4,160	6,273
1938	2,263	0	2,263	38	3,632	4	3,636	62	5,899	2,494	4,712	7,206
1939			2,401	40			3,654	60	6,055			
1940	2,251	1	2,252	37	3,796	14	3,810	63	6,062			8,067

"Plantation workers" and "independent cultivators" are broken down into males (M), females (F), and total (T). The category of "agricultural workers" is found in the consular population survey from 1914 onward, but this population does not appear to have been actually surveyed until around 1918. "Independent cultivators" includes such categories in the consular population survey as "agriculture," "cultivation," and "farming, gardening, livestock." Through 1920, the figures for dependents include dependents of people in nonagricultural occupations. The population surveyed was that of the entire geographical area under the jurisdiction of the Davao branch of the Japanese consulate general in Manila (later the Davao consulate), which extended somewhat beyond the borders of Davao.

Sources: For 1917–1938 and 1940, same as figure 1. For 1939, Taiwan Takushoku, Research Division, *Hiripin no sangyō to bōeki* [Industry and trade in the Philippines] (n.p.: Taiwan Takushoku, 1942), Appendix, p. 12.

provide land-clearing tools, food, and other necessities . . . it was very easy to become an independent cultivator."[11]

These new independent cultivators, however, were operating on a shaky economic base. The Japanese agricultural population of the Philippines shrank rapidly following such setbacks as the drop in the price of hemp that accompanied the end of World War I and the increased restrictions on Japanese land ownership imposed by the 1919 revision of the Public Land Act. It is clear from table 5 that there was a much greater reduction in the number of independent cultivators than in the number of plantation workers. It is thought that a significant percentage of the former reverted to the status of plantation worker instead of returning to Japan.

After a lull in the hemp boom after World War I, the agricultural population began to increase again in 1924. The main causes of this resurgence were improved hemp production thanks to the spread of the power-driven *hagotan* (hemp-stripping machine) and the establishment of a Davao shipping route by Ōsaka Shōsen in 1928 after the opening of the port of Davao in 1926.

The power-driven *hagotan* was developed by Ōta Kōgyō in 1920. At first driven by hydraulic power, it was later motorized, an improvement that resulted in a marked rise in production. Maximum production with manual stripping was ten kilograms of hemp per person per day, which severely limited the area of land an independent cultivator could manage. The power-driven *hagotan,* however, allowed fifteen to twenty kilograms to be stripped in an hour. This enabled one person to manage ten hectares, five times the former two hectares.[12] Accordingly, even if the unit price of hemp dropped, potential losses could be covered by increasing the total yield.

The opening of a Davao shipping route greatly increased traffic between Japan and Davao and contributed significantly to the rapid increase in the number of Japanese dependents in the late 1920s (table 5). The majority of these dependents belonged to households headed by independent cultivators; in 1930 the number of wives was equivalent to almost 40 percent of the number of independent cultivators, many of whom also had children (table 6). Clearly, by the late 1920s independent

Table 6. The Japanese Agricultural Population of Davao and Dependents (October 1, 1930)

Unit: No. people

| | | Dependents | | | |
Occupation	Working population	Wives	Male children	Female children	Total no. dependents
Abaca cultivation	2,865	1,069	675	724	2,468
Coconut palm cultivation	53	9	7	5	21
Vegetable cultivation	45	18	13	11	42
Coffee cultivation	4	1	2	1	4
Poultry raising	2	0	0	0	0
Silkworm raising	1	1	0	1	2
Agricultural labor	4,108	306	156	120	582

Source: Same as figure 1.

---

[11] Kamohara, *Dabao hōjin kaitakushi*, pp. 459–60.

[12] Furukawa, *Dabao kaitakuki*, p. 427–32.

cultivators were secure enough to support families. In addition, independent cultivators increased in number (table 5). Accordingly, the late 1920s can justifiably be
designated as the period in which a stable independent-cultivator system was
established.

In the early 1930s independent cultivators not only increased in number but also
constituted a growing percentage of the agricultural population. In the late 1930s
the number of independent cultivators decreased slightly but represented a higher
percentage of the agricultural population. As figures 3 and 4 show, the reduction in
the overall agricultural population was caused by the low price of hemp during
that period. Nevertheless, although the price fell even lower than at the beginning of the 1920s, the drop in the agricultural population was not as great as in the
1918–1923 period, thanks to the independent cultivators' firmer economic base.

There was a marked drop in the number of plantation workers at the outset of
the 1920s, and independent cultivators, whose number had grown so dramatically
during World War I, were even harder hit as their weak economic base crumbled.
But the independent cultivators of the late 1920s, who enjoyed a firm economic
base, were able to weather the low hemp prices that continued into the early 1930s
without a significant reduction in number, an indication of the emergence of a stable
type of independent cultivator. The number of plantation workers, however, decreased much more noticeably than at the beginning of the 1920s.

In summary, the Davao abaca plantations, the mainstay of Japanese agricultural activities in the Philippines, began to flourish during World War I because of
highly favorable hemp prices. Many of the Japanese plantation workers who
flocked to the area during this period were able to establish themselves as independent cultivators, thanks to high wages and financial support from the plantation companies. Due to their unstable economic base, however, many were unable to
weather the drop in hemp prices at the beginning of the 1920s, reverting to their
former status of plantation worker or returning to Japan. In the late 1920s hemp
production improved with the spread of the power-driven *hagotan*, and the resultant economies of scale enabled independent cultivators to compensate for low hemp
prices. They were also able to bring their families over from Japan. Thus was established a system of stable independent cultivators. Despite the drop in hemp prices
in the early 1930s, these cultivators remained in business, and when the price of
hemp recovered, the Japanese agricultural population increased again.

As we have seen, fluctuations in the Japanese agricultural population were the
result of economic factors, such as changes in the price of hemp and profits from
abaca plantations. Meanwhile, a system of stable independent cultivators gradually evolved.[13]

V. Analysis of the Commercial Population

As figure 4 shows, the Japanese commercial population (excluding prostitutes) of
the Philippines rose at the beginning of the second decade of the century, remained

[13] Of course, the advancement of Japanese farmers also represented economic exploitation of
Philippine society. Adequate treatment of this subject is necessarily curtailed by the limited nature of this paper's topic. For a discussion of post–World War II Davao that refers to prewar
economic exploitation, see Yoshiyuki Tsurumi, *Banana to Nihonjin: Firipin nōen to shokutaku no
aida* [Bananas and the Japanese: From Philippine plantations to the dining table] (Tokyo:
Iwanami Shoten, 1982).

Figure 5. The Value of Philippine Trade with Japan, 1907–1940

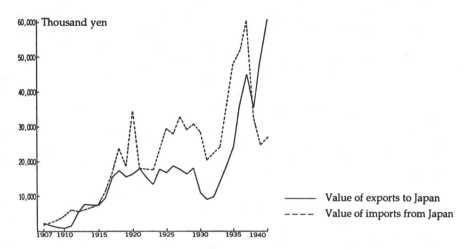

Value of exports to Japan
Value of imports from Japan

Source: Tōyō Keizai Shimpōsha, ed., *Nihon bōeki seiran* [Data on Japanese trade], reprint with supplementary material (Tokyo: Tōyō Keizai Shimpōsha, 1975).

flat overall while rising or falling by 1,000 to 1,500 people from the end of World War I to the early 1920s (actually, as we shall see below, the population curve flattened at the end of the second decade), and rose again in the 1930s.

Fluctuations in the Japanese population of Southeast Asia as a whole were governed by economic factors. In Singapore, trends in the commercial population corresponded very closely to trends in the value of trade with Japan. In the Philippines, however, fluctuations in the commercial population did not always directly reflect changes in the value of trade with Japan (fig. 5). Examination of the composition of the commercial population in each period will help elucidate this discrepancy.

Increases in the commercial population up to 1915 were the result of the strengthening of economic relations with Japan caused by the rapid expansion of bilateral trade and the settlement of Japanese immigrants on abaca plantations. Although the population registered a sudden drop in 1917, this was merely the result of a change in statistical categories in the consular population survey and can therefore be ignored. In 1917 a new category, "dependents of working people," was added, and dependents, who had formerly been listed and counted in the same column with heads of household, were moved to a separate column. Therefore the commercial population can be considered to have peaked for the first time in 1918; accordingly, occupational patterns in the Japanese commercial population that year should be examined.

The commercial population (excluding prostitutes) in 1918 numbered 1,540, of which 324 people fell into the category of "company and bank employees" and 283 into the category of "shop employees and clerks." These two categories together constituted 34 percent of the commercial population, the largest segment. The majority of these people are thought to have been involved in the import-export business and in wholesale and retail sales of Japanese goods. Statistics on the above are presented in table 7, along with statistics on general merchants and traders involved in transactions with Japan. As the table indicates, the number of people in these categories increased through 1918, in correspondence with increases in the

Table 7. Major Occupations of the Japanese Commercial Population of the Philippines, 1907–1940

Unit: No. people

Year	General merchants	Company, bank & shop employees, clerks	Traders	Total
1907	67	9	0	76
1908	71	9	0	80
1909	89	7	0	96
1910	138	18	0	156
1911	233	46	6	285
1912	281	62	6	349
1913	259	93	14	366
1914	255	111	17	383
1915	340	145	53	538
1916	343	166	62	571
1917	116	355	7	478
1918	129	607	15	751
1919	159	508	27	694
1920	162	496	10	668
1921	106	521	20	647
1922	125	578	19	722
1923	128	506	7	641
1924	125	570	14	709
1925	179	565	17	761
Year	Commodity merchants	Company, bank & shop employees, clerks	Traders	Total
1926	492	579	14	1,085
1927	230	763	22	1,015
1928	236	749	17	1,002
1929	300	838	14	1,152
1930	—	—	—	—
1931	369	1,250	22	1,641
1932	480	1,378	13	1,871
1933	529	1,366	14	1,909
1934	—	—	—	—
1935	517	1,649	7	2,173
1936	615	1,683	10	2,308
1937	504	1,675	16	2,195
1938	534	1,851	8	2,393
1939	—	—	—	—
1940	556	1,945	30	2,531

Source: Same as figure 1.

value of imports from and exports to Japan. This pattern exhibits the characteristic correlation between changes in the commercial population and economic factors.

In addition, the 255 Japanese classified as "cooks" and the 233 included in the category of "restaurants and bars" in the consular population survey should be considered. These two categories accounted for 32 percent of the commercial population, coming a close second to the categories of "company and bank employees" and "shop employees and clerks." The majority of restaurants and bars were small operations called *mizuya* (water shops), which sold ice water, juice, and other drinks to Filipinos, a fact borne out by the statistics from 1913 to 1915. The number of people working in restaurants and bars dropped from 217 in 1913 to 60 in 1914 and rose to 308 in 1915. In contrast, the number working in "tea shops" rose from zero in 1913 to 237 in 1914 and dropped to zero again in 1915. Moreover, the proviso "water shops" was added to the column headed "tea shops" in the 1914 consular population survey. This suggests that the majority of restaurants and bars sold ice water and that in 1914 such establishments were put into a separate category called "tea shops."

Thus, increases in the commercial population through 1918 were due to increases in the number of general merchants and traders and their employees, as a result of expanding trade with Japan. At the same time, a significant portion of the commercial population was made up of people involved in the service sector, such as cooks and others in the restaurant and bar business.

Examining subsequent population changes, we see that the commercial population peaked in 1918 and then decreased gradually until about 1923. This corresponded to a reduction in the value of trade with Japan, especially the value of imports from Japan. Despite a drop of about 50 percent in the value of imports of Japanese goods from 1920 to 1923, however, there was relatively little reduction in the commercial population. Moreover, since the 200 or more people classified as "cooks" through 1920 were reclassified as "domestic employees" in 1921, the actual reduction in the commercial population was even smaller than the statistics suggest.

In contrast to the large reduction in the Japanese commercial population of Singapore during the same period, the commercial population of the Philippines remained fairly stable. This does not mean that the commercial population of the Philippines was unaffected by economic factors. Rather, its relative stability was the result of two factors: the actual reduction in trade with Japan was less than it appeared to be in monetary terms, and the proportion of small businesses was much higher in the Philippines than in Singapore, where the majority of Japanese were employed by big trading companies and other large-scale businesses.

With regard to the first factor, the composition of imports from Japan changed significantly around 1920, as shown in table 8. Whereas such items as coal and cement constituted 20 to 30 percent of imports in 1910 and 1915, cotton goods took precedence from 1920 onward. This is confirmed by figure 6, which shows that the proportion of cotton goods in imports from Japan rose continuously in the early 1920s, eventually accounting for more than 50 percent of imports. Accordingly, while the total value of imports dropped drastically between 1921 and 1923, the decrease in the value of cotton goods was relatively small, and this decrease was due largely to reductions in unit price; as we see from table 9, the volume of cotton goods imported did not decrease so much. Imports of the main product, cotton-knit underwear, actually increased in volume during this period, and eventually the Philippine market absorbed about 20 percent of Japanese cotton-knit underwear exports. Moreover, as shown in figure 6, Japan's share of the Philippine cotton-goods market did not decrease between 1921 and 1923. These factors indicate that as far as the main items of merchandise in Japanese shops, cotton goods, were concerned, the effect on the Japanese commercial population of the decrease in the total value of imports shown in figure 5 was less than might be expected.

In addition, the mainstay of the Japanese commercial population handling such goods in the Philippines, unlike Singapore, was firmly established

Table 8. Major Items of Trade Between Japan and the Philippines, 1910–1935

Units: Thousand yen, % (in parentheses)

From Japan

1910		1915		1920	
Coal (lump)	1,067 (24)	Coal (lump)	2,039 (26)	Coal (lump)	6,437 (19)
Striped cotton cloth	394 (9)	Cotton knit undershirts & drawers	1,103 (14)	Cement	3,248 (9)
Cotton yarn (no. 20 & up)	332 (8)	Cotton yarn (no. 20 & up)	471 (6)	Cotton-knit undershirts & drawers	3,112 (9)
Potatoes	321 (7)	Cement	431 (6)	Gray shirting & sheeting	1,875 (5)
Cotton yarn (below no. 20)	228 (5)	Cotton-crepe undershirts & drawers	376 (5)	Cotton twill	1,314 (4)
Other	2,068 (47)	Other	3,351 (43)	Other	18,390 (53)
Total	4,410	Total	7,771	Total	34,376

From the Philippines

1910		1915		1920	
Hemp, jute, & Manila hemp	690 (88)	Hemp, jute, & Manila hemp	4,999 (68)	Sugar	7,533 (46)
Sugar	29 (4)	Sugar	1,844 (25)	Hemp, jute, & Manila hemp	6,214 (38)
Copra	22 (3)	Copra	220 (3)	Oil cake	949 (6)
Other	47 (6)	Other	245 (3)	Other	1,708 (10)
Total	788	Total	7,308	Total	16,404

From Japan

1925		1930		1935	
Cotton-knit undershirts & drawers	3,767 (13)	Other rayons	3,914 (14)	Cotton-knit undershirts & drawers	4,586 (10)
Coal	2,146 (7)	Cotton-knit undershirts & drawers	3,073 (11)	Calico	2,430 (5)
Cotton twill	1,294 (4)	Coal	1,700 (6)	Crepe & kabe-ori	2,311 (5)
Tenjiku cloth	1,042 (4)	Potatoes	834 (3)	Poplin	2,008 (4)
Gray sheeting	1,015 (3)	Gray shirting	789 (3)	Habutae silk	1,817 (4)
Other	20,041 (68)	Other	18,059 (64)	Other	34,906 (73)
Total	29,305	Total	28,369	Total	48,058

From the Philippines

1925		1930		1935	
Hemp, jute, & Manila hemp	12,917 (77)	Hemp, jute, & Manila hemp	8,317 (77)	Manila hemp	12,721 (53)
Sugar	2,522 (15)	Lumber	1,457 (14)	Other lumber	5,088 (21)
Leaf tobacco	239 (1)	Leaf tobacco	196 (2)	Iron ore	2,906 (12)
Other	1,022 (6)	Other	789 (7)	Other	3,234 (14)
Total	16,700	Total	10,759	Total	23,949

Items are listed in descending order of value. The figures for sugar represent the total value of the different grades listed in the original source.
Source: Ministry of Finance, *Dai Nippon gaikoku bōeki nempyō* [Chronological tables of Greater Japan's foreign trade].

Figure 6. The Value of Philippine Imports of Japanese Cotton Goods, 1916–1936

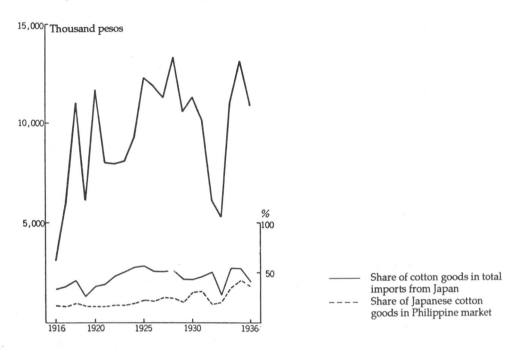

Sources: Milagros C. Guerrero, "A Survey of Japanese Trade and Investments in the Philippines: With Special References to Philippine-American Reactions 1900–1941," *Philippine Social Sciences and Humanities Review* 31 (March 1966): 28; Kamohara, *Dabao hōjin kaitakushi*, pp. 1,000–1,001. The statistics are originally from the annual reports of the Bureau of Customs of the Philippines.

Table 9. Philippine Imports of Japanese Cotton Goods, 1920–1923

Item	Value (¥1,000)				Unit	Volume			
	1920	1921	1922	1923		1920	1921	1922	1923
Cotton yarn (no. 20 & up)	1,079	321	454	508	Picul	4,589	2,677	3,447	3,862
Cotton-knit undershirts & drawers	3,112	2,325	2,740	2,655	1,000 dozen	509	584	717	746
Gray shirting & sheeting	1,875	631	439	222	1,000 yards	3,521	2,352	1,787	752
Cotton twill	1,314	339	385	791	1,000 yards	2,662	1,058	1,213	2,217

Source: Same as table 8.

Table 10. The Number of Japanese Companies in the Philippines

	1915		1921		1938	
Manila						
No. companies	23	(3)	88	(15)	115	(28)
No. employees	127	(37)	511	(256)	1,244	(944)
Davao						
No. companies	6	(1)	47	(30)	83	(38)
No. employees	48	(32)	1,991	(1,899)	1,798	(1,761)
Other						
No. companies	20	(1)	82	(7)	153	(20)
No. employees	58	(11)	320	(137)	852	(503)

"No. employees" refers to the total number of Japanese employees. Figures in parentheses indicate the number of companies with 10 or more Japanese employees and the number of Japanese employees in these companies. The figures for Davao in 1921 apply to the entire geographical area under the jurisdiction of the Davao branch of the Japanese consulate general in Manila.

Sources: For 1915, Ministry of Foreign Affairs, Bureau of Commercial Affairs, "Kaigai Nippon jitsugyōsha no chōsa" [Survey of expatriate Japanese businessmen]. For 1921 and 1923, Ministry of Foreign Affairs, Bureau of Commercial Affairs, "Zaigai hompō jitsugyōsha shirabe" [Survey of expatriate Japanese businessmen]. All figures are for the end of December.

individually owned businesses. The big trading companies in Singapore reduced their Japanese staffs when the value of trade fell, resulting in a sudden decrease in the Japanese commercial population. In contrast, as indicated by table 10, in 1921 very few trading firms and shops in the Philippines employed 10 or more Japanese. Unlike Japanese in Singapore, who could return to the main office in Japan if they were let go, Japanese in the Philippines would be unemployed and therefore were unlikely to return to Japan unless faced with insurmountable economic difficulties.

Due to the above two factors, the decrease in the Japanese commercial population of the Philippines in the early 1920s was slight. This phenomenon was governed by such economic factors as Japan's share of the Philippine market. It should be noted that even in 1923, when the Japanese commercial population decreased, the largest number of people involved in commerce (excluding prostitutes)—506, or 46 percent of the total—were still classified as company, bank, and shop employees and clerks, a higher proportion than in 1918. At the same time, although only 39 people were listed in the category of "restaurants, bars, rooms for rent, entertainment" in 1923, *mizuya* were apparently included in the category of "sale of other refreshments," which included 193 people. Moreover, the 230 cooks were classified as "domestic employees, cooks" and thus were excluded from the commercial population. Taking these factors into account, we see that the actual structure of the commercial population in 1923 differed little from that in 1918.

The commercial population increased gradually during the late 1920s, and more rapidly in the 1930s. Although the commercial population registered a decrease in 1926, no obvious cause, such as a reduction in the value of trade, can be identified. This suggests that some occupation formerly classified under commerce was reclassified that year, and the decrease can therefore be ignored.

The increase in the commercial population during the 1930s was clearly caused by the rapid expansion of trade with Japan. Although the value of trade decreased in 1931 and 1932, this did not result in a decrease in the commercial population, and for the same reasons as in the early 1920s. Through the rest of the 1930s expanding trade with Japan brought about significant changes in both the number and the nature of the Japanese commercial population of the Philippines.

As can be seen from table 7, from 1929 to 1940 the number of company, bank, and shop employees and clerks increased by 1,107, whereas the number of commodity merchants (including those classified as general merchants through 1925) grew by only 256. The proportion of company employees thus increased significantly, constituting 68 percent of the Japanese commercial population (excluding prostitutes) in 1940. This is corroborated by table 10, which shows that not only did the number of businesses and employees increase between 1921 and 1938, but so did the number of businesses in Manila employing 10 or more Japanese. In 1921 a total of 256 Japanese were employed by businesses with 10 or more Japanese employees, accounting for 50 percent of all Japanese employed by Japanese businesses in Manila; in 1938 this number increased to 944, or 76 percent. Moreover, whereas in 1921 only 104 of the 256 Japanese employed by businesses with 10 or more Japanese employees were engaged in commerce, in 1938 this number increased to 559 out of 944, or 59 percent of the Japanese employed by Japanese businesses in Manila with 10 or more Japanese employees. The proliferation of large trading firms and shops in Manila is particularly noticeable in comparison with the stagnation of the agriculture-based firms in Davao.

The increased business enjoyed by these large companies was due directly to the expansion of trade with Japan. Exports of hemp to Japan continued to increase, while the business of such companies as Mitsui & Co. and Daidō Bōeki, which handled hemp products, also expanded. Mitsui & Co. became involved in hemp exports around 1930 with the establishment of such facilities as a gunnysack warehouse in Santa Ana, Davao. Daidō Bōeki's predecessor, Itō Shōten, established a Manila branch in 1910. This became the Manila branch of Daidō Bōeki, establishing stronger ties with Furukawa Takushoku, when the trading company C. Itoh & Co. was reorganized during the recession that followed World War I. As a result of these developments, the number of Japanese employed by trading companies increased, as shown in table 11, in part causing the above-mentioned increase in the number of Japanese company and shop employees.

Table 11. Major Japanese Companies in Manila (Companies with Ten or More Japanese Employees)

	1915	1921	1938
Trading			
No. companies	1	2	4
No. employees	11	30	301
General merchandise			
No. companies	1	5	8
No. employees	10	64	168
Other types of commerce			
No. companies	0	1	4
No. employees	0	10	90
Fields other than commerce			
No. companies	1	7	12
No. employees	16	152	385

Sources: Same as table 10.

Table 12. Japanese Companies in Manila with Ten or More Japanese Employees: Company Name and Number of Employees

No. people

1921		1938	
Mitsui & Co., Manila Branch	16	Mitsui & Co., Manila Branch	74
Daidō Bōeki, Manila Branch	14	Daidō Bōeki, Manila Branch	69
		Osaka Bōeki	140
		Taihei Yōkō	18
Japanese Bazaar	10	Japanese Bazaar	35
Osaka Bazaar	17	Taiyō Bazaar	18
Taiyō Bazaar	14	Takahashi Shōten	35
Sun Star Bazaar	11	Ideal Bazaar	26
Takahashi Shōten	12	Inada Bros.	17
		Mayon Bazaar	15
		Nagasaki Bazaar	12
		Yokohama Shōkai	10
Yokohama Specie Bank, Manila Branch	10	Yokohama Specie Bank, Manila Branch	26
		Nakajima Shigeru Shōten	38
		Star Jitensha Shōkai	12
		Tokyo Grocery	14

Sources: Same as table 10.

Meanwhile, the value of imports from Japan rose rapidly at the start of the 1930s and remained fairly high thereafter; the number of general-merchandise and other companies selling Japanese goods increased accordingly. As table 12 shows, the number of employees of Japanese Bazaar, a typical general-merchandise firm, rose from 10 in 1921 to 35 in 1938. Osaka Bazaar also expanded its trading business, becoming Osaka Bōeki and increasing its staff to 140. The share of Japanese general-merchandise firms began to expand still more in 1931, when overseas Chinese stopped handling Japanese goods because of a boycott. The growth of Japanese enterprises in other cities in the Philippines during this period, shown in table 10, also deserves attention.

In short, growth of the Japanese commercial population during the 1930s was caused by expansion of trade with Japan, just as in the second decade of the century. In the 1930s, however, unlike the second decade, the number of company and shop employees increased far more than the number of small businesses. At the same time, the proportion of the Japanese commercial population involved in the service sector continued to shrink. Nevertheless, the proportion of companies large enough to warrant a head office in Japan remained smaller than in other parts of Southeast Asia, such as Singapore and Malaya.

Prostitutes have been omitted from this analysis of the Japanese commercial population in the Philippines simply for the sake of continuity, since they disappeared from the statistics in the 1920s. As already mentioned, however, there were far fewer prostitutes in the Philippines than in other parts of Southeast Asia during the early period of the Japanese presence, a fact in itself worthy of note, and the changes in their number thereafter should therefore be considered.

Tables 13 and 14 present consular population survey statistics on the number of Japanese prostitutes in the Philippines. Their number began to increase around 1900, rose to 300–400, then started to fall off rapidly around the end of the second

Table 13. The Number of Japanese Prostitutes in the Philippines, 1903–1930

No. people

Year	No. prostitutes	Year	No. prostitutes
1903	280	1917	258
1904	?	1918	233
1905	?	1919	123
1906	?	1920	72
1907	290*	1921	31
1908	226*	1922	21
1909	263*	1923	15
1910	432*	1924	5
1911	364	1925	28
1912	387*	1926	17
1913	431*	1927	3
1914	363	1928	0
1915	336	1929	0
1916	321*	1930	?

Figures followed by an asterisk represent the combined number of women listed in the categories of "miscellaneous occupations" and "unemployed" in the consular population survey; all other figures represent women listed in the category of "entertainers, prostitutes, serving women, etc.," in the survey.

Source: Same as figure 1.

Table 14. The Number of Japanese Prostitutes and Female Dependents in the Philippines, 1918–1921

No. people

Year	Prostitutes				Female dependents			
	Manila	Davao	Other	Total	Manila	Davao	Other	Total
1918	128	70	35	233	262	85	234	581
1919	12	70	41	123	298	85	216	599
1920	10	40	22	72	376	223	311	910
1921	0	14	17	31	365	385	227	977

Source: Same as figure 1.

decade of the century, dwindling to almost zero in the 1920s. Since prostitutes tended to be omitted from official statistics, however, these figures are not necessarily reliable if taken alone.

The accuracy of the statistics can be gauged by comparing them with records concerning Davao.[14] The first brothel was opened in Davao in 1910, but prostitution did not begin to flourish until the business boom of 1917, when thirteen brothels were in operation. In 1919, however, the brothels were moved in accordance with a government order. Moreover, owing to a drop in the market price of hemp, "economic recovery was impossible for half the brothels, and the number of prostitutes decreased drastically, to twenty-four or twenty-five."[15] In 1920 a branch of the Japanese consulate general was established in Davao, and at the same time an

[14] Kamohara, *Dabao hōjin kaitakushi,* pp. 132–39.

[15] Ibid., p. 136.

antiprostitution edict was issued. In 1923, however, there were still four or five brothels registered under Filipino names and about three Japanese restaurants. In 1925 the new governor of Davao took a stern antiprostitution line, and the local Japanese Society, fearing that prostitution would encourage anti-Japanese sentiment, resolved to eliminate it. As a result, all the Japanese restaurants were closed.

The above facts, considered in conjunction with tables 13 and 14, make it evident that the consular population survey statistics reflected the actual situation fairly closely. Some juggling of statistics seems to have taken place in response to the antiprostitution movement, such as classification of prostitutes as "dependents." In table 14, for example, the number of prostitutes in Manila suddenly dropped from 128 in 1918 to zero in 1921; the same year, 85 women were registered as dependents of the 191 people listed in the category of "restaurants, bars, rooms for rent, entertainment."

Nevertheless, it is unlikely that such juggling would affect the overall trend indicated by the statistics. Even if the peak number of prostitutes, 432 in 1910 (table 13), had continued unchanged to 1921, prostitutes would not have accounted for even half the total number of female dependents in 1921. Accordingly, it is unnecessary to revise my hypothesis that a large percentage of the Japanese female population in the Philippines at the beginning of the 1920s was made up of dependents.

The recession following World War I caused a major reduction in the number of Japanese prostitutes in the Philippines, and by the mid-1920s they had disappeared almost entirely as a result of the antiprostitution movement, which began around 1920.

In summary, the Japanese commercial population of the Philippines increased in the second decade of the twentieth century and in the 1930s as a result of the expansion of trade with Japan that occurred during these two periods. The commercial population remained relatively constant, despite a reduction in the value of trade with Japan in the early 1920s, because transactions were not greatly curtailed and because stable small businesses predominated. In the 1930s the proportion of company and shop employees rose as more large Japanese companies moved in. Nevertheless, the proportion of small businesses remained much greater than in Singapore and other parts of Southeast Asia. Prostitution was always much less developed than in other parts of the region, and after the postwar recession it lost its basis for further development, disappearing altogether with the antiprostitution movement of the 1920s.

Conclusion

From the above analysis it is clear that the pattern of Japanese economic penetration of the Philippines in the 1920s was governed by resources and markets, as was the case with regard to Singapore and Malaya. Moreover, over the course of time the agricultural and commercial populations were reorganized into large-scale businesses. Many abaca-plantation workers, who had increased in number rapidly during World War I, became independent cultivators but lost that status when hemp prices dropped during the recession at the outset of the 1920s. Quite a few even had to return to Japan.

The independent cultivators who emerged in the mid-1920s differed from their predecessors in that they had a more stable economic base, which enabled them to weather the depression at the beginning of the 1930s. Although they were called independent cultivators, in fact they functioned as tenants cultivating the land of agricultural companies. Their productivity was increased by the spread of the power-driven *hagotan* promoted by the agricultural firms, and their products were exported by the latter or by large trading firms. The development of these independent cultivators was thus dependent upon the capital resources of the agricultural companies.

As for the commercial sector, in the 1920s a system had developed whereby trading firms were importing Japanese goods to be sold in the Philippine market by retail businesses. Both types of businesses grew in scale. The export of Philippine products to Japan by large trading firms also increased.

In the Philippines, unlike Singapore and Malaya, the majority of Japanese engaged in the agricultural and commercial sectors were involved in independent small businesses, even though these were dominated by larger firms. The Japanese involved in agriculture were not hired plantation workers, as was the case in Malaya, but were independent cultivators; and the proportion of Japanese involved in commodity merchandising was much higher than in Singapore. Accordingly, although some reduction in population occurred during the recession at the beginning of the 1920s, the commercial population shrank less than in Singapore and Malaya. That the population remained stable during the depression at the beginning of the 1930s can be attributed to the stability of small-scale agricultural and commercial businesses.

This paper was originally published under the title "Senzenki Firipin ni okeru hōjin keizai shinshutsu no keitai: Shokugyōbetsu jinkō chōsa o chūshin to shite" [The pattern of Japanese economic penetration of the prewar Philippines, with special reference to the Population Survey by Occupation], *Asia keizai* [Developing economies] 26, no. 3 (March 1985): 33–51.

6

HIROICHIRŌ ISHIHARA AND THE STABLE SUPPLY OF IRON ORE

Yasukichi Yasuba

I. INTRODUCTION

Hiroichirō Ishihara, the eldest son of a farmer, was born in January 1890 in the village of Kichijōin, Kii County, Kyoto Prefecture. Kichijōin is now urbanized, but when Ishihara was born it was just an out-of-the-way hamlet of poor farmers. The Katsura River, flowing through the village, flooded every year. When the embankment broke, the villagers would be set to work repairing it, receiving 50 sen for a day's work. As a boy Ishihara often took part in such work.[1]

Though the villagers of Kichijōin lived "in the deepest poverty,"[2] Ishihara's family owned about two and a half acres of paddy, so Ishihara himself did not suffer deprivation. After graduating from Kyoto High School of Agriculture and Forestry, Hiroichirō helped on the family farm but before long, through the good offices of one of his teachers, Ryō Kimura, was hired as an agricultural technician by Kyoto Prefecture for a monthly salary of ¥12.50. He married Tomi, the second daughter of Hikojirō Ishihara, patriarch of the main Ishihara family. The couple had a daughter, thus laying the foundation for a stable life.[3]

Hiroichirō was ambitious, earning a degree from Ritsumeikan University's night school. But he was not satisfied with the prospect of remaining a low-level official if he could not qualify for the upper-level civil service examination. Excited by the enthusiasm for southern expansion then sweeping Japan,[4] and encouraged by Kimura, he decided to seek his fortune in Southeast Asia. When his younger brother Shinzaburō returned to Japan in 1916 for a visit after two years in Malaya, Hiroichirō left for Singapore with his wife, daughter, and two neighborhood youths he had persuaded to go along. At the age of twenty-seven, he embarked on

---

[1] Hiroichirō Ishihara, *Hachijū nen no omoide* [Eighty years of memories] (Tokyo: Ishihara Sangyō Kabushiki Kaisha, 1970), pp. 1–2; Ishihara Sangyō Kabushiki Kaisha, *Sanjūgo shūnenshi: Ochiboshū* [Thirty-fifth anniversary history: Gleanings] (Tokyo: Ishihara Sangyō Kabushiki Kaisha, 1962), p. 2.

[2] Tomekichi Yamashita; quoted in Ishihara Sangyō, *Sanjūgo shūnenshi*, p. 2.

[3] Hiroichirō Ishihara, "Ishihara Hiroichirō," in *Watakushi no rirekisho, dai 22 shū* [My career, collection 22], ed. Nihon Keizai Shimbunsha (Tokyo: Nihon Keizai Shimbunsha, 1964), pp. 11–12.

[4] Tōru Yano, *Nihon no nan'yō shikan* [Japan's historical view of the South Seas] (Tokyo: Chūō Kōronsha, 1979), pp. 92–95.

the Nippon Yūsen ship *Hitachi Maru,* traveling third class.[5] He had with him ¥5,000 that his father had raised by selling some land.[6]

From Singapore the party went to Panchor, Batu Pahat, in the sultanate of Johor, where Ishiraha's two younger brothers had a rubber plantation. There they built a house on stilts, with log pillars and a roof and walls thatched with atap. With the help of several Malay laborers, they cleared the surrounding jungle. Once they had finished clearing the land, they dismissed the workers and did the planting and weeding themselves. Their days were long and arduous. "The only recreation we had was the time we spent sitting on the veranda after dinner in the clear tropical moonlight, listening to the rustling palm fronds and talking about our aspirations."[7]

According to *Marai ni okeru hōjin katsudō no genjō* [The current state of Japanese activities in Malaya], published in 1917, the Ishihara rubber plantation covered only thirty acres. At that time Japanese-owned rubber plantations often ran to two hundred acres, so the Ishihara operation was very small.[8] Just when the rubber trees on the plantation had matured and were able to start producing rubber, World War I ended and the rubber market collapsed. Ishihara tried to make ends meet by taking on construction of a waterway planned by the Batu Pahat government, but this plan was scuttled by the war's end, as well.[9] He sold the plantation in 1918 and established a company in Singapore called Ishihara Yōkō, which imported bicycle parts and exported rubber and coconut, but it went bankrupt in 1919 and Ishihara was forced to return to Japan to seek new funds.[10]

II. Development and Import of Iron Ore

According to Ishihara's memoirs, when he arrived in Singapore in 1916 he learned that the walkways in the botanical garden had been filled in with chunks of limonite. He deduced that iron ore must be plentiful and "decided to make it my mission to search for iron ore and supply it to Japan, which lacked this resource, to contribute to the development of Japanese industry."[11] This account is dubious, however. If it were true, Ishihara should have been making more of an effort to find sources of iron ore while the ¥5,000 his father had given him lasted. In fact, while the rubber trees on the plantation were maturing, he and his brother did "spend a year crawling through hills and forests" from the center of Malaya to the east coast looking for iron ore,[12] but one wonders just how serious their exploration efforts were, since only in his later memoirs did Ishihara describe his searches for iron ore at length.

---

[5] Ishihara, "Ishihara Hiroichirō," pp. 12–14; Ishihara, *Hachijū nen no omoide,* p. 13.

[6] Earlier, his father had given ¥2,000 to Hiroichirō's two younger brothers. Ishihara, "Ishihara Hiroichirō," p. 9.

[7] Ishihara Sangyō Kabushiki Kaisha, *Sōgyō sanjūgo nen o kaiko shite* [Looking back on thirty-five years of business] (Tokyo: Ishihara Sangyō Kabushiki Kaisha, 1956), p. 4.

[8] Kōji Tsukuda, *Marai ni okeru hōjin katsudō no genjō* [The current state of Japanese activities in Malaya] (n.p., 1917), appendix, p. 13.

[9] Ishihara, *Hachijū nen no omoide,* pp. 21–25.

[10] Ishihara Sangyō, *Sōgyō sanjūgo nen,* p. 5.

[11] Ibid., preface.

[12] Ishihara, "Ishihara Hiroichirō," p. 15.

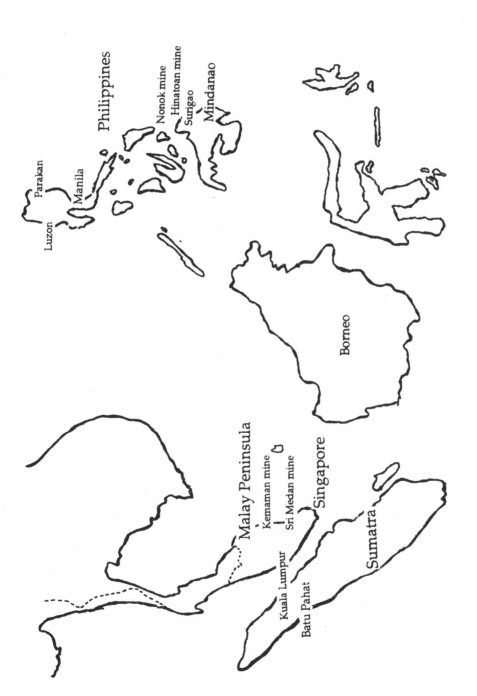

Hiroichirō Ishihara's Major Mining Operations in Southeast Asia, 1940

Developing iron mines was Ishihara's last gamble, following the failure of first the rubber plantation and then his business in Singapore. He received further financial help from his father and returned to Malaya, this time making a serious effort to find iron ore deposits. The iron mines on the Malay Peninsula developed by the company Ishihara established (today's Ishihara Sangyō) were at Sri Medan and Kemaman.

The first ore deposit that Ishihara discovered, in 1919, on the basis of information from a friend, was at Sri Medan, Johor, on the banks of the Simpang Kiri River. Ishihara described the circumstances as follows: as he tramped deep into the jungle,

> the way ahead suddenly became lighter. Proceeding in that direction as if drawn by the light, I found that the huge trees suddenly vanished and that I was in a large clearing. We decided to rest there, since we were tired from our trek, but as I started to sit down I saw some black rocks at my feet. The surface of the rocks was smooth and shone with a black gleam. I thought that was strange. Looking around, I saw that an area of about two or three hundred *tsubo* [1 *tsubo* = 3.954 sq. yds.] was filled with these gleaming black rocks. Without a word, I took my hammer from my belt to smash a rock; what a surprise when I saw that the broken surfaces had the characteristic metallic sheen of iron ore. 'Iron ore!' All three of us jumped up and shouted excitedly.[13]

The Sri Medan deposit was located in hills that began to rise about a quarter of a mile from the riverbank. They were "about a hundred meters high, with a total area of about four hundred acres. . . . The deposit was estimated to be around ten million tons, red iron ore with a 65 percent iron content."[14] Although Ishihara had made a rare find, he could not simply go into business then and there. He had to obtain mining rights, funding, and a market, and actually mine and transport the ore.

In regard to mining rights, Ishihara initially asked Matsuzō Nagai, director general of the Bureau of Commercial Affairs of the Japanese Ministry of Foreign Affairs, to help in notifying the authorities concerned. He was refused, however, since the consul general in Singapore feared provoking an international incident.[15] Ishihara then took it upon himself to negotiate with the Johor government; he asked not only for mining rights but also for permission to open a port at Batu Pahat, downriver from the Simpang Kiri River at the mouth of the Batu Pahat River.[16]

The British colonial authorities did not like the idea of opening a port. But in the economic downturn following World War I, revenues from rubber had fallen drastically and the sultan found the idea of the jobs that would be created in conjunction with developing the mine and the increase in export tax revenues that would be generated by the 50¢-per-ton tax on iron ore exports very attractive. After just one day of negotiations, the sultan personally approved the opening of a port at Batu Pahat in December 1920.

---

[13] Ishihara, *Hachijū nen no omoide*, pp. 28–29.

[14] Ishihara Sangyō, *Sōgyō sanjūgo nen*, p. 23.

[15] Ibid., p. 17.

[16] Ibid., pp. 16, 27–28.

In regard to a market for iron ore, a year before the opening of the port, at the end of 1919, Ishihara called on the head of Yawata Iron Works, Takeshi Shirani, without even a letter of introduction. He explained that he wanted to mine iron ore in Southeast Asia and that he had to find a way to supply it to Japan. As was Ishihara's wont, he linked the sale of iron ore to Japan's development. He must have been very persuasive, because Shirani promised to send technicians to Malaya immediately to conduct a survey. On the basis of their report, in February 1920 Shirani signed a contract to buy 50,000 tons of iron ore in 1921, 100,000 tons in 1922, and another 100,000 tons in 1923.

Ishihara later noted that he was "surprised at Shirani's boldness,"[17] but to Yawata, which imported 600,000 tons of iron ore a year at the time and which had begun obtaining iron ore from Karangbayangan, in the Philippines, in 1918, there was nothing particularly daring about contracting to import such amounts, especially since Ishihara's price was ¥5 lower than the going price of ¥30 per ton.[18] Actually, Ishihara's decision to supply large quantities of iron ore is surprising, considering that he did not know yet whether he would be able to open a port. If the port had not opened, the only way to ship the ore would have been through Singapore, which would have raised shipping costs by ¥1.50 per ton.[19]

Even so, Ishihara faced cash-flow problems until exports of ore began. Through the good offices of Koichirō Nakagawa, president of the Bank of Taiwan, whom Ishihara knew because Nakagawa had been the chancellor of Ritsumeikan University, the bank agreed to loan him a total of ¥1 million—a first installment of ¥350,000 and a second of ¥650,000. Things now looked as though they would go smoothly, but the situation changed just as Ishihara received the first ¥50,000 from the bank and started to develop Sri Medan. The Japanese economy had slowed with the end of World War I, and the bank suddenly lost its enthusiasm for further lending. Since one of its main borrowers was Suzuki Shōten, which was in financial straits, the bank had no choice but to cut back on new loans. The consul general in Singapore was also less than enthusiastic about Ishihara, so the bank stopped his loan.[20]

Again, however, Ishihara had a turn of good luck. Through an introduction from a man named Shioyama, the Osaka branch manager of Moritani Shōten, with whom Ishihara had dealt when he was doing business in Singapore, he met Kotarō Nagatome, a director of Kawasaki Dockyard, and was able to obtain the support of the company's president, Kōjirō Matsukata. Not only did Matsukata encourage Ishihara, but he also promised to offer enough Kawasaki Dockyard shares to secure the Bank of Taiwan loan. The bank then agreed to loan Ishihara a total of ¥750,000 (including the initial ¥50,000) and disbursed another ¥300,000. By ceding 50 percent of his mining rights to Matsukata, Ishihara gained his continued support.

Thus Nan'yō Kōgyō Kōshi (South Seas Mining Company), the predecessor of Ishihara Sangyō, was established as a joint-capital company (*gōshi gaisha*) with head offices in Osaka in September 1920. It had three members (*shain*): Ishihara,

---

[17] Ibid., p. 37.

[18] Ibid., pp. 31, 37; Yawata Seitetsu Kabushiki Kaisha, *Yawata Seitetsusho gojū nenshi* [A fifty-year history of Yawata Iron Works] (Fukuoka: Yawata Seitetsusho, 1950), p. 215.

[19] Ishihara, *Hachijū nen no omoide*, p. 51.

[20] Ibid., pp. 41–43.

Matsukata, and Matsukata's representative Shinkichi Tanaka.[21] Ishihara's brother Shinzaburō, as local supervisor, resumed clearing the forest, cleaning the river, and building a wharf as soon as he was cabled the ¥300,000.[22]

That money was soon gone, however. In December there was not enough cash to pay the workers' wages. Ishihara had returned to Malaya by then, and he asked his workers to wait two months for their pay, promising them plenty of food, beer, and whiskey in the meantime, in order to "send the iron ore that Japan needs." One can understand the Japanese workers responding to the slogan "Iron ore for the fatherland," but the three hundred Chinese and Malay laborers must have acquiesced either because they had been enjoying very good pay and benefits up to that point[23] or because they judged that being assured of food and liquor was better than being out of work in the high-unemployment period that followed World War I. It is true that the wages later paid by Ishihara Sangyō were relatively high,[24] but it is hard to believe that Ishihara was already trusted that much, so the latter supposition is probably correct.

At any rate, the work continued, the men working longer hours and taking no days off. In January 1921 the 7,000-ton Mitsui ship *Yūbari Maru* entered Batu Pahat port and loaded 3,000 tons of iron ore for Japan. Seeing this, the Bank of Taiwan came up with the remaining ¥400,000 of the loan, which finally put Nan'yō Kōgyō's operations on a stable footing. In fiscal 1921 the company produced 130,000 tons of ore against supply contracts for 50,000 tons. In September 1921 the sultan of Johor attended a banquet celebrating the first anniversary of the company and named the site of the mine Sri Medan (field of light). Formerly it had been known as Batu Medan (field of stone).[25]

Although Ishihara was blessed with good fortune on many occasions and had the help of many supporters, he and his employees did as much as possible themselves. In the beginning, mining, loading, and all other operations were carried out by completely inexperienced people; "we received no professional help in designing and building our facilities."[26] That these amateur efforts gradually led to technological improvements provides a clue to the secret of Japan's economic development.

As the company grew, of course, it began hiring specialists, and the pace of innovation picked up. In the mid-1920s a 500-horsepower electric generator and three endless conveyor belts were installed, and a canal from the river to the mountains was built. The company's fifteen tugboats and sixty barges enabled it to transport 2,000 to 2,500 tons of ore a day, or over 300,000 tons a year. The company eventually grew to have over 3,000 Japanese, Chinese, and Malay employees.[27]

---

[21] Ishihara Sangyō, *Sōgyō sanjūgo nen*, pp. 19–22.

[22] Ibid., p. 24.

[23] Ibid., pp. 30–31.

[24] Later sources frequently reported that the wages Ishihara paid were quite high. A number of examples are quoted in Hajime Shimizu, "Ishihara Hiroichirō ni okeru 'nanshin' no ronri to shinri" [Hiroichirō Ishihara's theory and psychology of "southern advance"], in *Kindai Nihon no Tōnan Ajia kan* [The view of Southeast Asia in early modern Japan], ed. Ken'ichirō Shōda (Tokyo: Ajia Keizai Kenkyūsho [Institute of Developing Economies], 1978), p. 9.

[25] Ishihara Sangyō, *Sōgyō sanjūgo nen*, pp. 33–36.

[26] Ishihara Sangyō, *Sanjūgo shūnenshi*, pp. 13–14.

[27] Ishihara, *Hachijū nen no omoide*, pp. 63–64; Ishihara Sangyō, *Sōgyō sanjūgo nen*, p. 36.

III. Expansion and Diversification

As already mentioned, the import price of iron ore from Sri Medan was initially ¥25 per ton. Prices fell with the end of World War I, however, and in 1925 the price was down to ¥11.50 on delivery to Yawata Iron Works. Of that amount, shipping costs totaled ¥4.50, which seemed very high to Ishihara.[28] The productivity of sea transport had improved greatly in the Meiji era (1868–1912), and shipping costs had fallen considerably,[29] though they could have been lowered even more if Ishihara had availed himself of government initiatives to encourage industry, which were being strengthened around that time.

Ishihara noted that "since freight rates fluctuate so much, my experiences over the past three years have shown that depending on a shipping company to export iron ore not only raises the cost of shipping but also keeps mine management unstable."[30] But though he was bothered by fluctuating freight rates, that did not lead him immediately to the "conclusion that the only way to ship iron ore is to own my own ships."[31]

At the time, because independent shipowners had greatly expanded their operations, there was intense competition among tramps in the seas around Japan. But since freight charges for shipping coal from Singapore to northern Kyūshū ranged from a high of ¥4.50 to a low of ¥2.80 in 1923 and 1924,[32] it is strange that Ishihara should have calculated the freight charge from Malaya to Japan, a route with few regular shipments, as ¥4.50. This suggests a lack of business acumen on the part of Nan'yō Kōgyō's shipping staff.

Of course, as Ishihara had explained to Shirani, obtaining an old ship cheaply would make it possible to ship iron ore from Malaya to Japan "for ¥3.50 to ¥4 per ton," thus permitting "a continued stable supply of iron ore at about ¥11."[33] Ishihara's true interest, however, lay neither in shipping ore in his own ships nor in ensuring a steady supply.

His real concern was that Nan'yō Kōgyō was having a hard time making ends meet with just the ¥750,000 borrowed from the Bank of Taiwan, especially when interest payments on the loan were taken into account.[34] But Ishihara's entrepreneurial genius lay in presenting convincing arguments for "a stable supply of resources," an idea he knew those with influence were partial to. Using this

---

[28] Ishihara Sangyō, *Sōgyō sanjūgo nen*, p. 166.

[29] The increased productivity of sea transport in the Meiji era was due mainly to improvements made on imported used ships. This, combined with lower prices for ships and a relative decline in seamen's wages, caused freight charges to fall. In the 1880–1909 period the cost of shipping coal from Nagasaki to Shanghai was one-sixth the import price of coal. See Yasukichi Yasuba, "Meijiki kaiun ni okeru unchin to seisansei" [Freight rates and productivity in Meiji-era shipping], in *Kindai ikōki no Nihon keizai: Bakumatsu kara Meijie* [The Japanese economy in the transition to the modern period: From the end of the Tokugawa shogunate to the Meiji era], ed. Hiroshi Shimbo and Yasukichi Yasuba (Tokyo: Nihon Keizai Shimpōsha, 1979).

[30] Ishihara, *Hachijū nen no omoide*, p. 74.

[31] Ibid., p. 75.

[32] Nippon Yūsen Kabushiki Kaisha, *Taishō jūyon nen kamihanki kaiun oyobi keizai chōsa hōkoku* [Research report on shipping and the economy in the first half of 1925] (Tokyo: Nippon Yūsen Kabushiki Kaisha, 1925), p. 12.

[33] Ishihara, *Hachijū nen no omoide*, p. 76.

[34] Ibid., p. 79.

argument, he gained the support of Shirani, Nakagawa, and other powerful men, and was able to obtain a low-interest government loan of ¥2.5 million to set up his own ore-shipping operation.[35]

Ishihara's true intent becomes clear when we see that he used only ¥1.4 million, less than half the loan, to buy ships. The remainder was used to expand his mining operations: he spent ¥210,000 to enlarge the facilities at Sri Medan, bought the Kemaman mine for ¥500,000, and repaid the ¥750,000 loan from the Bank of Taiwan. His entrepreneurial genius manifested itself further when he was able to get Kōjirō Matsukata to relinquish his share of the mining rights to Sri Medan on the condition that Ishihara would repay the Bank of Taiwan loan.[36]

Ishihara's second plan for the Malay Peninsula was set in motion when he bought the Kemaman mine, in Trengganu, in 1924. He purchased the mine from Sakuji Satō, who owned the mining rights.[37] By then development technology had improved a great deal, and construction at Kemaman proceeded rapidly. Permission to open a port at Kemaman was obtained the same year.[38] The Machang Sa'tahun mine at Kemaman yielded both iron ore and manganese. The ores were of high quality, the red iron ore containing 63 percent iron and the manganese ore containing 23 percent to 28 percent manganese and 25 percent to 35 percent iron.[39] Ishihara managed the construction operations himself. Because he used personnel who had helped develop Sri Medan, construction was completed in less than a year, and the first shipment of 230,000 tons of iron ore went out in 1925.[40]

By the late 1920s the mines were in full operation: Kemaman produced 100,000 to 200,000 tons of ore a year, and Sri Medan produced 800,000 tons a year.[41] In 1929 Ishihara increased the company's capital and renamed it Ishihara Sangyō Kaiun Gōshi Gaisha (Ishihara Industry and Sea Transport Joint Capital Company). In 1934 he restructured the company as a corporation (*kabushiki kaisha*), offered some of the shares to the public, and renamed the company Ishihara Sangyō Kaiun Kabushiki Kaisha. The company adopted its present name, Ishihara Sangyō Kabushiki Kaisha, in 1941, by which time further diversification had assured it of a durable financial base.[42]

Sri Medan, on the Malay Peninsula, was Ishihara's largest iron mine, but he also developed mines in the Philippines and on Hainan Island. The presence of iron ore in the Philippines had been known for some time. There had been talk of importing iron to Japan in 1920, but the American authorities had levied an export tax to prevent this.[43] After the Great Depression, however, the Americans changed their minds, and government representatives were sent to Japan to try to persuade Japan to buy iron ore from the Philippines. These negotiations failed, because the

---

[35] Ishihara Sangyō, *Sōgyō sanjūgo nen*, pp. 41–43.

[36] Ibid., p. 43.

[37] Ibid., pp. 44–45.

[38] Ibid., pp. 44–47.

[39] Ibid., p. 48.

[40] Ibid., pp. 46–47; Ishihara, "Ishihara Hiroichirō," p. 28.

[41] Ishihara, "Ishihara Hiroichirō," p. 28.

[42] Ibid., pp. 166–68.

[43] Toshiaki Tamiya, *Hompō tekkōgyō no kokusaiteki chii to sono dōkō* [The international status and trend of the Japanese steel industry] (Tokyo: Daidō Shoin, 1935), p. 75.

ore the Philippines wanted to sell was not suitable for steelmaking in Japan and because Japanese interests wanted a stake in the business, but Ishihara took advantage of the opportunity to set up operations in the Philippines.[44]

Mining rights to the Parakan mine, on southern Luzon, were already held by a local company, but Ishihara sent his brother Shinzaburō to see what could be done. To counter the strong discrimination against non-Americans, he set up a joint venture with the local company and proceeded to develop the mine, which began operating in 1938. In 1940 it produced 210,000 tons, but it had to be shut down in 1941 because of the worsening international situation.[45]

Another project of Ishihara's in the Philippines was the Hinatoan mine, on an island off the northeastern coast of Mindanao. Ishihara conducted an extensive mining survey of the area in 1938 and found a huge deposit of ore containing 48 percent to 53 percent iron. The size of the deposit was 200 million tons. However, since this mine would compete with the government-owned Surigao mine, on the northern tip of Mindanao, the Philippine government was unwilling to permit development of Hinatoan. On the pretext that some of the zoning markings were incorrect, the authorities refused mining rights in 1939.[46] Ishihara, having laid his groundwork carefully, did succeed in obtaining mining rights for Nonok Island, just six miles north of Hinatoan, but by then it was 1941, and the mine was left undeveloped, both because of the international situation and because of the quality of ore found there.[47] After the outbreak of the Pacific War, Ishihara began developing the Tazawa mine, on Hainan Island, on the orders of the Japanese military. He also developed a number of other mines in Southeast Asia.

In addition, Ishihara began to strengthen the management of Nan'yō Sōko (South Seas Warehouse), which had not been doing well, in 1930; went into the marine transport business, inaugurating regular runs to Java in 1931; and started developing bauxite mines in Malaya in 1936. These activities made him a leading practitioner of "southern advance." This was not enough for him, however: he also planned to set up a business in Japan that would maintain constant contact and transfer of personnel with work sites in Southeast Asia, providing health and recreational facilities for employees, education for their children, and other family welfare measures. The Ishihara Sangyō of today exists because of this approach.[48]

To realize his grand plan, Ishihara bought and began operating the Kamiyoshi gold mine, in Hyōgo Prefecture, in 1934. He also bought the Asahi gold mine, in Oita Prefecture, but the two mines were taken over during the war by Nippon Sankin Shinkō Kaisha (Japan Gold Production Promotion Company). The operations that provided the base for Ishihara Sangyō's postwar growth were a copper mine in Kumano, Wakayama Prefecture, and a copper smelter in Yokkaichi, Mie Prefecture. During the war these grew to be substantial enterprises, the Kumano copper mine employing more than three thousand people and the Yokkaichi plant more than thirteen hundred.[49]

---

[44] Ishihara Sangyō, *Sōgyō sanjūgo nen*, pp. 137–38.

[45] Ibid., pp. 139–46.

[46] Ibid., pp. 146–48.

[47] Ibid., pp. 148–49.

[48] Ishihara, *Hachijū nen no omoide*, p. 99.

[49] Ishihara Sangyō, *Sōgyō sanjūgo nen*, pp. 253, 257.

In the 1930s Ishihara began to expound his own brand of imperialist "southern advance," writing *Shin Nippon kensetsu* [Building the New Japan; 1934], *Tenkan Nippon no shinro* [Japan's course at the crossroads; 1940], and *Minami Nippon no kensetsu* [Building South Japan; 1942] and becoming involved in politics.[50]

IV. The Beginnings of the Japanese Steel Industry

As we have seen, Hiroichirō Ishihara started out with a rubber plantation, successfully developed iron mines, and expanded into many other fields of business. His proudest achievement was the development of iron mines, and he invariably referred to this in his writings. In an autobiographical essay, for example, he wrote:

> I was mining iron ore not only in Malaya but in two places in the Philippines and on Hainan Island as well and sending it at low cost in my own ships to Japanese steel mills. In the twenty-five years from 1921 to 1945, when the Greater East Asia War ended, I shipped a total of 18 million tons of iron ore, which accounted for 45 percent of the raw material Japan used for steelmaking in that period.[51]

Ishihara gained some recognition from the Japanese government for his activities; in 1930 he received the sixth-class Order of the Sacred Treasure, fifth degree. This was not a particularly prestigious honor, however, and Ishihara appears only as a minor figure in histories of the Japanese steel industry. For example, *Yawata Seitetsusho gojū nenshi* [A fifty-year history of Yawata Iron Works] states merely: "Iron ore began to be imported from the south, a new source of resources, in 1918. Ore came from Karangbayangan, in the Philippines, handled by Iwai Shōten, beginning in 1918 and from Johor, in Malaya, through Ishihara Sangyō's southern expansion, beginning in 1920."[52] No mention is made of Ishihara in relation to later imports of iron ore from Kemaman and other mines. And the volume on steel in *Gendai Nippon sangyō hattatsushi* [History of the development of modern Japanese industry] notes only that "in the second half of the 1920s imports [of iron ore] from the Malay Peninsula began to grow rapidly, overtaking imports from China in 1929 to become the most important source of iron ore for the Japanese steel industry."[53] While mentioning iron ore imports from Malaya, it says nothing about Ishihara Sangyō.

The disparity between these sources and Ishihara's own writings is great. That does not mean, of course, that a stable supply of iron ore was not important to the steel industry and to the Japanese economy before World War II. Imports of iron ore from Daye are given prominent mention in every history of the Japanese steel industry. Seiichi Kojima, for example, wrote: "In 1899 (officially, 1904) Yawata Iron Works made a long-term investment to secure supplies of the iron ore it needed from Daye, on the banks of the Yangtze River. . . . This arrangement between Yawata

---

[50] Shimizu, "Ishihara Hiroichirō."

[51] Ishihara, "Ishihara Hiroichirō," p. 30.

[52] Yawata Seitetsu, *Yawata Seitetsusho*, pp. 215–16.

[53] Ken'ichi Iida, Shūji Ōhashi, and Toshirō Kuroiwa, eds., *Gendai Nippon sangyō hattatsushi* [History of the development of modern Japanese industry], vol. 4, *Tekkō* [Steel] (Tokyo: Kōjunsha, 1969), p. 216.

and Daye underlay everything else and shows just how dependent Yawata was on Daye for iron ore in the early period." He also provided statistics.[54]

Over the long term, Ishihara undeniably played a very important role in assuring a stable supply of iron ore for Japan. Why, then, is he not given mention commensurate to his achievement in histories of the Japanese steel industry? To answer this question, it is necessary to review the history of this industry.

In Meiji Japan there was a strong feeling that "steel makes the state," that "steel is the mother of industry. If we do not develop a steel industry, no other industries will flourish, and we will not be able to raise an army. It is often said that the state of a country can be determined by the vigor of its steel industry."[55] Arguments for a policy favoring heavy industry were also heard: "This century is truly the century of steel. Demand for steel is growing in Japan, but our supply depends largely on foreign countries. Imports of steel the year before last, 1886, were valued at ¥3,244,542.55. . . . Of this . . . the value of unfinished products was about one-sixth that of finished products . . . so in the future we must produce about five times this amount. . . . It is definitely not a good idea to let foreigners profit from all this steel."[56]

The political opposition rejected the idea of building a government-managed steel mill, however, since doing so would expand the power of and create concessions for the so-called *hanbatsu* (clan faction) government of the time, dominated by the Satsuma and Chōshū clans. The chances for approval by the lower house of any proposal to build a government-run steel mill were nil until the Sino-Japanese War (1894–1895).[57] Except for a steel mill that the well-located Kamaishi mine, in Iwate Prefecture, managed to keep in operation, few privately operated enterprises succeeded, either, because of dubious profitability and the difficulty of obtaining financing.[58]

As with most cases of government intervention prior to World War II, plans for a government-operated steel mill were finally approved, despite opposition, to satisfy the military. During the Sino-Japanese War, when increasing the number of warships was the top priority, the lower house changed its stance, acknowledging that "in matters of national security and military preparedness, it is necessary to

---

[54] Seiichi Kojima, *Nippon tekkōshi: Meijihen* [History of the Japanese steel industry: The Meiji era] (Tokyo: Chikura Shobō, 1945), pp. 607–8.

[55] Kageyoshi Noro, "Tetsugyō shirabe" [Survey of the steel industry], 1891; quoted in Hiroto Saegusa and Ken'ichi Iida, eds., *Nihon kindai seitetsu gijutsu hattatsushi* [History of the development of steelmaking technology in early modern Japan] (Tokyo: Tōyō Keizai Shimpōsha, 1957), p. 108.

[56] *Chōya Shimbun,* July 6, 1888; quoted in Iida, Ōhashi, and Kuroiwa, eds., *Gendai Nippon sangyō hattatsushi,* vol. 4, p. 178.

[57] Ibid., p. 93. The Meiji oligarch repeatedly proposed the construction of steel mills, but the Liberal and Constitutional Progressive parties strongly opposed it every time. For example, at the fourth session of the Diet the opposition charged that "the clan-faction [*hanbatsu*] government continues to practice favoritism. . . . Officialdom has become almost exclusively a training ground for its own party." Saegusa and Iida, eds., *Nihon kindai seitetsu,* p. 146.

[58] In 1888, a group of Tokyo and Yokohama industrialists headed by Naomichi Shinagawa established Nippon Seitetsu Kaisha (Japan Steel Company). Because of the depression of 1894, however, the group was forced to disband the following year without having started construction.

protect vital installations, build gun emplacements, build more warships, improve weapons, build steel mills, and construct docks as soon as possible."[59]

With this shift in opinion as background, Takeaki Enomoto, then minister of agriculture and commerce, proposed building a government-run steel mill to the cabinet in 1894. After careful study by a research group on steelmaking operations, Yawata, in northern Kyūshū, was selected as the plant site and the decision was made to import iron ore from Daye.[60] The smelter was fired for the first time in 1901.[61]

Thus Yawata Iron Works began integrated manufacture of pig iron and steel in 1901 and was soon able to supply more than 50 percent of Japan's demand for pig iron (table 1). With the construction of many privately run integrated steel mills during World War I, production of pig iron passed the 500,000-ton mark and was soon able to satisfy more than 60 percent of domestic demand. Imports from India gradually increased, however, and with pig iron being shipped from Manchuria and Korea as well, the ratio of imports to demand gradually dropped.

Table 1. Domestic Demand for Steel, 1912–1942

(Annual average)

1. Year	2. Production (tons)	3. Imports (tons)	4. Exports (tons)	5. Net demand (tons) (2 + 3 - 4)	6. Net domestic production (%) (2 / 5)
1912–1915	274,022	207,387	317	481,092	57.0
1916–1920	507,729	284,869	7,345	785,253	64.7
1921–1925	578,899	405,349	6,011	978,238	59.2
1926–1930	1,009,471	619,186	4,620	1,624,037	62.2
1931–1932	964,052	572,478	910	1,535,619	62.8
1933–1935	1,686,278	890,802	866	2,576,213	65.5
1936–1940	2,725,395	1,015,888	850	3,740,434	72.9
1941–1942	4,354,549	831,378	1,908	5,184,018	84.0

Sources: Ministry of Commerce and Industry, Bureau of Mines, *Seitetsugyō sankō shiryō* [References on the steel industry], June 1934 survey, p. 2; Ministry of Commerce and Industry, Bureau of Metals, *Seitetsugyō sankō shiryō*, August 1943 survey, p. 3.

Pig iron from India was especially inexpensive. The average import price in the 1921–1925 period was ¥58.40 per ton, 16 percent lower than the average domestic price. The price differential widened even more later, so naturally enough imports of Indian pig iron grew rapidly. Moreover, private steelmakers still had little influence, and, since shipbuilders, machinery manufacturers, and other users of pig iron depended on imports for nearly half their supply, domestic steelmakers could not ask for protection through tariffs on imports.

Proponents of integrated steel production argued that importing pig iron was a mistake, for two reasons: though it might be cheaper to import pig iron to make steel, the pig iron needed to be reheated; and integrated steel manufacture

[59] Iida, Ōhashi, and Kuroiwa, eds., *Gendai Nippon sangyō hattatsushi*, vol. 4, p. 93.

[60] Ibid., pp. 23, 102, 112.

[61] Seiichi Kojima, *Hompō tekkōgyō no genzai oyobi shōrai* [The present and future of the Japanese steel industry] (Tokyo: Yūhikaku, 1925), p. 56.

produced useful byproducts, such as gas and tar.[62] If those advantages did exist, then pig iron produced through an integrated process should have been considered as of higher value. But as long as the advantages of using imported pig iron outweighed the disadvantages, there was no way that those advocating integrated production could prevail.

Opponents of integrated steel production were correct in their assertions that supporters "used as their final argument that 'integrated steel production is inevitable from the standpoint of national defense.'"[63] According to this defense theory, however, iron ore should be obtained "from Japan proper and Korea so that [there would be no interruption] in imports in an emergency."[64] From that viewpoint, it is clear that iron ore obtained from domestic sources and Korea was viewed in a completely different light from ore from Malaya or the Philippines.

Although the protectionists insisted that "tariff protection is not the issue,"[65] the 1917 Law for the Promotion of the Steel Industry was strengthened in 1926, effectively introducing protection. As amended, this law, which had originally exempted steel producers from expropriation and from income tax, tax on business profits, and tax on imported equipment for ten years, extended these exemptions to fifteen years and provided production subsidies of up to ¥6 per ton for steel produced in integrated mills and of up to ¥3 per ton for ordinary pig iron.[66] Shipbuilders and other users were granted generous subsidies. The amended law was the initial step toward supporting integrated steel production.

Not even this degree of protection enabled integrated production to grow much, however, and iron ore imports rose little after their drop following the end of World War I. Imports finally passed the 1.5 million–ton mark in 1926 and reached nearly 2 million tons in 1929. But at that point the Great Depression began, and both production and imports plunged again (table 2). While thirteen furnaces, with a combined production capacity of 1.35 million tons, remained in operation, nine furnaces, with a combined capacity of 800,000 tons, were shut down.[67]

During the economic downturn of 1928, the government had encouraged cartels in an attempt to "protect private industry." With the advent of full-blown depression, it was no longer able to counter arguments that production should be expanded

---

[62] Ibid., p. 151.

[63] *Tōyō Keizai Shimpō*, December 11, 1920.

[64] Kojima, *Hompō tekkōgyō*, p. 152.

[65] Iida, Ōhashi, and Kuroiwa, eds., *Gendai Nippon sangyō hattatsushi*, vol. 4, p. 199. However, the tariff on iron ore had been lifted in 1901, and this helped the production of pig iron. Tariffs on steel products were revised on numerous occasions. In 1912 tariffs were revised to 7.5 percent–10 percent for ingots, sheets, and plates; 15 percent for strips, rods, and wire; 20 percent for electroplated sheets, cast-iron pipes, and rails; and 25 percent for electric-wire supports and construction materials. Opposition to protective tariffs on these items was strong, as well. Thanks to the efforts of the shipbuilding industry, the average tariff was lowered from the 22.1 percent of 1906 to 19.1 percent. Yūji Tominaga, *Hompō tekkōgyō to kanzei* [The Japanese steel industry and tariffs] (Osaka: Osaka Shōka Daigaku Keizai Kenkyūjo [Osaka Commercial University Economic Research Institute], 1932), pp. 204–5.

[66] Tōa Keizai Chōsakyoku [East Asia Economic Research Bureau], ed., *Hompō tekkōgyō no gensei* [The current state of the Japanese steel industry] (Tokyo: Tōa Keizai Chōsakyoku, 1933), pp. 182–85.

[67] Iida, Ōhashi, and Kuroiwa, eds., *Gendai Nippon sangyō hattatsushi*, vol. 4, p. 307.

Table 2. Imports of Iron Ore from Various Regions, 1921–1942

Year	Region									
	Manchuria		China		British Malaya, Straits Settlements		Other		Total	
	Tons	Share (%)	Tons	Share (%)	Tons	Share (%)	Tons	Share (%)	Tons	Share (%)
1921			439,769	76.08	Included in "Other"		138,287	23.92	578,056	100.0
1922			644,730	78.77	Included in "Other"		173,780	21.23	818,510	100.0
1923			661,796	74.09	163,441	18.30	68,023	7.62	893,260	100.0
1924			800,157	75.12	264,933	24.87	42	0.00	1,065,132	100.0
1925			813,490	73.71	290,213	26.29	6	0.00	1,103,709	100.0
1926			502,747	63.41	290,053	36.58	30	0.00	792,830	100.0
1927			502,597	53.61	434,837	46.38	54	0.00	937,488	100.0
1928			877,841	54.29	738,502	45.67	631	0.04	1,616,974	100.0
1929			950,303	48.86	958,619	49.29	35,864	1.84	1,944,786	100.0
1930			790,566	40.06	997,891	50.56	185,202	9.38	1,973,659	100.0
1931			593,589	38.30	921,601	59.46	34,729	2.24	1,549,919	100.0
1932	6,182	0.42	557,092	37.58	877,886	59.22	41,249	2.78	1,482,409	100.0
1933	206	0.01	573,467	37.64	927,232	60.86	22,722	1.49	1,523,627	100.0
1934	3,307	0.16	825,461	38.72	873,395	40.97	429,753	20.16	2,131,916	100.0
1935	58	0.00	1,261,786	37.07	1,474,282	43.31	667,973	19.62	3,404,099	100.0
1936	66	0.00	1,251,908	33.12	1,691,432	44.75	836,703	22.13	3,780,109	100.0
1937	2,441	0.08	596,260	19.80	1,632,584	54.22	779,912	25.90	3,011,197	100.0
1938	2,800	0.10	147,208	5.17	1,600,144	56.24	1,094,855	38.48	2,845,007	100.0
1939	12,082	0.27	685,529	15.07	1,936,731	42.59	1,913,313	42.07	4,547,655	100.0
1940	46,841	1.00	1,174,968	25.05	2,041,366	43.52	1,427,052	30.43	4,690,227	100.0
1941	52,160	1.06	2,626,488	53.49	1,193,373	24.30	1,038,049	21.14	4,910,070	100.0
1942	86,476	2.30	3,539,531	94.19	76,887	2.05	54,800	1.46	3,757,694	100.0

From 1932 onward the figures for Manchuria include Guangdong.

Source: Ministry of Trade and Commerce, Bureau of Metals, *Seitetsugyō sankō shiryō*, survey of August 1943, p. 239.

by raising tariffs to discourage imports of pig iron.[68] The tariff on pig iron, which had been held down to 10 sen per 100 *kin* (approximately 132 pounds), or about 5 percent of the average import price of pig iron, was raised to 36 sen, or about ¥6 yen per ton. This was a tariff rate of more than 26 percent of the average import price.

As a result, although steel production grew substantially, imports of pig iron from everywhere but Manchuria failed to rise. Imports from India increased somewhat but never equaled the 410,000 tons reached in 1929. The ratio of domestic production to aggregate demand, which had been slightly more than 60 percent, rose to over 65 percent, and in the 1936–1940 period exceeded 70 percent on average.

V. The Significance of Iron Ore Imports From Malaya

The history of the Japanese steel industry before World War II, when pig iron was the main product, can be divided into five periods: the period before the establishment of Yawata Iron Works (through 1900); the period of near-monopoly by Yawata (1901–1913); the period when private companies were established because of World War I (1914–1919); the period of recession (1920–1932); and the period of protectionism (1933 onward).

Before the end of World War I it became clear that domestic deposits of iron ore were not as plentiful as the first hopeful estimates had indicated. In addition, the rapid rise in demand for steel accompanying the nation's military buildup temporarily increased the importance of ore from Daye. But the development of mines in Korea, Manchuria, and Southeast Asia after World War I led to a glut of the mineral until 1932 or 1933, and prices fell. The average import price per ton dropped from ¥24 in 1918 to ¥8 in the mid-1920s and stood at ¥9 in 1930.[69] Prices in general fell, of course, but while the prices of capital goods dropped about 28 percent between 1918 and 1930, iron ore prices tumbled 63 percent.[70]

To be sure, Ishihara Sangyō imported huge quantities of iron ore, mostly from the Malay Peninsula. But its imports shot up to around 60 percent of Japan's total iron ore imports only in the recessionary period, 1920–1932. Imports from Malaya continued to grow thereafter, but if the real purpose of integrated steel manufacture was to meet military needs, the supply from Malaya was not at all dependable. In fact, from 1941 onward the amount of ore imported from Malaya plummeted as the effects of the Pacific War began to be felt.

Understandably, Ishihara's achievements were dismissed as those of a mere successful speculator. Seen in that light, his undertakings could not be evaluated as a "great national endeavor" unless the southern region were integrated into the Japanese empire as "South Japan," in the way that the Korean Peninsula had been, and as Ishihara himself advocated.[71]

Looking at the great strides the Japanese steel industry made during and after World War II, one can argue that the "learning effect" of integrated steel production, which began well before the war, was considerable. If this argument is correct, Ishihara's role should be reevaluated, as well. Such an analysis, however, exceeds

---

[68] Ibid.

[69] Tominaga, *Hompō tekkōgyō*, p. 149.

[70] Kazushi Ōkawa et al., *Bukka* [Prices] (Tokyo: Tōyō Keizai Shimpōsha, 1967), p. 134.

[71] Hiroichirō Ishihara, *Minami Nippon no kensetsu* [Building South Japan] (Tokyo: Shimizu Shobō, 1942).

the scope of this paper, which endeavors only to explain why his operations were undervalued, based on arguments that actually prevailed in the prewar period.

This paper was originally published under the title "Ishihara Hiroichirō to shigen kakuho ron" [Hiroichirō Ishihara and the stable supply of resources], *Tōnan Ajia kenkyū* [Southeast Asian studies] 18, no. 3 (December 1980): 120–31.

THE JAPANESE COMMUNITY ABROAD: THE CASE OF PREWAR DAVAO IN THE PHILIPPINES

Reiko Furiya

INTRODUCTION

The largest concentration of Japanese in Southeast Asia prior to World War II was in Davao, on southeastern Mindanao, in the Philippines. In 1941 there were approximately 20,000 Japanese living in Davao (table 1),[1] which was the major focus of large-scale Japanese economic investment in Southeast Asia.[2]

Table 1. The Japanese Population of Davao, 1903–1941

1903	30	1913	700	1923	2,696	1933	12,742
1904	150	1914	1,250	1924	3,761	1934	13,065
1905	250	1915	1,550	1925	4,571	1935	13,535
1906	300	1916	2,450	1926	5,462	1936	14,029
1907	350	1917	5,300	1927	7,002	1937	15,000
1908	450	1918	7,350	1928	8,972	1938	16,100
1909	500	1919	7,000	1929	10,025	1939	17,300
1910	550	1920	5,533	1930	12,469	1940	18,600
1911	600	1921	4,268	1931	12,750	1941	20,000
1912	650	1922	3,209	1932	12,992		

The population figures for 1903–1919 are estimates. The figures for 1920–1941 are based on Davao consular population surveys, but the figures for 1937–1941 are approximate.

Sources: For 1903–1919, Kōji Kamohara, *Dabao hōjin kaitakushi* [History of Japanese development of Davao] (Davao: Nippi Shimbunsha, 1938), appendix. For 1920–1941, Yoshizō Furukawa, *Dabao kaitakuki* [A record of the development of Davao] (Furukawa Takushoku, 1956), p. 366.

Ever since the arrival of the first immigrants in 1903, the Japanese in Davao "remained strongly conscious of their national identity despite years of living and working with non-Japanese neighbors in a foreign country."[3] The settlers, controlled

---

[1] All figures for the number of Japanese in Davao are based on those in table 1.

[2] G. K. Goodman, *Davao: A Case Study in Japanese-Philippine Relations* (Lawrence, Kansas: Center for East Asian Studies, University of Kansas, 1967), p. 1.

[3] Cecil E. Cody, "The Japanese Way of Life in Prewar Davao," *Philippine Studies* 7, no. 2 (April 1959): 172–73.

by the Japanese consul and the Japanese Association,[4] "had transplanted a community from their homeland to Davao"[5] and showed no sign of assimilation with the Filipino population.[6] In the course of time thirteen Japanese elementary schools were established in the Davao area; these schools constituted "one of the most powerful agencies that stressed closer ties with the homeland."[7]

This paper attempts to clarify the role of Japanese schools in the formation of the largest prewar Japanese community in Southeast Asia. The first section outlines the early history of the community. Sections two, three, and four discuss the role played by Japanese schools, and section five touches briefly upon Japanese schools after the establishment of the Commonwealth in the Philippines.

1. The Origin of the Japanese Community in Davao

The Japanese community in Davao dates back to 1903. In 1898 sovereignty over the Philippines was transferred from Spain to the United States, and development of Mindanao was promoted. In 1903 discharged American soldiers began to settle in Davao, which had large areas of undeveloped fertile land, to operate hemp and coffee plantations. About 30 Japanese immigrants were hired that year as plantation workers, the first Japanese in the area.[8] The following year 180 Japanese were hired to work on hemp plantations, and 170 the year after. These immigrants had originally gone to the Philippines to work on the Benguet highway, linking Manila and Baguio, and had remained in the Manila area after it was completed. They were sent to Davao by Kyōsaburō Ōta, who later established the agricultural company Ōta Kōgyō.[9]

The majority of these immigrants were from impoverished farm villages. Rural Japan had been hard hit by the increase in land taxes following the Meiji Restoration of 1868, as well as by fluctuating rice prices, the influx of demobilized soldiers after the 1894–1895 Sino-Japanese War, and the 1898 crop failure. As a result, many men from rural areas became migrant workers.[10] Meanwhile, in 1903 immigration companies were permitted to recruit Japanese immigrants to the Philippines for the first time.[11] Thus the Japanese community in Davao was founded by migrant workers singing "If you want to make a buck, go to Benguet!"[12]

Like many Japanese in Southeast Asia, Kyōsaburō Ōta ran a general store catering to the Japanese community in Manila. He intended to launch a similar enterprise in Davao, but the Japanese population there was too small. Instead he

---

[4] Ibid., p. 176.

[5] Ibid., p. 173.

[6] Goodman, *Davao*, p. 102.

[7] Serafin D. Quiason, "The Japanese Colony in Davao, 1904–1941," *Philippine Social Sciences and Humanities Review* 23, nos. 2–4 (1958): 227.

[8] Yoshiyuki Tsurumi, *Banana to Nihonjin: Firipin nōen to shokutaku no aida* [Bananas and the Japanese: From Philippine plantations to the dining table] (Tokyo: Iwanami Shoten, 1982), p. 37.

[9] Yoshizō Furukawa, *Dabao kaitakuki* [A Record of the development of Davao] (Furukawa Takushoku, 1956), p. 356.

[10] Bill Hosokawa and Robert Arden Wilson, *Japaniizu-Amerikan* [Japanese Americans], trans. Kaname Saruya (Tokyo: Yūhikaku, 1982) pp. 38–40.

[11] Toraji Irie, *Hōjin kaigai hattenshi* [History of Japanese development overseas] (Tokyo: Ida Shoten, 1942), pp. 420–23.

[12] Ibid., p. 428.

bought some land from the Bagobo, a local people, in 1906 and established a hemp plantation,[13] hiring Japanese immigrants as laborers. The following year he established Ōta Kōgyō in accordance with the Public Land Act.

Ōta originated the method of plantation management known as the independent-cultivator system. Instead of cultivating the land himself, he left this entirely to Japanese immigrants. The company sold the hemp they produced, keeping 10 percent of the profits for rent and giving the remainder to the workers, whom he called "independent cultivators." Ōta's new style of management subsequently spread throughout Davao, becoming the predominant form of hemp-plantation management. Because working as an independent cultivator was much more attractive than working for wages on someone else's land,[14] Japanese immigrants who had formerly been scattered among various American- and Filipino-run hemp plantations flocked to Davao to become independent cultivators for Ōta Kōgyō. Meanwhile, about thirty stores catering to the Bagobo were set up by Japanese in Davao. Following Ōta's example, these entrepreneurs also established agricultural companies employing Japanese immigrants.[15]

Approximately 300 Japanese were living in Davao at the outbreak of World War I. The Japanese residents of that time "are aptly described as 'wanderers,' people drawn by the propaganda about southern regions carried prominently in newspapers and magazines as a tactic to deal with the recession following the [1904–1905] Russo-Japanese War."[16]

The hemp boom in Davao from 1915 to 1918, touched off by the war, greatly changed the size and nature of the Japanese immigrant population. The price of Davao hemp skyrocketed with the rapid rise in demand for hand-spun hemp fiber for braid thanks to the wartime prosperity in Japan and in demand for rope for naval use (table 2).[17] The Davao hemp yield was never very large, and Ōta Kōgyō monopolized its shipment and sale. With the sudden improvement in the market for Davao hemp, Japanese trading companies, which were now able to invest overseas, vied to establish agricultural companies and begin operating their own hemp plantations.[18] Sixty-five Japanese agricultural companies were set up from 1914 to 1918, including such well-known firms as Itō Shōten, established by a relative of Chūbei Itō, and Furukawa Takushoku, established by Yoshizō Furukawa with the support of Marubeni Shōten.[19]

This increase in companies was accompanied by a large influx of Japanese settlers. Until then Ōta Kōgyō had sent its executives to their home areas to recruit immigrants, but now it was possible to recruit on a much larger scale through immi-

---

[13] Tsurumi, *Banana to Nihonjin*, p. 36.

[14] Tōru Yano, *"Nanshin" no keifu* [The lineage of southern expansion] (Tokyo: Chūō Kōronsha, 1975), p. 104.

[15] Furukawa, *Dabao kaitakuki*, p. 357.

[16] Ken'ichirō Shōda, "Senzenki Nihon shihonshugi to Tōnan Ajia" [Prewar Japanese capitalism and Southeast Asia], in *Kindai Nihon no Tōnan Ajia kan* [The view of Southeast Asia in early modern Japan], ed. Ken'ichirō Shōda (Tokyo: Ajia Keizai Kenkyūsho [Institute of Developing Economies], 1978), p. 159.

[17] Tsurumi, *Banana to Nihonjin*, p. 42.

[18] Furukawa, *Dabao kaitakuki*, p. 375.

[19] Ibid., pp. 154–56.

Table 2. Davao Hemp Prices, 1915–1937

(Pesos per picul)

1915	2,000	1921	1,714	1927	3,700	1933	850
1916	3,100	1922	1,800	1928	2,577	1934	910
1917	4,000	1923	2,227	1929	2,604	1935	1,184
1918	4,925	1924	2,856	1930	1,882	1936	1,862
1919	3,600	1925	4,375	1931	1,262	1937	2,420
1920	3,925	1926	3,937	1932	786		

Prices are annual averages for grade F Davao hemp, except that the 1915 figure does not include December, the 1916 figure is for September through December, the 1918 figure does not include May and December, the 1919 figure does not include March, and the 1927 figure does not include December.

Source: Kamohara, *Dabao hōjin kaitakushi,* appendix.

gration companies.[20] In 1915 scheduled passenger ships to Australia began to stop at Zamboanga, on Mindanao, to facilitate immigration to the Philippines.[21] Thus the Japanese population in Davao grew rapidly, and Davao hemp, which had accounted for only 0.04 percent of Philippine hemp exports in 1910, rose to 13 percent of the total in 1919.[22]

The Davao Japanese Association was established in 1918. A Japanese Association had been formed twice previously on the urging of the Japanese consul in Manila, once in 1907, the year in which Ota Kōgyō was established, and once in 1916, but both times it had existed in name only. With the revision of the Public Land Act in 1919 a Japanese Association was formed once again to protect the interests of Japanese settlers.[23] This did not result immediately in the organization of the Japanese community under the aegis of the Japanese Association, however. The number of Japanese immigrants fluctuated in correspondence with changes in the Japanese domestic economy and the price of hemp, and the community in Davao was still made up largely of migrant workers. The price of hemp dropped drastically in 1918 and 1919 in the postwar recession. Poor economic conditions continued for several years thereafter, bottoming out in 1923.[24] The number of Japanese immigrants, which had risen to more than 7,000, dropped below 2,700.

On January 17, 1923, the worst year of the recession, in a document titled "Concerning the Establishment of a Japanese Elementary School in Davao and Its Accreditation as an Overseas School," the chief of the Davao branch office of the Manila consulate general appealed to the minister for foreign affairs, Kōsai Uchida, to establish a Japanese elementary school.[25] At a board meeting on July 8 that year, the Japanese Association decided to build a school in Davao to commemorate the wedding of the crown prince. Groundwork for the school's estab-

---

[20] Ibid., p. 228.

[21] Kōji Kamohara, *Dabao hōjin kaitakushi* [History of Japanese development of Davao] (Davao: Nippi Shimbunsha, 1938), p. 119.

[22] Tsurumi, *Banana to Nihonjin,* p. 43.

[23] Furukawa, *Dabao kaitakuki,* pp. 381–85.

[24] Kamohara, *Dabao hōjin kaitakushi,* p. 147.

[25] Telegram from Kadori Naruse, chief of the Davao branch office of the Manila consulate general, to Minister for Foreign Affairs Kōsai Uchida dated January 17, 1923, "'Davao' Nippon kokumin gakkō" [Davao school for Japanese nationals], Ministry of Foreign Affairs record I5-0-2-7-1, Diplomatic History Archives, Ministry of Foreign Affairs.

lishment was undertaken by a seven-member task force led by Yoshizō Furukawa and including Naotarō Inoue, president of Ōta Kōgyō, and other prominent figures. Practical details were concluded at a special board meeting on August 5, and the opening ceremony was held in the presence of the chief of the Davao branch office of the consulate general on April 1 the following year.[26]

The establishment of the school marked Davao's transition from a center for migrant workers, which it had been since 1903, to a more permanent settlement. The role of Japanese schools in this transition is described in the next section.

2. The Creation of a Stable Immigrant Community

The decision to establish a Japanese school in Davao in 1923, the worst year of the recession, indicates the function that the school was initially expected to perform. The recession, which began at the end of 1918, was accompanied by a mass exodus of Japanese immigrants. This dealt a lethal blow to the owners of companies that had expanded their hemp plantations during the wartime boom. With the hemp crop standing neglected as the harvest season approached, plantation owners sought to avert ruin by employing Filipino laborers and by improving production through use of the newly invented power-driven *hagotan* (hemp-stripping machine) to alleviate the labor shortage. But when the use of Filipino labor proved unsuccessful,[27] employers shifted their focus to inducing Japanese immigrants to settle on a long-term basis. At the first signs of recession in 1918 the prominent businessmen leading the Japanese Association strove to promote the settlement of Japanese immigrants by submitting a petition to the foreign minister through the Davao branch office of the Japanese consulate in Manila, urging that the limit on accompanying family members be expanded from immediate family to include relatives in the fourth degree.[28]

The problem of children's education was a natural concomitant of the increased number of married settlers. This can be clearly seen in the changing male-female ratio of the Japanese community. The number of females per one hundred males increased steadily, from seven in 1920 to fifteen in 1925 and forty-four in 1930 (table 3). There were many public elementary and middle schools established by the American colonial government under the system of free compulsory education, in which American teachers taught an American curriculum. The Japanese, however, did not send their children to these schools, since "almost all are one-room schools under the charge of a single teacher and are aimed primarily at educating savage tribes."[29] There were also some private Japanese schools, but the majority of Japanese "did everything they could to scrape together the money" to return to Japan.[30]

The importance of educational facilities in promoting the growth of immigrant communities, as pointed out by Kiyoshi Inoue,[31] a well-known contemporary writer

---

[26] Kamohara, *Dabao hōjin kaitakushi*, p. 151.

[27] Ibid., p. 147.

[28] Ibid., p. 109. The Manila consulate was raised to the status of consulate general in May 1919.

[29] Telegram from Naruse to Uchida dated January 17, 1923, "'Davao' Nippon kokumin gakkō."

[30] Kamohara, *Dabao hōjin kaitakushi*, p. 151.

[31] "If we boldly aspire to venture across the sea to the four corners of the earth, we must regard the entire world as the Emperor's domain. There is definitely meaning in the way foreigners set out immediately to build schools, temples, and cemeteries to set their minds at ease. While

Table 3. The Japanese Population of Davao, by Gender, 1920–1936

Year	Male	Female	Total	Year	Male	Female	Total
1920	5,162	385	5,533	1929	7,881	2,114	10,025
1921	3,842	422	4,265	1930	8,631	3,838	12,469
1922	2,854	352	3,206	1931	8,290	4,466	12,755
1923	2,444	249	2,693	1932	9,557	3,435	12,992
1924	3,276	482	3,758	1933	9,138	3,604	12,742
1925	3,962	600	4,562	1934	9,130	3,935	13,065
1926	4,629	824	5,452	1935	9,255	4,280	13,535
1927	5,859	1,144	7,002	1936	9,270	4,759	14,029
1928	7,197	1,775	8,972				

Source: Kamohara, *Dabao hōjin kaitakushi*, pp. 746–47.

on the South Seas, was widely recognized, and it is clear from the following comment that the official in charge of the Davao branch office of the consulate general also held this view: "The basis of overseas colonial development is long-term settlement. Needless to say, the most effective method is to acquire permanent residence rights and to provide education for children in order to eliminate settlers' fears for the future."[32] Thus the objective of the Davao branch office of the consulate general and the leaders of the Japanese Association in establishing a Japanese school was to encourage the long-term settlement of Japanese immigrants.

Education continued to be the most important criterion for creating a stable community. Efforts to set up a well-equipped Japanese school sprang from the perception that "the establishment of education, in other words, eliminating parents' worries regarding their children by providing schools to which they can entrust them while concentrating on their own work, is the surest guarantee of the success of immigrant Japanese enterprises."[33]

Thus the establishment of a Japanese school was viewed by both consular officials and the leaders of the Japanese Association as fulfilling an important role in the transformation of the Japanese community in Davao from a group of migrant workers to a stable settlement. These expectations were, in fact, fulfilled. After 1923 there was no further decrease in the Japanese population of Davao, and immigrants "began to dream of becoming permanent or semipermanent settlers operating their own enterprises."[34]

With the progress of Japanese settlement and the formation of the Japanese Association, Japanese schools were to fulfill another important function. The role of Japanese schools in the formation of the Japanese community in Davao is discussed

---

Japanese educators and religious leaders must be stimulated in this respect, I also fervently hope that the government and overseas Japanese will become aware of the importance [of such activities]." Kiyoshi Inoue, *Nan'yō to Nippon* [The South Seas and Japan] (Tokyo: Taishōsha, 1913), p. 56. This work is typical of Japanese publications on the South Seas in the Taishō era (1912–1926). See Yano, *"Nanshin" no keifu*, pp. 70–71.

[32] Telegram from Naruse to Uchida dated January 17, 1923, "'Davao' Nippon kokumin gakkō."

[33] Telegram from Akira Saitō, chief of the Davao branch office of the Manila consulate general, to Minister for Foreign Affairs Giichi Tanaka dated June 10, 1927, "'Davao' Nippon kokumin gakkō."

[34] Telegram from Saitō to Minister for Foreign Affairs Kijūrō Shidehara dated June 11, 1926, "'Davao' Nippon kokumin gakkō."

below, first with regard to the organization of the community and second with regard to the replication of Japanese culture.

3. The Organization of the Japanese Community

The Early Japanese Community and Japanese Schools

Davao changed from a temporary work site for migrant workers to a stable settlement, but this did not of itself signify the formation of a Japanese community. Since the majority of Japanese in Davao were migrant workers from impoverished farm villages, they had little interest in forming a Japanese community in Davao under the aegis of the Japanese Association.

Moreover, ever since the establishment of a cultivators' association in 1919 there had been conflict between the independent cultivators and their employers, that is, the leaders of the Japanese Association. Independent cultivators contracted for the use of public land leased by agricultural companies, a practice criticized by Filipinos as violating the Public Land Act, which prohibited the lease of public land to individuals. To avoid censure, the cultivators' association, which had been established to protect the land rights of such companies as Ōta Kōgyō and Furukawa Takushoku and to facilitate intercompany communication, drafted a sample contract, which it distributed to each plantation in order to standardize contracts between companies and independent cultivators. Independent cultivators were thereby designated as mere contract workers, and provisions concerning the transfer of contract rights and the sale of hemp were less favorable than before. Consequently, Japanese Association membership remained so low that in 1920 "extraordinary measures," including sanctions, were imposed to sustain the association.[35]

Japanese schools played an important role in the Japanese Association's control and organization of Japanese immigrants. In 1923 it was decided that a Japanese school would be established through the following procedures. Funds for building and maintaining the school would be obtained by soliciting contributions from the Japanese community. Since the minimum annual maintenance cost for the first few years would be six thousand pesos, one thousand contributions of fifty cents each would be collected each month. Japanese residents of Davao who were independent cultivators or storekeepers would contribute one or more units depending on the scale of their business.[36] Through such measures funds to cover school construction and maintenance were obtained from a broad spectrum of the Japanese population of Davao.

The community split, however, over the location of the school. One group consisted of the leaders of the Japanese Association, a "privileged class,"[37] and the

---

[35] The following measures were stipulated: "1. Plantation owners are responsible for collecting membership dues from all members living on their plantations. 2. All members will obtain membership cards from plantation owners. 3. Plantation owners are not permitted to contract work to or in any way employ Japanese who do not possess membership cards. 4. Sanctions will be applied by other plantation owners against those who violate items 1 and 3." Kamohara, *Dabao hōjin kaitakushi*, p. 511.

[36] Ibid., p. 515.

[37] "The Japanese Association was often criticized as the monopoly of a privileged class." Ibid., p. 521. The association's leaders consisted primarily of the managers of large companies, such as Furukawa Takushoku and Ōta Kōgyō.

consular officials in Davao; the other group comprised local branch members of the Japanese Association, primarily independent cultivators in Mintal. The former group advocated building the school in Davao, where the consular branch office was located,[38] and insisted on construction of only one school, for the following reasons:

1. The economic capacity of the Japanese community in Davao is insufficient to maintain two schools.
2. Not only is the establishment of one good school preferable to the establishment of two mediocre schools, but also one school is more convenient when applying for accreditation as an overseas school.
3. If a branch school or detached classrooms are established at the outset, it will be difficult to handle similar requests that may arise in future.
4. School fees will be relatively lower for one school than for two.

The latter group advocated building the school in Mintal because of "the large number of children living in the area and [because] parents cannot afford to board their children in a school dormitory."[39]

Following the decision to build the school in Davao, the latter group organized a supporters' association to raise funds to establish a separate school in Mintal, and the private Mintal Japanese Elementary School opened on April 21, 1923.[40] The Mintal school supporters' association asserted that "if it is impossible to obtain government subsidies unless the founders are a Japanese Association, we will withdraw our membership from the present Japanese Association and form a new association."[41] The group also tried to obtain subsidies from the government general of Taiwan.[42]

To the consular officials and the leaders of the Japanese Association, who wished to bring the Japanese community under the unified control of the Japanese Association, the Mintal school supporters' association was indulging in "unreasonable behavior by local Japanese upstarts."[43] The consular officials strove to place the Mintal school under the direct control of the Japanese Association by monopolizing the authority to award subsidies and forcing the Taiwan government general to stop subsidy payments on the grounds that these interfered with the policy of establishing schools administered by Japanese Associations and financed by the Ministry of Foreign Affairs.[44]

---

[38] Furukawa, *Dabao kaitakuki*, p. 406.

[39] Telegram from Naruse to Minister for Foreign Affairs Keishirō Matsui dated July 1, 1924, "'Davao' Nippon kokumin gakkō."

[40] Kamohara, *Dabao hōjin kaitakushi*, p. 623.

[41] Telegram from Naruse to Shidehara dated November 15, 1924, "'Davao' Nippon kokumin gakkō."

[42] Telegram from Naruse to Shidehara dated December 26, 1934, "'Mintaru' Nippon kokumin gakkō" [Mintal school for Japanese nationals], Ministry of Foreign Affairs record I1-5-0-2-7-33, Diplomatic History Archives, Ministry of Foreign Affairs.

[43] Telegram from Naruse to Shidehara dated November 15, 1924, "'Davao' Nippon kokumin gakkō."

[44] Telegram from Naruse to Shidehara dated December 26, 1924, "'Mintaru' Nippon kokumin gakkō"; telegram from Vice-Minister for Foreign Affairs Katsuji Debuchi to Director General

The Foreign Ministry did not in fact care whether the recipient was the Japanese Association or the school supporters' association, but left all decisions concerning the allocation of subsidies to the chief of the Davao consular branch office,[45] who thus gained authority over payment of subsidies. By proposing that all additional subsidies for the next fiscal year be allotted to the Mintal school, he was able to persuade the supporters' association to place the Mintal school under the jurisdiction of the Japanese Association.[46] Moreover, aware that most of the Japanese in Mintal were independent cultivators under contract to Ōta Kōgyō, he appointed the company's president, Naotarō Inoue, to be the official of the Japanese Association responsible for resolving the issue.[47] In this way the Mintal school came under the association's control.[48]

Cooperation between the consular branch office, which held authority over the allocation of subsidies, and the leaders of the Japanese Association prevented a rift in the association and facilitated unification of the Japanese community under its leadership.

THE EXPANDING JAPANESE COMMUNITY AND JAPANESE SCHOOLS

In 1924 the Davao economy began to pick up again. Improved conditions led to an increase in the number of Japanese immigrants, and also to a change in the nature of the community with which the Japanese Association dealt. Once again control of the Japanese community, which had seemed assured after the earlier conflict, was proving difficult. Let us examine the role of Japanese schools in the formation of this expanding and changing community.

The price of hemp began to rise again in 1924 (table 2). This was accompanied by an influx of Japanese immigrants who settled as independent cultivators on plantations scattered throughout the Davao area.[49] At the same time, with the improved production resulting from the power-driven *hagotan*, invented during the recession, "many hemp-plantation nouveaux riches appeared in Davao."[50] As a result, influential independent cultivators began to emerge as leaders of the Japanese Association.[51]

As independent cultivators grew in number and rose in status, they formed their own organizations to foster mutual friendship and protect their interests. In 1928, for example, 230 independent cultivators from eight plantations in the Catigan area formed the Catigan Independent Cultivators' Association; the following year 160 independent cultivators in the Davao area formed the Four-Plantation Federation of Independent Cultivators; and in 1930 some 300 independent cultivators

---

Fumio Gotō, Government General of Taiwan, received February 17, 1925, "'Mintaru'" Nippon kokumin gakkō."

[45] Telegram from Shidehara to Naruse dated December 25, 1925, "'Davao' Nippon kokumin gakkō."

[46] Telegram from Naruse to Shidehara dated November 15, 1924, "'Davao' Nippon kokumin gakkō."

[47] Telegram from Naruse to Shidehara dated February 2, 1925, "'Mintaru' Nippon kokumin gakkō."

[48] Furukawa, *Dabao kaitakuki*, p. 407.

[49] Ibid., p. 376.

[50] Kamohara, *Dabao hōjin kaitakushi*, p. 169.

[51] Ibid., p. 521.

formed the Five-Plantation Federation of Independent Cultivators, a major organization of the time. More than thirty other organizations of independent cultivators were established on various plantations.[52] Thus independent cultivators not only rivaled the leaders of the Japanese Association, who included the managers of such companies as Furukawa Takushoku and Ōta Kōgyō, but also represented different areas of Davao.

In 1930, affected by the onset of the Great Depression, the price of hemp began to fall. In 1931 a severe drought and forest fires heavily damaged the hemp plantations.[53] In addition, increased production of sisal hemp forced down Davao hemp prices.[54] Davao was plunged into a severe depression. This aggravated the rift between the leaders of the Japanese Association and the local branch members, as well as conflicts among the local branch members themselves.

One bone of contention was the question of membership dues. Independent cultivators, who constituted the majority of the Japanese Association's membership (table 4), paid the minimum dues. Consequently the issue of dues was a major concern of both the leaders of the association and the independent cultivators, that is, the local branch members, and a constant source of conflict between the two groups.[55]

Table 4. The Number of Independent Cultivators, 1913–1941

1913	200	1921	1,944	1928	3,000	1935	4,500
1914	400	1922	1,204	1929	4,000	1936	4,400
1915	600	1923	815	1930	5,000	1937	4,300
1916	700	1924	1,101	1931	4,900	1938	4,200
1917	1,600	1925	1,138	1932	4,800	1939	4,100
1918	3,000	1926	1,419	1933	4,700	1940	4,000
1919	4,000	1927	2,000	1934	4,600	1941	4,000
1920	2,880						

Source: Furukawa, *Dabao kaitakuki*, p. 425.

Another bone of contention was the issue of whether to increase the number of Japanese schools. Following the economic recovery of 1924, the port of Davao was officially opened in 1926, and the number of female immigrants increased. The number of children in local branches increased correspondingly. Many of these children were unable to commute to either the Davao or the Mintal school and boarded at one or the other. With the Great Depression, the local branch members wished to establish new schools to save money by eliminating boarding fees. The leaders of the Japanese Association, however, opposed the construction of more schools because of the cost entailed.[56] The local branch members' dissatisfaction with the leaders of the Japanese Association mounted.

In 1932 it was finally decided to build a school in Bankas, but members of the local branches in the Bankas area disagreed over the school's location, and

---

[52] Ibid., pp. 771–74.

[53] Ibid., pp. 212–19.

[54] Ibid., p. 526.

[55] Kamohara, *Dabao hōjin kaitakushi*, p. 529.

[56] Letter from Japanese Association Chairman Torajirō Takuma to Ministry of Foreign Affairs Secretary Eiji Wajima dated September 26, 1935, "'Davao' Nippon kokumin gakkō."

members of the Manambulan and Twin Rivers branches, among others, withdrew from the Japanese Association. This issue ignited a conflict among the local branches, fanning the flames of discontent with the Japanese Association leaders and of conflict among local branch members and bringing the Japanese Association to the verge of disintegration. As Kamohara stated, "the situation was quite out of control."[57]

Prior to the general meeting of the Japanese Association in 1933, there was furious campaigning for the election of the local branch officers, who would in turn elect the Japanese Association officers. On the day of the general meeting, members came from every branch to observe the election of the association officers. The budget deliberations at the regular meeting of local branch officers, held in this confrontational atmosphere, were "hostile" and marked by "furious debate."[58]

Conflict arose again in 1934, when the local branch members advocated minimum dues of two pesos during budget deliberations, whereas the Japanese Association officers proposed dues of three pesos. Voting resulted in adoption of the local branch members' proposal. In response, the association officers resigned en masse, and it was two-and-a-half months before new officers were elected. The consular officials,[59] who so far had cooperated with the Japanese Association, changed their policy in view of the disorder within the association, discarding the two-school policy and deciding to permit the establishment of schools wherever local branch members expressed such a desire. Accordingly, schools were built in Manambulan, Bankas, Tugkalan, and Lasang in 1934 and in Calinan, Bayabas, and Digos in 1935.[60] The land for these schools was obtained from companies managed by prominent independent cultivators who supported the schools' establishment.[61] The construction of schools independent of the Japanese Association signified a shift away from unified control of the Japanese community by consular officials and Japanese Association leaders and the local branch members' independence from the association.

A brief explanation of the system of overseas accredited schools is necessary to clarify this point. This system derived its legal foundation from the 1905 Law Concerning Retirement and Survivors' Benefits for Employees of Overseas Accredited Schools (Law 64). Employees of schools designated by the government as "schools established for overseas Japanese" were entitled to the same retirement and survivors' benefits (combined under the term "pension" in 1923) as employees of public schools in Japan.[62] Moreover, under Ministry of Education Ordinance 37 (October 25, 1919), "Concerning School Entrance and Transfer of Pupils and Graduates of Over-

---

[57] Kamohara, *Dabao hōjin kaitakushi*, p. 526.

[58] Ibid., p. 527.

[59] The Davao branch of the consulate general had been upgraded to a consulate in 1932.

[60] Kamohara, *Dabao hōjin kaitakushi*, pp. 523–30.

[61] "'Bayabas' Nippon kokumin gakkō" [Bayabas school for Japanese nationals], Ministry of Foreign Affairs record I1-5-0-2-7-25, Diplomatic History Archives, Ministry of Foreign Affairs; "'Karinan' Nippon kokumin gakkō" [Calinan school for Japanese nationals], Ministry of Foreign Affairs record I1-5-0-2-7-34, Diplomatic History Archives, Ministry of Foreign Affairs.

[62] Sōsuke Watanabe, ed., *Zaigai shitei gakkō kankei shiryō* [Sources on overseas accredited schools], vol. 1, *Zaigai shitei gakkō ichiran (1906–1945)* [Summary of overseas accredited schools, 1906–1945] (Tokyo: Kokuritsu Kyōiku Kenkyūjo [National Institute of Educational Research], 1982), preface.

seas Accredited Elementary Schools," pupils and graduates of overseas accredited schools were granted equal status to pupils and graduates of public schools in Japan, established under the Elementary School Order.[63] To become an overseas accredited school it was necessary to notify the foreign and education ministers of the school's organizers and its maintenance and management methods, in accordance with the "Regulations Concerning the Designation of Overseas Accredited Schools" (Ministry of Foreign Affairs and Ministry of Education Ordinance of September 6, 1923).[64]

Japanese immigrants wanted the same education for their children, in terms of both system and curriculum, as that offered in Japan. As far as the school organizers were concerned, the purpose of establishing a Japanese elementary school in Davao in 1923 was to encourage Japanese immigrants to settle there permanently. They were not especially concerned with replicating the curriculum and teaching methods used in Japan. The head of the Davao branch office of the consulate general was of the opinion that Japanese children should rely on the education of the host country. But since most Japanese immigrants at that time were migrant workers who intended to return home eventually, they desired schools with equal status to those in Japan. The demand for such schools was so strong that it was feared the collection of school fees would be affected by the possibility of transfers from local schools to schools in Japan.[65]

As discussed below, even after Japanese immigrants began to show a tendency to settle, it was necessary to hire teachers with formal qualifications from Japan because of the immigrants' insistence on curriculum and teaching methods identical to those in the homeland.[66] For these reasons the Japanese schools established in Davao had to obtain official recognition as overseas accredited schools.

School organizers had to apply for accreditation through the consul. Thus, in addition to his control over subsidies, he exercised control over accreditation.[67] Accordingly, as long as the consul supported the leaders of the Japanese Association, who advocated a policy of only two schools, it was impossible for local branch members to establish accredited schools. Local branch members were obliged to pay dues to the Japanese Association to help maintain the Davao and Mintal schools run by the association and send their children to one or the other. The association, meanwhile, justified its control of the Japanese community by declaring the provision of education for the children of Japanese immigrants to be one of its major missions.[68]

---

[63] Sōsuke Watanabe, ed., *Zaigai shitei gakkō kankei shiryō* [Sources on overseas accredited schools], vol. 2, *Zaigai shitei gakkō ni kansuru hōseido to shochōsa* [Legal systems and surveys pertaining to overseas accredited schools] (Tokyo: Kokuritsu Kyōiku Kenkyūjo [National Institute of Educational Research], 1983), p. 26.

[64] Ibid., p. 27.

[65] Telegram from Naruse to Uchida dated January 17, 1923, "'Davao' Nippon kokumin gakkō."

[66] Telegram from Saitō to Shidehara and Minister of Education Ryōhei Okada dated September 12, 1925, "'Davao' Nippon kokumin gakkō."

[67] For example, when the administrators of the Tugkalan school applied for certification as an overseas accredited school, the consul requested the foreign minister to postpone approval for fear that conflict between the Tugkalan and Bankas branches would recur. Telegram from Consul Ichitarō Shibata to Minister for Foreign Affairs Naotake Satō dated April 19, 1937, "'Davao' Nippon kokumin gakkō."

[68] Kamohara, *Dabao hōjin kaitakushi*, p. 539.

From the above it is clear that the consular officials' changed stance concerning the two-school policy resulted in the local branch members' independence from the Japanese Association. In the face of this situation, the Japanese Association was forced to modify its policy to avoid disintegration. It no longer insisted on a limit of two schools, a policy that had caused much dissatisfaction, but worked instead to bring the schools that were already being established in other areas under the association's control. Schools with more than forty pupils were recognized as accredited schools, for which the association would defray all expenditures. The other schools were designated as private schools, which were eligible for subsidies.[69]

Subsidies were of vital importance for small local schools.[70] In October 1935 the consul whose shift away from the two-school policy had caused friction with the Japanese Association was transferred[71] and a "softer" consul took his place,[72] so that once again the consulate and the Japanese Association began to cooperate. Moreover, new schools under the jurisdiction of the Japanese Association were now to be regarded as branches of the overseas accredited schools in Davao and Mintal, thereby receiving equal status.[73] Local schools thus found it more profitable to place themselves under the control of the Japanese Association than to operate independently.

Table 5. The Number of Pupils in the Thirteen Japanese Elementary Schools, by Grade, 1938

School	1st grade	2d grade	3d grade	4th grade	5th grade	6th grade	Total
Davao	73	48	37	26	22	15	221
Mintal	77	68	41	39	36	30	291
Calinan	66	64	37	13	11		191
Manambulan	34	25	24	24	19		126
Lasang	12	9	6	7	6		40
Daliao	60	49	30	19			158
Bayabas	28	22	11	13			74
Digos	11	17	9	18			55
Bankas	6	7	8	2	14		37
Tugkalan	28	14	11	14	15		82
Catigan	18	8	6	7	4		43
East Lasang	20	12	7	4	3		46
Wañgan			U n k n o w n				

Source: Kamohara, *Dabao hōjin kaitakushi*, pp. 622–32.

On June 1, 1935, the Calinan, Lasang, and Manambulan schools offered their school buildings and all other facilities to the Japanese Association and transferred administration to the association. The Bankas and Tugkalan schools followed suit on January 1, 1936, as did the Bayabas and Digos schools on February 4

[69] Letter from Takuma to Wajima dated September 26, 1935, "'Davao' Nippon kokumin gakkō."
[70] Telegram from Shibata to Minister for Foreign affairs Hachirō Arita dated December 12, 1936, "'Davao' Nippon kokumin gakkō."
[71] Furukawa, *Dabao kaitakuki*, p. 303.
[72] Ibid., p. 387.
[73] Telegram from Shibata to Hirota dated December 3, 1935, "'Davao' Nippon kokumin gakkō."

and the Daliao school on June 1.[74] The largest of these schools, Calinan, Lasang, Manambulan, and Daliao (table 5), became overseas accredited schools at the time of transfer to the Japanese Association's jurisdiction.[75] Thus the local branch members remained within the Japanese Association as a result of changes in the administration of the schools.

This did not resolve all the conflicts between Japanese Association leaders and local branch members or among local branch members themselves, however. Trouble continued to erupt. In 1937, owing to a land dispute between association leaders and local branch members, the latter demanded the resignation of the acting chairman of the association, and the officials of the association resigned en masse. The arbitrators of the dispute—Yoshizō Furukawa and Ōta Kōgyō President Yasaku Morokuma—together with the consul proposed reorganizing the Japanese Association and appointed a committee to draft a proposal.

Several reforms were undertaken on the basis of the committee's findings. The centralized system, under which the association had exercised direct control over all projects, was changed to a decentralized system emphasizing local autonomy. At the same time, the well over one hundred local branches were reorganized into thirteen branches centered on the school districts of Davao, Mintal, Calinan, Manambulan, Lasang, Digos, Bayabas, Bankas, Tugkalan, Daliao, Catigan, Wañgan, and East Lasang. Each branch office, located in the school, was in charge of school administration and maintenance as well as overall branch administration. The headquarters of the association, responsible for fostering friendship among members and protecting their rights and interests, was essentially "reduced to parasitic dependence on the branches."[76] The Davao Japanese Association was now organized around the Japanese schools.

The Japanese community in Davao was made up largely of migrant workers in the early period, and of independent cultivators later. Controlling this community presented many difficulties for the consul and the leaders of the Japanese Association. Through the establishment of Japanese schools they succeeded in giving this immigrant community a more settled character, and through manipulation of school subsidy payments and the system of accreditation of overseas Japanese schools they were able to maintain control and organize the community. After being decentralized the Japanese community was reorganized according to school districts. Thus the schools played a major role in the organization of the community. They also functioned to replicate Japanese culture. The next section deals with this aspect of the schools by examining school regulations in Davao and contemporary attitudes toward education.

4. THE REPLICATION OF JAPANESE CULTURE

As discussed above, the establishment and administration of Japanese schools fulfilled the important functions of stabilizing and organizing the Japanese community. This was made possible by the immigrants' strong desire to educate their children according to the Japanese school system and curriculum, an indication of the strength of the immigrants' attachment to their homeland.

---

[74] Telegram from Shibata to Hirota dated March 5, 1936, "'Bayabas' Nippon kokumin gakkō."

[75] Furukawa, *Dabao kaitakuki*, pp. 407–10.

[76] Kamohara, *Dabao hōjin kaitakushi*, pp. 536–49.

Japanese immigrants considered their children to be showing a "tendency toward total assimilation, understanding the languages and customs of the various races in Davao [better than their own]."[77] The emphasis in education therefore was on preventing assimilation, and there were even plans to organize trips to Japan.[78] Education that was strongly oriented toward the homeland communicated this orientation to children born and reared in Davao and made possible the replication of Japanese culture.

School regulations were drawn up with the establishment of the Japanese school in Davao in 1923.[79] According to Article 1, the purpose of the school was "to provide education to Japanese children in and around Davao based on the objectives set forth in the first article of the Elementary School Order." Teaching plans for each grade level and weekly class plans also followed the enforcement regulations of the Elementary School Order (Article 11). To facilitate transfers to schools in Japan,[80] January 1 was designated as the first day of school (Article 5). National textbooks were to be adopted as school texts (Article 10). The school was to employ teachers licensed as elementary school instructors under the overseas accredited school system.

Not everything, however, was the same as in Japan. There was some attempt to adapt the curriculum and other aspects of the schools to the Philippines. The Davao school regulations included English as a subject (Article 11), and a Filipino English teacher was employed.[81] Geography included a brief survey of the Philippines. The principal was empowered to adapt the science curriculum, adding or subtracting material (Article 10). Philippine national holidays and Davao festival days were school holidays (Article 7).

Most children of local branch members lived too far from the Davao and Mintal schools to commute and therefore boarded at school. The effect of boarding on promoting the assimilation of Japanese culture was well recognized.[82] Eighteen pupils were enrolled upon the establishment of the Davao school, while twenty-five were enrolled in the Mintal school. The staff of each school included a principal who was also an instructor, a dormitory matron, a school doctor, and a Filipino English teacher.[83]

Following the economic recovery of 1924 the number of Japanese immigrants increased, and the higher proportion of female immigrants resulted in an increase in the number of children. This was accompanied by the establishment of new schools and the expansion of existing facilities. The Davao school became an overseas accredited school in 1926, and a new school building was constructed in 1930. By 1937 the school had 242 pupils and 10 staff members. The Mintal school was certified in 1927, and several additions were built. By 1937 it had 325 pupils and 11 staff members.[84] As discussed above, eleven other Japanese schools were estab-

---

[77] Ibid., p. 661.

[78] Ibid., pp. 679–80.

[79] Telegram from Naruse to Matsui dated July 1, 1924, "'Davao' Nippon kokumin gakkō."

[80] Furukawa, *Dabao kaitakuki*, p. 411.

[81] Kamohara, *Dabao hōjin kaitakushi*, p. 623.

[82] Ibid., pp. 649, 675.

[83] Telegram from Naruse to Matsui dated July 1, 1924, "'Davao' Nippon kokumin gakkō."

[84] Kamohara, *Dabao hōjin kaitakushi*, pp. 623–24.

lished. In 1937 these thirteen schools had a combined total of 1,420 pupils, 48 Japanese staff members, and 9 Filipino staff members.[85] Moreover, as the number of graduates increased, supplementary education was offered at both the Davao and Mintal schools.[86]

From the above it is clear that the education provided by Japanese elementary schools in Davao was the same as that offered in Japan aside from a few adaptations to local conditions. Education of children born and raised in Davao was oriented toward Japan, thereby allowing the replication of Japanese culture in Davao.

5. Conclusion

The role played by Japanese schools in the formation and development of the Japanese community in prewar Davao has been analyzed above. This community, which comprised a handful of migrant workers at the turn of the century, began to grow significantly around the time of World War I, expanding to include many Japanese immigrants and Japanese-run agricultural companies. The managers of such agricultural companies as Ōta Kōgyō and Furukawa Takushoku, together with the consul, established elementary schools in an effort to encourage immigrants to settle. Subsequently these schools played an important role in the Japanese Association's control and organization of the increased number of immigrants.

The consul, who had authority over subsidy allocations and school accreditation procedures, and the Japanese Association worked hand in glove to manipulate and organize the immigrants. This was facilitated by the immigrants' strong attachment to Japanese culture. The schools, by adopting the same system and curriculum as schools in Japan, transmitted this attachment to the immigrants' children, replicating Japanese culture in Davao. Thus the schools fulfilled an important role in the formation of the Japanese community—a community that, organized around the schools, grew with Japan's economic expansion in Southeast Asia.

In addition to schools, the immigrants established hospitals, newspaper companies, banks, Buddhist temples, and Shintō shrines.[87] As a result, Davao became a "Japanese village," a community "in which, although they were living in a foreign land, the Japanese could strut about as if they owned the place."[88] The Japanese maintained their sense of national identity, showing no sign of assimilation with the Filipino population.

The Philippines entered a turbulent period in the 1930s. During the worldwide depression touched off in 1929, opposition to US sovereignty over the Philippines increased in the United States. In 1934 the Philippine legislature accepted the Tydings-McDuffie Act, which provided for a ten-year commonwealth in preparation for independence. A constitution was adopted and a general election held, and the Commonwealth was established in 1935.

The constitutional convention debated the fundamental principles of the new Philippine nation-state. One key issue had to do with protection of the nation's

---

[85] Ibid., pp. 620–21.

[86] Ibid., pp. 622–24.

[87] Goodman, *Davao*, p. 6.

[88] Kamohara, *Dabao hōjin kaitakushi*, p. 663.

economic profits. At that time, the Philippine economy was dominated by the United States, China, and Japan. Policy measures to foster national industries and curb the influx of foreign capital were adopted. Another major issue was the question of a national language. Under US rule English and Spanish had been the official languages, and English had been the language of education. There was no language common to all Filipinos, however. It was decided to foster a national language based on indigenous languages, and instruction in Tagalog commenced in junior high schools and teacher training schools in 1940.

Burgeoning Philippine nationalism led to mounting criticism of exploitation by Japanese capital, centered on the Japanese community in Davao.[89] There were impassioned anti-Japanese speeches in the constitutional convention, and warnings that Davao must not become a second Manchuria.[90] In 1934 the Public Land Act was revised to restrict Japanese land ownership. Under the amended law noncitizens could no longer acquire land.[91] Land use under the independent-cultivator system was declared illegal the following year, and an order invalidating land leases was issued.[92] Thus the independent-cultivator system, the traditional method by which Japanese immigrants had acquired land, was made illegal. In 1940 a law restricting immigration was passed. The annual number of Japanese immigrants to Davao, which had been about 2,700, was limited to 500.[93] The Japanese community, which had grown under the control of the consul and the leaders of the Japanese Association, thus lost its vested rights and was barred from further expansion.

Under the Naturalization Law of 1939 Japanese immigrants could become Philippine citizens for the first time. To do so, however, they had to meet certain criteria concerning length of residence and property and had to be able to speak one of the major indigenous languages, as well as English or Spanish. In addition, throughout the necessary period of residence, applicants' youngest children must have been enrolled in public schools teaching Philippine history, politics, and civics or in private schools accredited by the Office of Private Education of the Philippines. The length of residence required for naturalization was halved for Japanese who worked for the Philippine government, who were married to Philippine nationals, or who had brought new industry or inventions to the Philippines.[94] The new law, though too early for economic independence, represented a compromise by the Philippines as it strove to achieve nationhood.

Jintarō Uehara, the chairman of the Japanese Association and the Okinawan Association and a member of the Davao Elementary School Construction Committee,[95] stated the following opinion of the Naturalization Law: "The acquisition of citizenship is vital for second-generation development, but certain changes in the

---

[89] Setsuho Ikehata and Shigeru Ikuta, *Tōnan Ajia gendaishi* [Modern history of Southeast Asia], vol. 2 of *Sekai gendaishi* [Modern history of the world] (Tokyo: Yamakawa Shuppansha, 1977), pp. 122–28.

[90] Goodman, *Davao*, pp. 33–36.

[91] Kamohara, *Dabao hōjin kaitakushi*, p. 422.

[92] Furukawa, *Dabao kaitakuki*, p. 469.

[93] Joseph Ralston Hayden, *The Philippines: A Study in National Development*, 2d ed. (New York: Macmillan, 1947), p. 691.

[94] Hayden, *The Philippines*, pp. 728–29.

[95] Kamohara, *Dabao hōjin kaitakushi*, p. 1,498.

school regulations will have to be considered. At present English is the only foreign language taught; no other knowledge concerning the Philippines is offered."[96]

As already mentioned, the Japanese schools had always provided largely the same education as that available in Japan, but when it became impossible for Japanese to continue to own land except by acquiring citizenship under the Naturalization Law, the addition of education concerning the Philippines was considered. The Japanese schools, which had performed a central role in the formation of the Japanese community in Davao, were thus compelled to adopt a new approach under the Commonwealth.

On December 8, 1941, however, Japanese troops invaded the Philippines as the Pacific War commenced. On January 2 the following year Manila fell, and the next day the Philippines came under Japanese military rule[97] and Davao became a naval base.[98] That year the Ministry of Greater East Asia was established, and overseas accredited schools throughout the region came under its jurisdiction.[99] Thus the Japanese schools in Davao became overseas accredited schools under the Ministry of Greater East Asia before any changes in the school regulations could be effected.

This paper was originally published under the title "Senzenki Dabao Nihonjin shakai no keisei to Nihonjin shōgakkō " [The formation of the Japanese community in prewar Davao and Japanese elementary schools], *Kokusai kankeiron kenkyū* [Studies on international relations] 5 (March 1986): 73–87.

---

[96] Jintarō Uehara, "Hiripin no dōkō to Davao" [Trends in the Philippines and Davao], in *Dabao kaitaku no kaiko to tembō* [Recollections and prospects of the development of Davao], ed. Chihiko Konishi (Tokyo: Nan'yō Keizai Kenkyūjo [Institute of South Seas Economies], 1941), p. 16.

[97] Ikehata and Ikuta, *Tōnan Ajia gendaishi*, vol. 2, p. 130.

[98] *Sekai daihyakkajiten* [World encyclopedia], vol. 18 (Tokyo: Heibonsha, 1958), p. 307.

[99] "Dai Tōashō zaigai shitei gakkō kisoku" [Regulations for overseas schools accredited by the Ministry of Greater East Asia], Ministry of Greater East Asia Ordinance 1, November 1, 1942, in Watanabe, ed., *Zaigai shitei gakkō kankei shiryō*, vol. 2, p. 42.